Marshall
County
Public Library

Henry Billeman

26 Sept. 2008

The Shellman Story

Hanging the Preacher

by

Henry A. Buchanan

Bloomington, IN   Milton Keynes, UK

authorHOUSE®

AuthorHouse™
1663 Liberty Drive, Suite 200
Bloomington, IN 47403
www.authorhouse.com
Phone: 1-800-839-8640

AuthorHouse™ UK Ltd.
500 Avebury Boulevard
Central Milton Keynes, MK9 2BE
www.authorhouse.co.uk
Phone: 08001974150

First published by AuthorHouse 8/21/2008

ISBN: 978-1-4259-8490-8 (sc)

Printed in the United States of America
Bloomington, Indiana

This book is printed on acid-free paper.

INTRODUCTION

The events I am about to tell you about here took place a half century ago. To you who have not yet reached your fiftieth birthday, it will seem like ancient history, and the world I will describe will be rather strange to you. But to me it is like yesterday because I remember it so vividly, and what happened in Shellman, Georgia, then changed the course of my life; what has happened to me since then could not have happened if I had not been in that little town fifty years ago.

I confess to you that I had not heard of Shellman, Georgia until very shortly before I went there to be the pastor of the Baptist Church. I had grown up on some unprofitable farms near Macon, Georgia. And if God had not singled me out and said "Go preach" I never would have heard of Shellman. But because He did and I said "Where?" the name of Shellman was heard all over the country but that did not make the people who lived in Shellman happy.

Shellman is a small town in Southwest Georgia. Wealth and local prestige marked Shellman in the nineteen fifties. I was told by one long term resident there that Shellman had a very high rate of both college graduates and alcoholics. During the three years I lived in Shellman, I found the alcoholics to be fairly comparable to the college graduates, and in some cases more interesting. An alcoholic lawyer from Cuthbert, which is the county seat only twelve miles away, came to me for counseling, and he explained his problem in this way. "I am a trial lawyer, and when I win a case in court I drink to celebrate. And when I lose, I drink to commiserate."

The reason the Shellman Baptist Church learned about my existence is that I had made a good impression on Dr. Spright Dowell who was President of Mercer University, my alma mater. I had married in my senior year at Mercer, and President Dowell had arranged for me and my bride, MarthaLee, to live in a big old house on campus called Stagger Inn, on condition that we would try to have a good influence on the other students there who had earned that name for the house.

At graduation time Dr. Dowell had a reception for the graduates. It was a hot day in June, 1945, well before the time of air conditioning. I was the only male graduate who showed for this event in shirt sleeves. The Prexy thought this might be the sign of some native intelligence, and. he remembered me in the years afterwards.

In the meantime, President Dowell had some personal contact with Shellman. He had gone there to persuade an aging wealthy resident, Riley Curry, to make a gift to Mercer to endow a Chair of Christian Studies. His conversation with Mr. Curry was overheard by the black manservant in the house. This man later related what he had heard in these words: "Y'all know? Mister Riley Curry done bought hisse'f a muhcy seat in Heab'n. He done paid a hunnert thousan' dollars fer it."

Now you have some of the major players in this drama about to take place in Shellman, and the only other thing you need to know now is that President Dowell, the man who had dispensed a mercy seat in heaven at the price of a hundred thousand dollars, knew that I was graduating from the Southern Baptist Theological Seminary with a Doctorate in Theology, and he told some influential person in the Shellman Baptist Church that I would be just the man to fill their pulpit.

THE SHELLMAN STORY is told here at two levels. There is the narrative covering the events of my Shellman ministry which began under favorable auspices, and after three years of felicity, ran afoul of deeply rooted Southern traditions in the area of race relations. This conflict flared when the U.S. Supreme Court outlawed racial segregation in public schools. It reached its climax with an overwhelming vote to oust me from the pulpit of the Shellman Baptist Church.

In between the initial outbreak of hostilities, and the final rupture of our relationship, there was the hanging. But I must not hasten you on to this event.

The second level of THE SHELLMAN STORY is an attempt to explain how a boy brought up on those same Southern traditions held sacred by the people of Shellman, how that boy, when he had become a man of thirty years, could come to Shellman with a Gospel that would throw the town into turmoil because what he preached was in conflict with the Southern tradition.

So I reached back into my boyhood, and I came up with the people, black and white, who touched my life at a tender age, and caused me to become the man who would fire off a revolution, and be hanged for it in Shellman.

First, there's Sunshine, The homeless black waif who came to live with us because his own Pa was "tard a feedin' 'im." Then there was Dump, the teen age black girl who angered both me and my dog, White Lightnin', and brought down Mama's wrath on all of us.

Uncle Seeb, the black farmer/preacher, and Aunt Hattie, his wife who was wise beyond anything scholars can teach; these were the black people who molded the pliable clay of my boyhood. Uncle Babe, my white Uncle who voiced the feelings of my own people. They all had their influence, even without knowing it.

Mama and Papa. Did they know? And Miss Florrie, my school teacher, and the school bus driver, Fred Powers, who threatened to put me off the bus into the hornets' nest of black anger I had aroused by throwing corn out the window of the moving school bus, yelling "Black Nigger! Black Nigger!" at the black children walking to their dilapidated school house.

There were others. Little Seeb and Ra'Lee, Tobe, my cousin Mutt, and some even whom I failed to recognize in my impetuous rush to grasp life's opportunity by the forelock. The reader will meet these people, these denizens of my boyhood; they are the ghosts, the spirits, the angels both good and bad, who hovered over the Shellman battlefield like the Olympian gods and goddesses before the walls of Troy.

CHAPTER ONE

This is a true story. It is as near the truth as a man can get when he is the principal character in the story. It is what happened in Shellman when I was pastor of the Baptist Church in the years 1951-1954. It is a story of both tragedy and glory. Tragedy because the Shellman Baptist Church had its opportunity to realize its true destiny as the embodiment of Christ in the great racial revolution that enveloped the nation, and failed the test. But of glory because the remnant, the core, the small group of people within the church, rose to the challenge and met it with courage and devotion.

It was a hot Saturday in July, 1951. I had driven alone from Louisville, Kentucky, to this Southwestern corner of Georgia, and Claron Wooten, a local merchant and farmer, met me and welcomed me to the town. "You will spend the night at Truitt Martin's house, and preach at eleven in the morning." It was to be a "trial sermon" for the church members to determine whether the man Doctor Dowell had recommended could actually deliver the goods. I felt confident that I could, for had I not spent ten years in learning all that a preacher needs to know in order to preach the gospel effectively to both the saints and those still wavering at the door of the Kingdom?

Truitt and Mary Laura Martin were a pleasant and friendly young couple. They lived in a big old house on a quiet tree lined street. I was to learn that all streets in Shellman were quiet and tree lined except when the train passed through the center of town. But the Martin home was special. I slept on a feather bed, and awakened early on Sunday morning with the feeling that eyes were staring at me. There were, in fact, three pairs of eyes. They belonged to a mother cat and two furry gray kittens in a basket, and they were curious about the man who had shared their bedroom with them.

At breakfast, a ham, eggs and grits affair to fortify a young preacher for the day ahead, I mentioned the cats, and said that I had already named the kittens Romulus and Remus in honor of the founders of Rome. My hosts offered to give the kittens to me. I said "If the church calls me to be pastor, I will take Romulus when I come." Truitt was a deacon of the church, and I believe, a member of the Pulpit Committee, and whether he saw an opportunity to get rid of a cat, I cannot say, but after the church heard my sermon, the members of the Pulpit Committee told me that they wanted me to come as pastor, and they took me to see the rambling old house that MarthaLee and I were to live in. It was a good house, much bigger than anything we had ever lived in before, and right next door to the church. There was room for Romulus, who was waiting for me when MarthaLee and I arrived a short time later.

I don't think that Sunday morning sermon was anything spectacular, and I don't know how they came to this quick and apparently unanimous decision about me, but I learned later that they had set one pre-condition on which they would not call me. They had decided, sight unseen and unheard, that they would not call me if my wife came with me on the trial visit. Some unpleasant experience with a preacher's wife must have been in their history, but in this case they were short sighted, for MarthaLee was the better part of the bargain, and after they met her they confessed that they had been afraid that If she came with me it would mean that I was dependent on her for my decision. What they did not know was that I went back to Louisville and asked her what she thought before I made my decision. After I gained her consent, I gave them mine.

So while the people in Shellman believed I was wrestling with the Lord in Prayer over whether to come to Shellman, and claim Romulus, I was trying to win MarthaLee over to the idea of living and working in Shellman. She was against it. I had made application for the Air Force

Chaplaincy and was waiting for the appointment to come through. It was slow in coming and I was for going to Shellman. The Chaplaincy would carry the rank of First Lieutenant but I had been a Second Lieutenant in the ROTC, and I had learned that no matter what rank I attained, there would be somebody with a higher rank above me, and I did not like to be under authority. It was something I had shaken off when my father died, and I was not eager to put my neck under the yoke again. What I was to learn in Shellman was that the deacons feel that they hold a rank above that of the pastor, but that discovery was three years away, and I said "Yes" to the church in Shellman and "No" to the Chaplaincy when my appointment did come through.

We called a mover to load and carry our meager furnishings, drove to Shellman, and arrived there two weeks ahead of the moving van. We slept on the floor while we waited, but Romulus was content to sleep there with us, and when the van, which had gone by way of Texas, finally arrived, Mrs. Wooten was there with us. She saw the pitiful little bit of furniture being unloaded, and said "Is that what you have been waiting for?" It had seemed to us to be enough when we were living in one room on campus at the Seminary, but in the church parsonage it did not make much impression. I got the impression that by Shellman standards we might just as well continue sleeping on the floor.

We drove to Atlanta and bought a desk and two chairs, then settled into being the first couple in the Shellman Baptist Church. The School Board hired MarthaLee to teach the second grade in the Shellman Elementary School. The local Lions Club invited me to become a Lion, then saddled me with the job of Scoutmaster for the Boy Scout Troop which the Lions sponsored. I found that sleeping on the ground, under a pup tent was a rough way to go, but I felt that I was helping the boys develop character, and I really enjoyed being out in the woods with them. The Mercer Extension School invited me to teach a class in a nearby town and I was glad to show how much I had learned in my many years in school. D.K. Bynum, a young deacon and treasurer of the church, gave me a fine pointer pup, and I was free to hunt birds on any of the farms in the neighborhood. Life was good, and it was paying to serve Jesus.

In fact, two outlying country churches, Friendship Baptist and Brooksville Baptist asked me to hold services on Sunday afternoons. I accepted their offer, and was able to get double use of my Sunday morning sermons. Whether they were better or worse the second time around I never knew, but I was brought into close contact with the farmers and became the object of their generosity. One farmer, J.O.E. Jackson, a member of the Friendship congregation, drove his pickup truck into town one hot August morning, stopped at the house, and said "You're welcome to come out to the farm and pick all the blackeye peas you want."

I said "Thank you, but I already have."

"I didn't see you out there." Evidently he watched the pea patch closely.

But thinking of the heat in that pea patch, and recalling that peas were Ten cents a can at Mister Land grocery, I said "But I have already picked all the peas I want to pick." I had, in fact, done that years before on the farm in Bibb County, near Macon, Georgia.

Romulus had become a celebrity in the church. Not admired by all, but known by all. He had grown up from a lovable grey Maltese kitten to become a mean and ornery cat. I loved him though because he was a lot of company when I worked alone at my desk, and he liked to ride with me in the car when I made pastoral calls. MarthaLee did not like him because he shed hair on the floor, and when she had to sweep it up he would fight the broom. Mrs. Alma Martin did not like Romulus either. Miss Alma did not like any cats, and Romulus did most to earn her dislike. On warm Sunday evenings he would slip in the open church doors and attend the evening service. Miss Alma was the church organist, and Romulus' favorite place to lie and watch me preach was the top of the church organ. When he leaped up there, Miss Alma went into hysterics and hit a wrong chord.

Once when Miss Alma had come to see me at my office in the church owned home to discuss the music program for the following Sunday, Romulus met her at the door. He became trapped between the door and the screen, began yowling and spitting. Miss Alma fled in panic, and I don't remember what the musical selections were for the Sunday worship service. I remember that Romulus became known as "the preacher's cat", a term of opprobrium comparable to "preacher's kid" in those situations where the preacher has mean children. MarthaLee and I had no children yet, but Romulus was carrying his part of the load very well.

The church was paying me thirty six hundred dollars a year, and that was a handsome salary for a preacher back then. Allowing for inflation, it would be a livable wage today, with a house to live in. MarthaLee's teaching salary helped too, so I was able to pay off my school debt which went back to Mercer days when the Men's Bible Class, of the First Baptist Church in Macon helped to pay my tuition, with the understanding that I would repay it in order to enable another impoverished but worthy student to attend Mercer University. I viewed it as a sacred trust and I paid it off during those three happy years at Shellman. And they were happy years. The people thought I was a wonderful preacher, and wondered when some larger church would steal me away from them. One Sunday we had visitors at the morning worship service, and they commented favorably on my humility. I thought this surely put me in the class with Moses, if not with Jesus himself, and I was right proud of it.

So things went well with me and the people in Shellman and in the two little country churches until the Supreme Court of the United States struck down enforced racial segregation in the public schools of America. Brown versus the School Board ended my pastoral honeymoon in Shellman, Georgia.

CHAPTER TWO

Brown versus the School Board did not take me entirely by surprise, although my early childhood had not prepared me for racial integration. On the farm we had Negro neighbors, and my brothers and I played with the black children, but always with the assumption that we were not social equals. Except when it came to playing marbles. Then we discovered that we still were not equals, but they were superior to us. One Sunday morning we had slipped away from the house and had a game of "winnants" going with Black Seeb's boys, and to make a long game short, Little Seeb had cleaned us out, even taking our "shooting toys." Then we heard Mama calling us to dinner, which was the noonday meal, and when we ran home, all sweaty and red faced, Mama demanded to know where we had been and what we had been doing.

When she learned that we had been shooting marbles with the black children, and "winnants" at that, "winnants" being a form of gambling, and on Sunday, she handed us a bar of Octagon soap and said "Go wash the nigger off yourselves before you sit down at my table to eat." Already knew that white folks don't eat with black folks. Now I knew that they don't play with them either, and if they slip around and do it on Sunday, they must wash away the pollution of their breach of the racial code.

There was also the incident of the school bus. White children rode to school on a big yellow bus, and black children walked in the dust that was thrown up by the passing bus. On one memorable occasion I loaded my pockets with shelled corn and when we passed the black children on the edge of the road, I threw it at them, yelling "Black nigger. Black nigger."

The school bus driver stopped the bus and threatened to put me off in the midst of the angry black children who might have beaten me to death if he had carried out his threat. I was thoroughly chastened, frightened, and afterwards I restricted my corn throwing to the task of feeding the chickens, but it was not until I moved from Macon to Louisville, Kentucky, that I made the discovery that the social mores governing race are not the same everywhere.

I was attending classes at the Seminary in the mornings and working at John Hunt's Gulf station in the evenings, and a black man drove in for gasoline. While I was pumping gas into his tank, he asked me if he could use the rest room, and I told him that we didn't have a rest room. When he drove away, John Hunt said to me "Why did you tell that man that we don't have a rest room?"

"Because we don't have a rest room for blacks." I looked at John as if he had asked a question, the answer to which was self evident.

"We have a men's room and a women's room. That's the only distinction we make here." Now that was a revelation to me, something they had not taught me in college, nor in the first year at the Seminary, although I was to gain a social consciousness on the subject before my studies at the Seminary were completed. On the brink of graduation six years later, some of the students were saying that they didn't know how they were going to handle this new knowledge when they went back to their deep South home states to preach. But I knew what I was going to say because John Hunt had opened my eyes in my first year there. "I will tell it like it is ... in the Gospel," I said, and I did when I got to Shellman where I opened up more than the men's rest room.

I had been the popular and much admired preacher at the Baptist Church in Shellman for two and a half years when the first crack appeared in the door of, not the men's rest room, but the school house.

The rumbling had begun, not in Shellman, Georgia, but in Washington D.C. where the question of racial separation in the schools was before the Supreme Court of the United States.

In Shellman, Georgia the Methodist minister, Reverend Frank Gilmore, a middle aged, mild man, with a pleasant wife and three children, was to be away on the Sunday of January 24, 1954, and this freed up the Methodist congregation to stay home or go somewhere else. Many of the members of the Methodist Church chose to attend the Baptist Church where I was preaching, and they, along with the Baptists, heard my first sermon on the developing racial crisis in America.

My own consciousness of the approach of trouble had been growing for several months, but there had been no open discussion of the matter in Shellman. White children attended the Shellman schools where MarthaLee taught the second grade. Black children attended the school for blacks where, it was assumed, they were taught all they would ever need to know in order for the men to do the work in the white man's fields, and for the women to do the work in the white woman's kitchen. Education in Georgia was said to be "separate but equal."

There were no visible storm clouds, in the sky over Shellman, but I had chosen for my sermon topic The Church's Three Horizons, and the Methodists had come to hear me because the Methodist minister was out of town. I do not know what they expected to hear, but what they did hear was not what they expected.

I am going to give you that sermon here just the way I gave it to the Baptists and Methodists in Shellman on Sunday evening, January 24, 1954. But I have to tell you first that a preacher can say whatever he wants to say to people as long as they don't expect anything to be done about it. It is, indeed, considered courageous for him to "lay it on the line" where the ideals of the gospel are being set forth, but foolhardy for him to start meddling with the time honored traditions at the level of action. But here is the sermon. I had written it all out. I read it just as I had written it. I preserved it just as I had written and spoken it. And God preserved it years later when most of my sermons that had been preserved over twenty years were destroyed in a house fire.

Well, not all of it. But not all of it was burned either. So here is what was saved, and it describes what I was thinking as the dark storm clouds gathered and I wondered whether in the mixture of blessings and curses to come, the Church might have the vision and the courage to measure up to her destiny, and cause the good to outweigh the evil. Having described the three horizons of the Church's vision, I proceeded to the application:

"Now let us apply this principle to a matter confronting us all, and posing for the Church the peculiar problem of setting the truly Christian example in the face of possible hostility. The problem: Equal citizenship rights among all races making up our society. There is at present before the United States Supreme Court the question of abolishing the practice of racial segregation in the schools of the United States of America.

"The Georgia Legislature, acting under the leadership of Governor Herman Talmadge, has prepared and passed legislation which will, they hope, enable Georgians to get around the issue in case the Supreme Court renders a decision against segregation. Now let us bring our three horizons into play.

"Looking at the matter on the horizon of our immediate situation, it is not a pleasant prospect. Many white people in the South have deeply rooted prejudices, prejudices rooted in a history of which we may only dubiously be proud. It is only by denying principles even we now hold to be just, that we can take any pride in the history of slavery in the South. But the prospect of sending white and colored children to the same school in Georgia and in Shellman is not a happy one for the white people; it is questionable whether it appears very bright for the Negroes. Neither, however, is the prospect of losing our local school because our enrollment is so low; nor the prospect of the additional financial burdens which our expanding two-school system places on us. On the local horizon, the end of segregation will mean that the whites will have to swallow pride and prejudice, and admit the Negro into a new kind of fellowship

- the fellowship of learning and of playing together, since sports are a major part of modern education.

"Or, we here in Georgia will lose our public school system, at least in name, by a ruse which is nothing more than an attempt to beat the devil around the bush.

"Now, however, let us lift our eyes, and look at the scene which appears on the world horizon. Here we see such powerful and influential members of the colored races, which are, incidentally, predominant in the world today, as Ralph Bunche, Negro, of the United Nations Organization; Madam Pandit, Indian leader and representative to the U.N.O.; General Chiang Kai Shek, Christian Nationalist; Mao Tse Tung, communist Chinese leader, determining the course of the nations of the world. Moreover, to the world we proclaim that America is the land where full freedom is the heritage of every law abiding citizen. Finally, the Christian Church in its world wide missions, preaches and practises a fellowship of full acceptance of all races on the mission field.

"Indeed, on the world horizon our position of segregation seems indefensible and even inexpedient, and threatens to brand us as hypocrites in the eyes of the world. To the world we say in effect, that we are willing for Ralphe Bunche to speak for us in the assembly of the nations, but we are not willing for Ralph Bunche's child or grand child to sit in the same classroom with ours.

"We point with pride to George Washington Carver and to Booker T. Washington, and say these men have made incalculable contributions to the field of science and teaching, but we are unwilling for our children to learn from them. Now that we are taking the issue out of Shellman, and out of Georgia, and even out of the Southland, we are beginning to see the absurdity of our narrow gauge thinking.

"Still, there is another horizon, the cosmic, the eternal horizon on which God Himself looms with His judgment upon human actions. Here the eternal rightness or wrongness of our position maybe seen. Here all our false pride is stripped away, and the matter stands naked before the eyes of the eternal God, and is judged on the basis of its merits alone. And what will God say to our desperate efforts to maintain our myth of superiority and to justify our position of separateness?

"We know quite well what His verdict is. He will say that He is completely color blind; that He created and loves all alike; that Christ died for the Negro as well as for the white; that with Him there is but one way of dividing men, the righteous and the wicked. That wicked, proud and selfish men are black with the blackness of sin; that the righteous are those whose robes have been made white in the blood bath of humility and obedience; that He has not decreed that the disciples of the Teacher of Galilee should be segregated according to their color as they sit at his feet.

"God will say to us in the cosmic situation, as He has said to us in the historic situation of the War of 1861-1865, that we are wrong, that our position is morally indefensible, that if we continue to try to preserve ourselves we shall lose our lives, that only by dying - by the death of the old man of pride and prejudice and narrowness of heart - may we gain eternal life, the life of God."

How can you measure the impact of a sermon on people? Most don't argue publicly with the preacher unless they see what he is saying as a threat to them. He can say what he wants to say as long as people think nothing will happen to them as a result of what he says. They think, Maybe he doesn't believe what he is saying himself, or doesn't really mean it. And too often he does not. Did the Methodists and Baptists who heard me that evening believe they would have to adjust to a new way of life? Did they believe the storm would strike them? If so, there was very little visible evidence of it because most of them told me they enjoyed the sermon. Some even complimented me on my courage in speaking out on such a sensitive subject.

But most of them? I don't think they believed that I meant what I was saying. Or that I really believed what I was saying. They had grown accustomed to hearing idealistic preaching from the pulpit, then going on with their normal way of life. Maybe they thought for three years I had been warning them of storms that never struck them. Why should they believe that this storm was going to blow their houses away and carry their children away into a land they had never dreamed of?

At any rate, the Methodist minister was back in his pulpit the next Sunday. I was back in my pulpit the next Sunday. I was still the darling of my flock. I was as humble as Moses. Maybe even a little like Jesus himself. And for the next four months of that year 1954, Shellman was a quiet little town. The farmers were planting another crop of peanuts and cotton. MarthaLee was teaching the little children in the second grade to read and write and do arithmetic and be decent members of society. I was leading the Boy Scouts in the Pledge of Allegiance to the Flag of the United states of America.

Then on May 17, 1954, the axe was laid to the root of the tree.

CHAPTER THREE

Mrs. O'Malley's cow kicked over a lantern in the early morning darkness, and started the great Chicago Fire. That's according to legend. And it sounds reasonable enough to me. I wrote a letter to the Editor of the Atlanta Journal/ Constitution, and got hanged, after setting off a conflagration that swept first through Shellman, then the Southland of the nineteen fifties. That too, is legend, but legend is what this story is. For Herman Talmadge was Governor of Georgia, and the Supreme Court of the United States handed down an unpopular opinion on race. And I had preached a sermon based on an obscure Old Testament text. I called the sermon "Where is the Non-Conformist Today?" and nobody would have needed to look beyond my pulpit to find him.

Let's begin with the Supreme Court, for on May 17,1954, the nine justices said that the principle of racial segregation in the public schools is contrary to the Constitution on which our democratic way of life in this country is built. This came as a great blow to the people of the South who had considered the separation of white and black races into two strata to be normal. White people were better than black people. White people were good to black people as long as black people stayed in their place. And everybody knew where black people's place was. Separate from, and below, that of white people. This applied to the public school system. White children were hauled to brick school houses in big yellow school buses; black children walked, if they went at all, to clap board leaky roofed shanty type buildings, sometimes located adjacent to a Negro church house and graveyard. The Supreme Court of the United States said this was wrong and would have to stop. The people heard what the Court said and they were stunned into sullen silence.

Except for the Governor of Georgia. That was Herman Talmadge and he was not silent. He spoke up and said black children would not go to school with white children in the State of Georgia as long as he was Governor. He aimed to finish out his term of Governor too, just as his father, Eugene Talmadge had finished both of his terms as Governor, happy and successful in keeping the races apart.

I was not silent either. I found that story about the prophet Micaiah and I preached a sermon about him in the Shellman Baptist Church and this is it:

"Micaiah was a non-conformist. He would not say what people wanted him to say. He would not speak good of an evil king, so he was branded as a subversive. He would not agree with the great majority of the religious leaders, so he was branded as a heretic. In matters both political and religious he was a nonconformist, so Micaiah was hated by the king and despised by the prophets

"We are living in a political, religious and social climate that produces the prophets who speak favorably by the hundreds, but it's a rare bird who appears in our day to speak out against the kings and governors who want their actions sanctioned by God, or at least by the people, and it is a rare bird who will contradict the four hundred who with one accord speak favorably to the ruler."

Now I am going to interrupt my own sermon to tell you that people in Georgia were beginning to speak out about the Court's decision. On May 23,1954 The Atlanta Journal & Constitution, in its Views of the News, carried a report from newspaper editors in twenty seven Georgia towns. All of them, without exception, expressed the view that their people rejected the Supreme Court's decision on segregation. Their reports covered the attitudes of men in various walks of life, particularly teachers, jurists, and the man on the street.

Now I will return to my sermon on Non-conformity, because it is important for the reader to know that I said all this to my Shellman congregation before I wrote anything to the newspaper, The sermon continues now:

"It is not hard to see that any man who favors the recent Supreme Court decision on segregation is a non-conformist in Georgia. King Ahab has spoken and his four hundred prophets have said "Amen, go up, for the Lord will give it to you." Ramoth Gilead is the white man's exclusive territory and the governor and his puppet legislature are determined to have it.

"But where is the non-conformist in God's program of world revolution? He is at the very center of all the change going on in human thought and human action today. Therefore he is at the forge of tomorrow's accepted patterns of thought and conduct. Tomorrow's conformists will stand where he stands today; the difference will be in their attitude, for they too will defy all change and will thus rob the non-conformist's labors of their spiritual reward. With drawn swords tomorrow's conformists will defend the lines whose exponents today will lose their heads to those same swords.

"When a few bold voices such as Henry Ward Beecher, Charles Sumer, and John Brown, began to speak out against human slavery in the last century, Southern governors and their courts of 400 clergymen came to the defense of the ignominious practice, and went up to take Ramoth-Gilead, but they did not return in peace.

"What will be the outcome of today's crisis? Ahab will not listen to Micaiah. He will listen instead to the 400 who tell him to go up to Ramoth Gilead and triumph. Micaiah will be smitten on the cheek, and perhaps even thrown into prison and fed with a scant fare of bread and water, but Ahab will be slain by an arrow shot at a venture, and the people will turn and flee in terror and dismay.

"And now what has the non-conformist to say in this hour of crisis?"

Again, I must interrupt my own sermon to say that all this talk of Ahab and Ramoth-Gilead might have sounded like so much Bible spouting to some of the people there in church. On the other hand, they were well aware that political fever was running so high that there was even a movement afoot to retain Herman Talmadge in office another term beyond the constitutional limits on account of the segregation crisis. So the people knew very well that I was talking about the governor when I said King Ahab and that I was the non-conformist prophet.

"First, that Ramoth Gilead, the ground of the white man's rule, will not again be ours, and we are wasting ourselves in trying to retake it. White superiority is a shattered myth, and to organize crusades to regain it is to go on a fool's errand.

"Second, that if we would show ourselves superior, then let us excel in Christian grace and charity. Let us show that we are the superior Christians that we claim to be by giving willingly to others what the law would force us to relinquish. Let us accept in the bonds of Christian love, as brothers in Christ, those whom the law would force us to admit to our schools. Let us show that we are better than the world by preferring those who are weak and lowly and of a mean estate. What credit is it to us that we love fellow white Christians? Even the pagans love their own people. Let us learn to love black people if we would show ourselves superior in a Christian sense of the word.

"Third, as to separateness, let us separate ourselves from what is evil and degrading rather than from people who have a different skin color. There is plenty within ourselves, plenty of selfishness and greed and dishonesty, and obscenity, and immorality and profanity, and drunkenness and uncleanness within our own race, to separate ourselves from. There is enough in our own practices that smell to high heaven without our getting worked up over someone else's body odors. Let us indeed be a separate people, but let Christ be the line that separates, not skin color.

"Fourth, the non-conformist would say that he sees no reason why a real teacher who loves to teach should object to having people come and learn from him just because the would-be pupil is black. Do you not teach your colored farm workers how to operate farm machinery, or are you above that? Nor do I see any reason why a person who really wants to learn would refuse to be taught by a person of a different color. Did not colored "mammies" teach you how to dress yourselves when you were children? And do you not even now entrust your children to colored maids who are in fact tutors for the first three or four years of their lives? Did not some old "darky" teach you how to "bait a hook to catch a catfish" when you were a boy? Why is it so objectionable when the same process of teaching and learning is transferred to the class room?"

By this time you would think I was finished speaking, or they with listening. But no, I still had another point to make, and I made it, and it is prophetic. Of what? At least, prophetic of what was going to happen to me.

"Fifth, and finally, the non-conformist would remind you that he is fully cognizant of the risk he takes in sounding this word of warning, but he did not choose the office because he thought it would make him popular. Rather, he was called and sent to perform the office because the Spirit of the Lord must have a mouth to speak the truth amidst the noise and clamor of the courts of the world. Doubtless, some of you will turn from this house and will say to one another "See. Did I not tell you that he would not prophesy good concerning me, but evil?" But I was not sent to sing sweet sounding words to your ears - I was not sent to tell you that you are doing fine, and the Lord will prosper you in whatever you set your hand to do, and give you the victory in whatever battle you choose to fight. Rather I was sent to proclaim to you the whole counsel of God, and to speak the truth without favor, and without fear of any man. If I have failed to do that, then may the Lord judge me whether I am a true prophet or a false, and if false, then may the Lord. close my mouth forever. But if I have spoken the truth, then let every man hear and take heed."

As I look back on this event of fifty years ago and think of the way people felt about the race issue, I am a little bit surprised that I walked out of the church alive. I am more than a little bit surprised that nobody spoke a word of adverse criticism to me about what I had said. I am even astounded that one wealthy lady remarked to me as she left the church: "I agree with you wholeheartedly, but I am afraid I would not be able to take a public stand." And that she never did take a public stand does not surprise me at all. And it will not surprise the reader that I went beyond saying what I said to the church. Indeed, the very next day I wrote that letter to the editor of the newspaper. And I chose the Atlanta paper that covers Dixie like the dew.

What inspired me to write the Letter to the Editor was the appearance of all those other Letters to the Editor. All of them were expressions of anger and rebellion against the ruling of the Supreme Court, They were from politicians, school teachers, everyday citizens who had their backs up over the decision. In two pages of letters there was not one that had a kind word for the nine old men on the Supreme Court. Not one that seemed to me a reasonable approach to the issue of racial integration of the public schools. It appeared that we were going to fight the Civil War over again.

So I wrote my Letter to Editor Childers in which I summarized the sermon I had preached in the pulpit of the Baptist Church in Shellman. The sermon had not drawn any fire when I preached. When it appeared in the Atlanta paper a week later and was delivered to the front porches of the residents of Shellman, The people of Shellman saw their pastor's name attached to a Letter to the Editor of the Atlanta paper, and they were incensed. Here's the Letter.

The Editors: Your coverage of Georgia's reaction to the recent decision of the Supreme Court on segregation in the Public Schools certainly reflects the feeling of the majority of Georgia's people and their leaders. There is, however, a minority voice.

The unpleasant truth is that the Supreme Court has rendered a just decision, and we must accept it or perish simply because it is right. It is not the Supreme Court that is playing politics in this case, but the political leaders of Georgia. Our hot-headed Governor and his puppet legislature are leading the people of Georgia into a trap from which we will not escape whole. For the governor's madness will foster and encourage violence on the part of men who are ruled by their passions and prejudices rather than by reason and regard for justice. Where then will our people be? They will be like sheep without a shepherd, scattered upon the mountains, set upon by ravening wolves and falling into pits of destruction. And scanning the political scene, one sees not a single candidate for the governor's office who proposes to face the reality that an abominable tradition has come to an end, and we have entered a new era of social justice.

We stand in danger of losing our public school system, but what is worse of losing the respect of decent minded men throughout the world for the sake of carrying a senseless crusade to defend the shattered myth of white superiority, and to preserve a tradition of separateness grounded in the ignominious practice of human slavery, the darkest blot ever made on the white man's escutcheon. If there were any validity to our claims to a living Christian faith, we would have already granted to our black brothers, of our own volition and desire, the privileges which the law now requires that we give them.

For why should the true teacher, who loves to teach above all else, object to sharing what he knows with students of another race? And why should a person who really wants to learn refuse to be taught by one of a different color? For that matter, is there any reason - prejudices aside - why white children and black children cannot learn together in the same classroom?

They are going to have to live in the same world, and not in the roles of master and slave. Can the true teacher shut up the wells of his knowledge to one who is thirsty, simply because his skin is black? And does the one who is suffering from thirst refuse the water of life because it is offered to him in a black pail? Or would the thirsty turn away unsatisfied simply because others of a different color wait beside the same fountain? Education is primarily a matter of mind and heart, of a mind that is free to learn and free to teach the Truth; of a heart that is free to love and free to give of itself without restraint and without fear; of a spirit that knows no bounds of color when it stands in the presence of the mystery of life.

But our school teachers are no longer free; they have sold their birthright for bread, and have bartered their soul for the security of a job. For with one accord they have submitted themselves to the tyranny that is seated in Atlanta; they have with the docility of sheep signed away their personal freedom in an oath of loyalty that has made them the vassals of the state and the pawn of the concentrated power that is able to insert or strike out at will any requirement that the governor my see fit to make.

Does it not seem strange that the same administration that uses the scare of Communism to extract an oath of undeviating allegiance from the teachers now raises the flag of rebellion against the Supreme Court of the United States? Education has become a gubernatorial plaything in Georgia, and before the governor will give up his toy, be will dash it upon the floor and break it into pieces. For "Ahab" has decided to take "Ramoth-Gilead" (cf I Kings 22, The Old Testament) and his "four hundred prophets" have spoken favorably to him, saying "Go up and triumph," but if he returns at all in peace from this fool's errand, then the Lord has not spoken by me.

I added a Post Script: I hope that you will see fit to publish this in your paper, but knowing how great a storm of wrath it may bring down upon your head, I will not feel harshly toward you if you do not.

The editor did publish my letter but it did not bring the storm down on his head; the storm came on mine. And the letter he published was cut down from its original great length. Here it is:

The Editors: Your coverage of Georgia's reaction to the recent decision of the Supreme Court on segregation in public schools, certainly reflects the feeling of the majority of Georgia's people and their leaders .. There is, however, a minority voice ...

The unpleasant truth is that the Supreme Court has rendered a just decision, and we must accept it simply because it is right. It is not the Supreme Court that is playing politics in this case, but the political leaders of Georgia ...

Scanning the political scene one sees not a single candidate for governor who proposes to face the reality that an abominable tradition has come to an end.

We stand in danger of losing our public school system, but what is worse, of losing the respect of decent-minded men throughout the world ...

Why should the true teacher who loves to teach above all else, object to sharing what he knows with students of another race?

For that matter, is there any reason - prejudices aside - why white children and colored children cannot learn together in the same classroom? They are going to have to live in the same world ...

When I saw my letter in print, my first reaction was, He has emasculated it. In fact, I drove to Atlanta, confronted Editor Childers, and told him that. He looked at me with a serious but kindly mien, for he must have thought that my youthfulness and lack of experience had led me into a path of folly, and he said "Quite the contrary. I might have saved you from being badly hurt, even getting shot."

He pointed out to me that he had removed. the more volatile aspects without changing the essence of what I had said. When I got home again in Shellman, I found that he had left plenty in the letter to get me in trouble with the people there. It would, in fact, get me hanged. What puzzled me was that I had said all of it and much more directly to the people in Shellman. From the pulpit I had confronted them with the challenge in much stronger terms. And they had not raised an eyebrow nor spoken a word of protest. But when it appeared in the newspaper, the most prestigious newspaper in the Southeast, over my name, and the name of Shellman, it was a different matter. It was as if I had spoken for Shellman, and Shellman did not believe the way I had spoken.

So Editor Childers had left plenty in that letter to get me hurt, and I would soon begin to feel the pain.

Still, I was going to have more to say on the issue because I believed that I was right, that God was speaking through me to the people on the racial issue. And there was radio.

But before I can tell you about Brown vs. The School Board, I must tell you about Sunshine. Sunshine and the Snipe. For this is one of the earliest of my boyhood memories. And unless you see the boy I was, at five, you cannot truly see the man I was at thirty. If I had been born in Brooklyn; if I had gone to Yale, and then to Union Theological Seminary, the people of Shellman might have believed that, misbegotten, misguided and misinformed as a born and bred Yankee might well be, then I might have said and written the things I said and wrote in Shellman. But for a native son of Georgia, brought up by respectable parents who occasionally went to the local Baptist Church, and always maintained a strict line of demarcation between themselves and black people, for such a man to say and write the things I was saying and writing was inconceivable.

Had I not attended the all white public schools of Bibb County? Graduated from all white Mercer University? And held a Doctor's Degree from all white Southern Baptist Theological Seminary? And even served as student pastor of all white Baptist churches in Georgia, Kentucky and Indiana? Then for such a man to drop down like a meteor from the sky, right into the pulpit of the all white Shellman Baptist Church, and say and write the things I was saying and writing demands an explanation. That explanation will be found in the place least suspected: my boyhood in the home of my Mama and my Papa.

To understand this, the Reader must be told that both my Mama and my Papa had two codes of racial justice which neither of them even suspected were contradictory. Mama believed that there is an uncrossable line drawn between white people and black people, and that for either to cross that line will result in contamination of the white person and endangerment for the black one. But she also believed that for a white person to do or say anything damaging to the person or the self image of a black person was a mortal sin on the part of the white person committing such an act, punishable by God at the Judgment Day, if not sooner.

Papa believed that all "niggers" were by nature, and by some special edict of God, inferior to all white men, and were required to show by their conduct that they knew and accepted that. He also believed that some black people were worthy of respect as long as they stayed within the lines drawn by the white man's social order. Some were even worthy of being rescued by him from other less worthy blacks, and he did not hesitate to be the arbiter of this justice, especially if the victim was a small black boy, which brings us to the story of Sunshine.

For in this complicated social order into which I was born, and in which I grew to manhood, there were also black people, especially Seeb and Hattie whom I was taught to call Uncle Seeb and Aunt Hattie, and they had a profound influence on my development from a boy of four or five when Sunshine came into my life, until I was a man of thirty who believed that God had selected him out of the general herd, educated and trained him for a special role in life, and then set him down in Shellman, Georgia, as the pastor of the Shellman Baptist Church there to reveal His Will for people in the matter of racial justice.

I will treat more fully and explicitly the influence of the, black people who played a special role in the family life of the boy I was. But for the moment they must wait while I give my attention to Sunshine, whose story is the story of my very early boyhood when I learned how a little white boy relates to a little black boy, and how Papa's and Mama's values came into conflict without either one of them consciously suspecting that they held any contradictory racial views.

The Reader will, I hope, realize that in these flashbacks to my boyhood, I am Alfie, which is an appropriate rendering of my middle name, Alfred. At age four or five I was too little to go about over the red dirt farm eight miles from Macon, Georgia, bearing on my shoulders the names of England's two most prominent kings. So Alfie I was until I reached that age well enough known by black people to be called Mist' Alfie.

I hope The Reader will also accept the fact that this is not the first time these tales have been told. I have, in fact, embedded them in my autobiographical Alfie Stories which have not been accorded the recognition I think they deserve. They are my stories though. Nobody else owns them. I can't plagiarize myself, and I claim an old man's privilege of repeating myself in telling again the tales of the halcyon days of my boyhood, since they are necessary for you to see the boy I was in order to understand the man I became. So after teasing your interest in Sunshine all this while, I Will tell you now Sunshine's hunt for the Snipe in which I, as the little boy Alfie, played a minor role, with Mama and Papa playing the leads.

SUNSHINE

"You better never do nuthin' to git sent to the chain gang for, Sunshine." I was very serious. "Because Tex told me they will put dogs on you if you try to run away." Tex was my Hero in Black and White Stripes. He was the only white man on the chain gang and he drove a big dump truck and drank water from the bucket at our well.

Sunshine's eyes became as big as saucers at this news, but he was not daunted by the threat; he had already been threatened with the chain gang by his Pa. I had opened up a whole new dimension of it for him though and he put up a brave front. "Shucks! Ah run so fas' them ol' dawgs never ketch me."

I wished Sunshine had been there when Tex stopped for water and told about the "nigger boy they put the dogs on" but Papa had taken Sunshine with him to pull some weeds out of the corn. I would have begged to go too if I had not been watching for Tex's dump truck. Still I hoped Sunshine would be more careful not to get sent to the chain gang.

But the chain gang stopped work at sundown, and there was no use for me to watch for Tex any longer. Besides, Papa had come home from the corn field and Sunshine had come with him, so Sunshine and I were playing together in the corn crib when Papa called "Sunshine! You come here to me!" Papa's blue eyes were dancing with mischief which Mama noticed with suspicion. Then Papa turned to Mama. "Where's Sunshine at? I want 'im."

Mama was feeding some day old corn bread to her chickens. She crumbled the corn pone and threw it onto the ground where the hens, six

Rhode Island Reds, four Buff Orpingtons, and eight Barred Rocks called Domineckers, were jostling one another for the crumbs. "I sent Sunshine to the crib for two ears of corn but Alfie went with him, so I imagine they have got up a game and forgot what they went after." Mama studied Papa's face and became certain about the mischief "What do you want with Sunshine?"

"Never mind." The hint of mischief had become certainty. "I want 'im." He called louder "Sunshine! You heah me! Come 'ere!"

Sunshine appeared, like a genie out of a bottle. He was holding an ear of corn in each hand. "Heah Sunshine is." A happy, grinning black boy announced himself. He was echoed by an equally happy, grinning, expectant white boy who trotted at Sunshine's side. I was that little white boy.

"Here's Sunshine, Papa!" I announced, as if I had delivered Sunshine to Papa on demand. "What do you want with Sunshine, Papa? Here he is."

Both Sunshine and I stood looking up at Papa, but casting glances at Mama too. Sunshine's face showed a generous expanse of white teeth and eyes contrasting with the blackness of his skin. My own big brown eyes were set in a round white face with a blush of pink in it that denoted recent exertions in the game Sunshine and I were playing in the corn crib. Sunshine's thin black wrists extended from the made-by-Mama flour sack shirt sleeves. His ankles showed below the already outgrown overalls. Mama said "Give me the corn, Sunshine. It took you an awful long time to pick up two ears of corn."

"Yes 'm" Sunshine said, but he kept looking at Papa. Sunshine was older and taller than I was. Wiser in the ways of the world, a harsh, demanding world, which had taught him fast. He was skinnier and weighed less than I did. And he was black. He gave the two ears of corn to Mama and said "Me an' Alfie, we got to playin' an' I fergot."

I repeated "Here's Sunshine, Papa. I told 'im you wanted 'im." I idolized Sunshine, but Sunshine was a black idol, and a black idol had to do what his worshiper wanted. Sunshine was my dark shadow. I was the bright effulgence of Sunshine's ebullient person. Now Sunshine turned his ebony face up to Papa, ready to do whatever Papa commanded. I turned my cherubic face up to Papa, ready to be included in whatever Papa wanted Sunshine to do.

"Sunshine," Papa said. "You go back to the corn crib and git me a croaker sack. Make haste now. We're goin' on a snipe hunt."

Sunshine stared at Papa, uncomprehending. "Make haste!" Papa spoke impatiently "Dark'll ketch you while you're standin' there." Sunshine turned and ran toward the corn crib. Mama looked reprovingly at Papa, then began shelling the corn for the chickens.

"Can I go too, Papa?" I was torn between running with Sunshine to the corn crib and staying to beg permission to go on the snipe hunt. "Can I go On the snipe hunt with you, Papa?"

"You can't go this time," Papa reached for the two ears of corn that Mama was shelling. He, rubbed them together vigorously, and the corn flew in every direction; the hens ran in every direction to pick it up. "You'll hafta wait till you're bigger before you can go snipe huntin'." My face fell before this rejection. "But you run an' help Sunshine find a croaker sack." I turned toward the corn crib, and Sunshine, but the joy was gone.
"Aw shucks, I wanta go snipe huntin' too, if Sunshine goes." When I was out of earshot, Mama turned suddenly on Papa. "You ought to be ashamed of yourself. He's just a child. Just a homeless child. It doesn't matter if he IS black. You ought to be ashamed."

Papa might have felt shame under Mama's words, but he didn't admit it. "It ain't gonna hurt 'im." Papa finished shelling the corn and threw the cobs on the ground. "He WAS homeless. And he IS black. But it 'AIN'T gonna hurt 'im."

Yes, Sunshine was homeless. That is, he was homeless that morning when he appeared on the back doorsteps. It was only a few days after Sandy, the mostly Collie dog, took up at our house. Quite early in the morning. Papa had just finished breakfast and be had gone onto the porch to roll a cigarette and smoke while he made up his mind about what had to be done that day. And there was the little black boy sitting on the bottom doorstep, with Sandy crouching happily beside him and trying to lick his face. The little black boy was trying to push Sandy away to keep him from licking his face but not trying very hard.

Not trying to push Sandy all the way away. When Papa looked at him there on the doorstep he seemed to be all elbows and knees, both of which showed through the tattered shirt and overalls with patches on top of patches.

He was all eyes too. His eyes seemed to fill his face. Luminous. Expectant. Waiting, fixed on Papa. "Well" Papa said, taking out his little bag of Bull Durham. "Where'd you come from, Sunshine?"

It was on impulse that Papa called him Sunshine. But Papa was like that. He would look at somebody for the first time and give him a name. Always a name that would fit. Because Papa seemed to know what to call somebody the first tine he ever saw him. If Papa had been in the world at the time of the Creation and the Lord had run all the creatures past him the way He did Adam, Papa would have known just what to call each one of them. He would have reeled off their names without even having to study about it. So when Papa saw a little black boy in tattered overalls and a face shining up at him, Papa said "Well, Where'd you come from, Sunshine?"

"Ah run away fr'm home," the newly dubbed Sunshine replied. His big eyes were searching Papa's face, pleading, wondering. "Can Ah stay heah?" Sandy's tail now thumped the doorstep; his tongue dripped saliva; he turned to lick Sunshine's face.

"How come you run away from home, Sunshine?" Papa sifted a thin wafer of paper from a package, and started to pour tobacco into it when he had cupped it with his fingers. "Does your Pa know where you've run off to?" Papa sat down on the top doorstep and began twisting the paper full of tobacco into a cigarette. He studied Sunshine's face closely, but he didn't seem to be the least bit surprised to find Sunshine sitting on his doorstep. Nor was even surprised by Sunshine's request to stay.

"He don' keer." Sunshine dodged Sandy's tongue and looked down at his knee, which was showing through a hole in his overalls. "My Pa say he don' keer where Ah goes." He hesitated, picked at the threads around the edges of the hole in the knee of his overalls. "Pa say he tard a feedin' me."

Papa struck a match on the doorstep. He held the flame to the twisted paper at the end of his cigarette. It caught. He drew in the smoke. Shook the flame from the match and threw it onto the ground. "All right Sunshine. You can stay here."
Papa drew in some more smoke and let it out through his nostrils. "You can stay here till your Pa comes for you. But you'll hafta mind me. You hear?"

Sunshine heard. "Yassuh. Ah minds you." He was eager to please. "Ah minds You good."

Papa called Mama from the kitchen. She stood on the porch looking at Sunshine. She said "Another stray. Yesterday a stray dog. Today a stray child. What will tomorrow bring?"

Papa said to Mama "This un' here is Sunshine. He's gonna stay. At least until we put some meat on his bones. Or till his Pa comes to take 'im back."

Mama said "He looks half starved."

"I s'pect he could clean up any biscuits you had left from breakfast." Papa examined Sunshine's head for lice. "Only thing is, I'm skeered if he stands up them overalls'll fall off 'im." Satisfied there were no lice, Papa turned Sunshine's head loose.

Mama said "You come in the kitchen, Sunshine." And she said to Papa "You'll have to fix up a place for him."

"I'll take keer of that." Papa flipped the used up cigarette onto the ground. "I can fix him a place in the smokehouse, but there ain't no hurry about that. It's just now sunup and he ain't goin' to bed till dark. But you better feed 'im quick before he starves to death. He says his own Pa got tired of feedin' 'im. It musta not took much to make his Pa tired, from the looks of the boy."
I stared in wide eyed wonder at the new arrival, and moved closer to establish my claim on Sandy, who in two days had become my dog.

Papa got together everything he thought he would need to fix a place for Sunshine in the smokehouse. Hammer, saw, nails, boards. He kept sending me for little, things he had forgotten, and when it was all assembled, and Papa had laid out his plans, he sent me for a match. Run and tell your Mama to send me a match." Then he started rolling a cigarette, and when he had it about ready, I came back with a match which I held up proudly to Papa, but he said "it takes two to make a match Son." It was my second arithmetic lesson, Papa style. The first one was: "Oughts ought, and nine's a figger; all for the white man and none for the nigger."

I ran back to Mama who was already lighting a fire under the washpot to boil water for Sunshine's disinfection. "Did that one go out?" she asked.

"No'm. But he won't strike it till he has two. Papa says it takes two to..."

"I know." Mama had heard it before. She gave me another match, and turned back to Sunshine saying "Lordy Mercy!" Sunshine was eating the last biscuit from the breakfast batch. His face showed utter contentment but Mama put an end to it. "Get your clothes off, Sunshine. They're going in the pot and you're going in the tub." She unwrapped a new bar of Octagon Soap tore the coupon from the wrapper and stored the coupon in her apron pocket."Get them off!" she said to the embarrassed little black boy. "I don't guess you're any different from the four boys already running around here. Only the color of your skin. Get those rags off!"

Papa stepped outside the smokehouse, looked at naked Sunshine, and said "Good idea. Clean 'im up. If every stray in the county is gonna take up here we'll hafta keep the washpot boilin' in self defense."

Papa went back inside the smokehouse, sawed and hammered for two hours, built a bed frame of two by fours, nailed on the slats to support a mattress, shaped a table of rough boards on four sturdy legs, and fastened it to the wall for extra support. He built a small wooden box, open at the top, for Sunshine's, clothes and anything else he might accumulate. "I'll make a lid for it later," he told me, "if I see anything in it that needs coverin' up."

"Papa," I asked, "is this gonna be Sunshine's room all by hisself?"

"Yes, Son. He's come to live with us now and he'll hafta have a place of his own here in the smokehouse. Till his Pa comes for 'im anyway."

"How come Sunshine can't stay in the house with me, Papa. How come he couldn't sleep with me?"

"Sunshine's black. That's how come. Black folks don't sleep with white folks."

I was thoughtful. "Papa, will Sunshine's Pa come an, take him back?"

"I wouldn't be surprised." Papa struck the head of a nail a couple more times. "About the time we put some meat on his bones."

Sunshine had slipped in and was squatting on the floor beside me. Sandy had come inside too, and he was thumping his tail on the floor. I said "Papa, Can I stay out here with Sunshine sometimes? Mama has done cleaned 'im up. Can I sleep out here with him sometime? Till his Pa comes and takes 'im away from us?"

Papa sat down on the table, testing its strength. It didn't sag. He reached two fingers inside the bib pocket of his overalls, took out the little sack of Bull Durham. Then a cigarette paper. Poured the tobacco into the cupped paper. Rolled it. Twisted it at each end and put one end between his lips. Found that second match. Struck it on the table top and held the flame to the cigarette. Shook the match out and dropped it onto the floor. Drew the smoke into his lungs and expelled it.

I watched, my mouth standing open. Sunshine waited, rolling white eyeballs now at me and then back at his own bare feet extending from the overalls which had belonged to Junior until an hour ago when Mama decided to burn Sunshine's rags rather than try to get them clean. Sandy thumped the floor with his tail, looked up at me and Sunshine, then fixed his eyes on Papa and smiled.

Papa had been about to repeat what he had said about black folks and white folks not sleeping together. Now he smoked and looked steadily at me and Sunshine, one white with a pink bloom on him and one black with a shine on him. He was thinking. Then he said "It'd be a mighty long way for you to hafta run in the middle of the night if you was to wake up and take a notion you wanted to crawl in the bed with your Mama an' me." Papa stubbed out the cigarette; it had burned down so short it almost burned his hard, callous fingers when he took it out of his lips. He exhaled the last of the smoke.

I remembered then how good it felt, how warm and safe, in the bed between Mama and Papa. Sometimes I would fall asleep there while Papa was telling me a story. Then I would awaken in my own bed, alone, afraid, wet. I would crawl out of my own bed and find my way back, in the darkness, to the big bed, crawl in between Mama and Papa, and then I would no longer be afraid and alone. Still wet but I would try to forget the wet and would fall asleep again, safe, happy. In the morning Papa would wake up when the first streak of light touched the Eastern sky. He would call out to Mama, and say "God A'Mighty! Now how did this youngun wind up in our bed? And wet too!"

"You sure you wanta sleep out here with Sunshine insteada with your Mama' an' me?" Papa waited for my decision, his blue eyes twinkling.

I kicked my bare feet one against the other. I ducked my head, then looked back at Papa. "I'm glad we got Sunshine, Papa. But I ruther sleep with you an' Mama."

Sunshine had stayed on with us, sleeping alone in the little bed Papa had built for him in the smokehouse. He had put a little meat on his bones with Mama's cooking, which he ate alone in the kitchen where Mama fixed a plate of food for him because he could not eat at the table with us. He had became my dark shadow and my sometimes obedient idol. And now Papa planned to take him on a snipe hunt. And Mama had said to Papa "You ought to be ashamed of yourself."

And while Mama was endeavoring unsuccessfully to make Papa ashamed of himself, Sunshine and I had gone to the corn crib where we found a croaker sack, which is just a burlap feed sack. Then Sunshine came dragging the croaker sack with Sandy hanging to it with his teeth bared, growling and shaking it in mock battle and providing a full measure of enjoyment for both me and Sunshine, but Papa called out a warning, "Sunshine, you be keerful you don't tear a hole in that croaker sack. If there's a hole in it the snipe will run right through it and git away!"

Papa's word of warning brought Sunshine back to the business at hand, which was the snipe hunt. He stopped and tried to get the burlap bag out of Sandy's jaws, but Sandy knew a good thing when he had sunk his teeth into it, and he settled back onto his haunches and growled and shook his head from side to side. Sunshine held on, but he looked up at Papa and said "How we gon' ketch dat ol snipe anyhow? How we gon' do it?"

"We'll run 'im in that croaker sack unless you aim to let that damn' dog run off with it." Papa reached for the contested sack, got hold on it, and Sandy renewed the struggle with greater zest because now he had a real contest with a worthy opponent. But Papa was in no mood for foolishness with a dog, and he clapped Sandy sharply on the ear with the palm of his open hand. Sandy turned loose and dodged a second blow.

Sunshine, without Sandy for a counterforce fell over backwards with the burlap bag clutched in his hands. Papa snatched the bag and spread it out on the ground.

"Now look here, Sunshine," Papa said in severe tones. "You hold the sack open like this." He opened the mouth of the sack. Sunshine, Sandy and I watched enraptured, but Papa addressed himself to Sunshine alone. "You'll be down in that big gully that runs through the cotton patch at the other end." Papa waited until Sunshine's face showed that he understood where he would be. "Then me an' Mister Charles will drive the snipe down the gully to you. When he runs in the sack, you close it like this." And Papa clamped the mouth of the bag shut and twisted it making the bag jump about as if there were some living thing in it. "We've got 'im! Git away Sandy!" for seeing the bag jump about, Sandy had come back to renew the struggle, but Papa swatted him again. Sandy dodged the main force of the blow and stood back, his ears standing alert but drooping slightly at the tips.

"You think you can do that now, Sunshine?"

Sunshine dropped on to the ground, distended the mouth of the bag and imitated Papa's movements, even to making its imagined contents jump about inside. "Shucks! Ah ketch dat ol snipe f'r sho. He ain't gonna git away from me."

I had stood sullen and silent throughout this demonstration of bagging the snipe. Now I turned to Mama and said "I wanta go too. I could hold the croaker sack as good as Sunshine. Make Papa let me go too."

Mama said nothing. She put her hand on my shoulder and turned judgmental eyes on Papa. "Not this time," Papa said. "This time's for Sunshine. your time will come." But seeing Mama's eyes, Papa amended this statement. "Your time may come." And because he saw that I was about to cry, "Tell you what Son. You stay here with your Mama an' wait up for us because we'll come in all hot and tired and thirsty an' we'll need you to help us take the snipe outta the croaker sack. Takin' 'im can be a bigger job than runnin' 'im in there."

I was not mollified; I clung to Mama and snuffled, but Mama said "Stop acting like a baby now. You don't want Sunshine to see you acting like a baby."

I hated Sunshine at that moment, and I determined never to sleep with him even if Mama and Papa agreed to it, because Sunshine was going on the snipe hunt and Papa wouldn't let me go. Then Papa remembered something. "Sunshine, You run and fetch the lantern, and don't you try to light it either. I ketch you strikin' matches and settin' somethin' afire around here and I'll put you in a croaker sack with the snipe an' dip the two of you in a tub of cold water." Papa thought this ought to mollify me but it didn't.

Sunshine dropped the croaker sack and ran to get the lantern. As soon as he dropped it, Sandy grabbed the bag again and began shaking it, but with nobody on the other end, the challenge was gone, so Sandy soon lost interest and turned to watch Sunshine, debating in his canine mind whether to chase after him or to stay with the white folks. I decided that I didn't hate Sunshine enough to let him have all the glory of bringing the lantern to Papa, so I ran after Sunshine and this settled the issue for Sandy; he ran after me.

The lantern was hanging on a nail driven into one of the two by four studs holding up a partition between the milking stalls. Sunshine stood on tiptoe, then climbed the stud to get it down. "Wusht Ah had me a match," he said just as I drew up breathless. "Ah strack it an' light dis ol' lantern an' see ef it give off anuff light f'r me to see dat ol' snipe."

"You better not!" My hostility had returned "You heard what Papa said about strikin' matches." But Sunshine was too elated over the prospect of going snipe hunting to let even the threat of being dipped in a tub of cold water dampen his spirits. He laughed wildly and dashed away, swinging the lantern.

I was still concerned that Sunshine might try to light the lantern, and I ran beside him all the way back to Papa. I was going to tell Papa what

Sunshine had said but Mister Charles had arrived and he seemed concerned about something Mama was saying to him and Papa about the snipe hunt.

What Mama was saying was that she didn't approve of what Papa and Mister Charles were planning to do to Sunshine because it wasn't right, and God would surely punish them for it. "If not in this life, then surely at the Judgment Day." Mister Charles was a regular church goer and he was feeling nervous under Mama's stern words, but he had given Papa his word on the matter and he didn't want to back out. Papa was defensive.

"It 'ain't gonna hurt 'im," Papa was talking loudly because he was under attack. "I ain't never heard tell of nobody gittin' hurt on a snipe hunt." Sunshine had now arrived with the lantern in hand, and he stopped with his mouth wide open to listen to what was being said. "Here, Sunshine. Give me that lantern. What took you so long? Did you git lost between here and the barn?"

Sunshine started to defend himself by making an excuse. "Hit dark in dat ol' barn widout no light." But Papa wanted to get away from Mama's eyes, and he grabbed the lantern and shook it vigorously to determine if it had any kerosene in it. Then he opened the lantern and ran his finger along the oil soaked wick. He struck a match, giving Sunshine a warning glance to let him know that he was not allowed to strike matches. He applied the flame to the wick; it caught and flared up. Papa adjusted it and closed the chimney.

"Chimney's nearly as black as you are, Sunshine, but there ain't time to clean it now. You can do that in the mornin'. I 'reckon we don't need a bright light. It might skeer the snipe before we're ready to jump 'im."

Mister Charles was eager to get going because of Mama, and he said "You grab the croaker sack, Sunshine, and don't drag it on the ground thataway. You'll drag the bottom outta it and the snipe will run right through it and git away from you."

Sunshine pushed out his lower lip and set his jaw in a determined line. "Ol snipe ain' gonna git away from me. Now you git away, Sandy, and quit tuggin' at dis yere croaker sack. Ol snipe come runnin' down at me an' Ah ketch 'im so quick he don' know who got 'im."

Mister Charles laughed, glanced back once more at Mama who had wrapped her arms about me and still giving Papa and Mister Charles a disapproving stare. "Well, you see that the snipe don't high ball it right past you before you're ready for him. Looks like it might frost tonight and if that snipe has frost on his tail feathers he's gonna be hard to hold."

"Ah hol' 'im awright." Sunshine balled up the burlap bag to keep it away from Sandy. "Don' you worry none 'bout me holdin' him, Mister Charles. Ah hold him come frost or no frost. Ah ain't turnin' no ol' snipe aloose."

Sandy was still watching for a chance to grab the bag away from Sunshine, and Papa said "Here, Alfie, you hold onto Sandy till we're clean outta sight, and don't turn him loose even then. We don't need him skeering up the snipe before we're ready." I held onto Sandy, but more to reduce my own sense of loneliness than to keep Sandy from running up the snipe before Papa was ready for the snipe to run. I silently hoped the snipe would get away from them.

I hugged Sandy close and it helped a little but a great loneliness settled over me. I sat on the doorstep, hugging Sandy and watching the dim and blurry silhouettes of the snipe hunters as they walked away into the gathering darkness, but the greater darkness was inside me; the tears flowed down my cheeks

Into the dying evening of early October the snipe hunters walked. Papa and Mister Charles and Sunshine. Papa walked with long swinging strides, swinging the lantern as he went. Mister Charles matched Papa's stride, but he was breathing rapidly. His gum rubber boots clunked on the hard ground. Sunshine danced alongside, ahead of them, behind them, clutching the, balled up burlap bag, the croaker sack that was to entrap the snipe.

I watched them as they walked away. Self pity overwhelmed me. Tears rolled down my cheeks. Sandy whined and licked my face, wiping the tears away with his tongue. Mama stood up, straightened her dress, looked down at me. "No sense sitting here all night. Come on in the house. It's getting chilly ... Sandy can come with you."

That was a big concession to my grief.

Mama's own bitterness then came to the surface. "Or he can go traipsing off after the snipe hunters." Sandy came inside with me and curled up on the floor near Mama's feet.

Darkness settled in over the snipe hunters. Dried and broken corn stalks rustled and rattled in a rising breeze. Dry, brittle grass crunched under Papa's heavy brogan shoes and Mister Charles' gum rubber boots, rustling quietly under the light tread, the soft touch of Sunshine's ragged tennis shoes. As if by some dark work of magic, a canopy of black velvet fitted itself over a sky that had glowed with a pale rose light a short while ago. Stars appeared in the black velvet. A crescent moon hung in their midst. The light of the stars and of the moon was like distant sparklers in the black velvet canopy. On the path that led across the cotton patch was the light of the swinging lantern, flickering and wavering beside Papa's rapidly moving legs.

They walked to the mouth of a large gully running across the cotton patch and into the cow pasture. Two strands of barbed wire separated the cotton patch from the cow pasture. Open, empty cotton bolls hung from the bare stalks. In the nippy autumn air their sharp points pricked Sunshine's legs through his thin overalls. "Well, here we are!" Papa announced in a voice slightly affected by the memory of Mama's disapproval. He held the lantern up level with his own face. Light and shadow played across his countenance. "Here's the big gully. Here's where you're gonna ketch your snipe, Sunshine."

At home, Mama lifted the tall glass chimney from the Aladdin lamp. She was careful not to disturb the fragile mantle as she put the flame of the match to the wick. The mantle heated slowly, then glowed with an incandescence that made me glad that they had carried the old stinking lantern off with them on the snipe hunt. When she was confident that the lamp would not overheat, and the flame would not run up and destroy the mantle, Mama picked up the little shirt she was making for me. She looked at it, then laid it down. Started to thread her needle. Her hand trembled and it was difficult for her to see the eye of the needle.

She drew the thread across her moistened lips. She tried again with the stiffened thread; it went through the needle's eye. "Well!" Mama said, as if she had finally accomplished a tedious task. She knotted the thread.

I stood quietly at Mama's elbow. My eyes followed the jerky movements of the thread. Then I searched her face. "You reckon they'll ketch the ol' snipe, Mama?" Gazing intently into Mama's immobile face, I asked "You reckon sunshine will ketch the snipe in the croaker sack when Papa and Mister Charles run it down the gully?"

Mama drew the knotted thread tight, jerked it. Her lips were tightly compressed. She started to work the buttonhole. "They'll catch their death of cold, and that's all they'll catch." Her tone carried the unspoken hint that the fulfillment of her prophecy would be evidence that a righteous Providence was watching over the affairs of men, even on a snipe hunt. "You're better off right here."

"But I wanted to go." I leaned against Mama's shoulder. "I wish I could go."

I was fighting for control of my voice. Then, "Mama, how come Papa took Sunshine an' wouldn't let me go?" Mama carefully laid the shirt aside. She carefully buried the needle's point in the cloth, and took me in her arms.

"Don't cry about it Son. They won't even be able to see anything in the dark."

"Papa got the lantern, Mama," I snuffled and buried my face in, Mama's breast.

****

"This is the place, Sunshine." Papa held the lantern as high as he could reach. It's movement caused the shadows to flow over the sides of the gully. "Now you stay right here and hold that sack open. You heah? Point it up the gully. That's where the snipe's comin' from. We're goin" up there an' flush 'im out. We'll drive 'im right down the gully and it's your job to ketch 'im. You do just like I showed you. Keep your eyes open. Hold still and don't make no racket. The snipe'll make enough racket for the both of you."

Sunshine hunkered down in the gully. He spread the burlap bag the way Papa had shown him. He picked up a dead twig and propped the mouth of the bag open. His black face glistened as the light of Papa's lantern's rays struck it. Then as Papa started to move away, the intense face disappeared in the gully, merged with the darkness of the night. "Are you ready, Sunshine?" Papa asked.

"Ah's ready for 'im," Sunshine replied bravely although his voice didn't sound as confident as it had when they were at the house.

"Well, don't let the snipe git past you. You heah me?"

"Yassuh, Don' you worry none 'bout ol' snipe gittin' past me. Ah ketch 'im." Now his voice quavered a little.

"All right. Just remember, keep quiet. And no matter what happens, don't move from that spot where you're at. You heah?"

"Ah be right heah an' Ah have ol' snipe all bunched up in dis heah croaker sack when you'n Mister Charles come back." Sunshine shook out the sack, rearranged it, propping it open with his arm cocked on his elbow. As Papa and Mister Charles moved away, Sunshine muttered "Wusht

Alfie was heah." But he did not say it loudly enough for Papa and Mister Charles to hear him.

Papa and Mister Charles walked away, the lantern swinging between them. The gully grew darker and lonelier. Sunshine watched the receding light of the lantern. Fear came upon him and grew like some fungus as Papa and Mister Charles entered a small pine thicket at the edge of the cotton patch, and the light disappeared completely and Sunshine knew that he was alone in the darkness.

The darkness settled on him like a shroud. He opened his mouth to breathe. He gripped the edges of the burlap bag and listened intently to the night sounds. A gust of wind stirred a dry leaf at the lip of the gully. The leaf fluttered like a small bird caught in a snare. A small clod of dry dirt, loosened by Mister Charles' boot when he had passed, gave way now under its own weight, crumbled and rolled down the embankment in delayed action. Far off, a dog barked, and finished on a howling note. Then a new sound, unfamiliar, unidentifiable, high and keening, rose on the night air.

Sunshine raised his head at the sound; he, held his breath; he felt his skin prickle. His scalp tingled. His short, tightly curled hair was charged with electricity. The sound rose in pitch and volume. It was joined by a second sound. The second sound attempted to blend with the first, then pulled apart from it, moaning and transforming itself into a piercing screech.

Sunshine moaned involuntarily in cadence with the sound. He gripped the croaker sack with clenched fists. His nails bit into the flesh of his palms. The sound rolled down the gully, surrounding and engulfing him. His eyes stared into the darkness. He became aware of his own moaning. It was now the only sound in a silent universe. He bit his lips to stop the moaning. Raising his head, he peered over the gully's edge. A light burned in the window of the house he had left less than an hour ago.

The light in the window drew his eyes as a magnet draws an iron filing. Then the sound came again, screeching and moaning in concert on the frosty night air. It rolled down the gully toward him, then stopped. He held his breath, waiting. His eyes grew ever larger, searching the darkness, searching for the light in the window. Cold sweat bathed his face. His hands trembled; they lost their grip on the burlap bag. Tremors passed through his small body, jerking him up from the ground.

The dread hovered over him silently. Then the sound burst upon him again. Closer. Rising out of the darkness in the gully. Rolling along its embankments. He bolted from the gully. His eyes found the light in the window. The light gave wings to his feet. He ran with the wings of urgency, yet it seemed to him that be stood still, not moving in a world that passed by him.

He was suspended in the darkness, and the darkness filled him with terror. In the moving darkness the stiff brittle cotton stalks moved past him while he stood poised, elevated on the wings of time. His feet struck the floor of the front porch. He flung himself against the door. His mouth stood open. Screaming. But no sound came. The door flew open. Jerked open from within. He tumbled in at Mama's feet. "Mama!" I cried. "It's Sunshine! Mama!"

I was on the floor beside Sunshine. Staring into Sunshine's distended, bulging eyes. "Sunshine! Sunshine!" I gasped. "Is it the snipe?!"

"Shet de do'" Sunshine pleaded, gasping. "Shet de do." He gasped again. "Fo dat ol snipe git in heah!" I moved toward the door, but cautiously. Sandy, bristling and barking aggressively, plunged and skittered through the open door to attack whatever might be on the other side. Sunshine collapsed onto the floor again breathing stertorously. "Shet de do'!"

Mama closed the door with a swift, decisive movement. She bent over Sunshine. Lifted him and cradled him in her arms. Sunshine held onto Mama for endless minutes, trembling and shaking. When the tremors stopped, he breathed deeply. He looked at me and stood up. "Ah be awright now. Ah be awright." He grinned at me. Sheepishly. "Dat ol' snipe. He be gone now. Long gone."

Papa and Mister Charles were on the porch now. They were stamping their feet and talking loudly. Sandy was barking a greeting to them. I crouched beside Sunshine, looking into Mama's face. Papa flung the door open wide and the light from Mama's Aladdin lamp flowed out onto the porch. Papa raised the smoky lantern and squinted his eyes against the brightness of the lamp. He raised the smoky glass chimney to the lantern, ran his finger over the crusty, blackened wick. "Light went out on us right after we jumped the snipe."

Then, "What became of you, Sunshine? I told you to hold the croaker sack. Did you see the snipe?"

Sunshine stared back at Papa "Ah seen 'im awright. He come barrelin' down on me lickety split an' he run clean over me. Ah hol' out mah croaker sack an he jus' run right off wid it."

"Hunhh!" Papa was taken aback by Sunshine's response. "Musta been a big 'un." Papa looked now at Mister Charles but Mister Charles didn't offer any help. Papa went on talking. "He was makin' a God awful racket when he come outta that pine thicket. Could you tell whichaway he went, Sunshine?"

"Nassuh. He make so much racket Ah deaf an' blind. Ah can't see which-away he went."

Papa looked more closely at Sunshine. "How come your overalls all tore out the way they are, Sunshine? Did you git hung up in a barb wire fence?"

Sunshine glanced down at his torn overalls. The light from Mama's Aladdin lamp gleamed on his ebony cheeks. The skin was stretched tightly over high cheek bones. The whites of his eyes stood out, dominating his whole face. "Ah didden see no bob wahr fence. Ah jes, see dat ol' snipe runnin' off thew de pasture wid dat ol' croaker sack over his head."

Chapter Four

"It is my time to speak on the Bethel Hour," I said. "And I will speak." The Bethel Hour was a Saturday morning radio program sponsored by the Baptist churches of the Bethel Baptist Association. The radio station, WDWD, was in Dawson, a larger town located about ten miles East of Shellman. Ministers of the local Baptist churches took turns speaking on the program. My time had come up, and I printed an announcement in the church bulletin that I would make "a major policy address." This had alerted the members of the church and they were not happy to learn that I was going on radio with my message on race relations.

Four of the deacons of the Shellman Baptist Church - Claron Wooten, C.T. Martin, Earl Edwards and Manry Stewart, came to me and said "You are just going to add fuel to the fire. We don't think you ought to do it."

The Methodist minister, Frank Gilmore, and the pastor of the Rehoboth Baptist Church, a young man named E.A. Cline, also tried to dissuade me. They wanted me to know that they loved me and that they had no quarrel with my position, but they felt that it would be unwise for me to speak on the radio. "You will just make matters worse." But they promised to pray for me. I think they were praying that I would not stir the already troubled waters in Shellman.

MarthaLee turned her big brown eyes on me beseechingly, but she would not say "Don't do it." I don't know whether it was because she knew it would not stop me or if she felt that I must do what I felt I must do. She stayed home and listened to me on the radio.

"I have received a threatening call," the station manager James Woodall, informed me when I arrived. "The caller urged me not to let you speak." He did not say what the caller had threatened to do. I thought that short of burning down the radio station, the only thing the caller could do was turn off his radio. Mister Woodall said "You can speak on the radio here any time you want to."

This was not the only threat that had come out of Dawson. A grocer there had said that he would not sell groceries to me or to anybody who supported me, Fess Johnson, friend and supporter in the Shellman church, usually bought his groceries there. "But when I heard that," he said to me, "I told him where he could put his groceries."

So on Saturday morning at ten o'clock, on June 6, 1954, I went on the radio at Dawson with just about everybody in the area listening. Some of them were hoping I would not say anything to make matters worse. Some, no doubt, were hoping I would say something that would expose me to open attack. Still others who did not know me at all, were listening just to learn what I did have to say because there were plenty of rumors going the rounds. Only MarthaLee knew what I was going to say because I had read the speech to her at home. But I was in the position of the Negro preacher I had been to hear in Shellman before the trouble arose. He stood before the church and said "Brethren and sistern, I'se ti'ed. I drove all the way up heah from Florida this mawnin' an' I'se tied."

The congregation responded "It don't make no never mind. It's yo' time to preach. Preach on." He did, and when they thought be had preached long enough, they stood up, started singing, and drowned him out. He stopped preaching.

I was not tired. I had driven only ten miles from Shellman to Dawson.

But I admit that I was deeply troubled and anxious about the effect my speech would have on my listeners. I had prepared it very carefully, writing and rewriting it, timing it to fit into the allotted thirty minutes, reading and rereading it to MarthaLee, I was certain that my words would say what I wanted to say. I realized that people would hear what they wanted to hear. Now here is the radio address: THE ROLE OF THE CHURCH IN THE TROUBLED AREAS OF LIFE. I give it to you, patient reader, just as I gave it to the people listening to me.

"This is a troubled hour. But I would not trade places with those who have preceded me, nor would I be willing, if I were able, to deep freeze this hour for generations of the future. I welcome the challenge of this hour though I dread its terrors, in the realization that if I am true, those who have gone before me may rejoice that they have not lived and died in vain, and that those who shall follow me not be ashamed of their heritage. But the trials of our time will not be dealt with effectively by men who are related only to the procession of human forces that have crossed are now crossing, and will yet cross the stage of history. Rather, they will be met, endured, and transformed into victories by men who are directly and vitally related to the divine forces that shape our destiny. For whenever we speak of a Christian's responsibility in life's crisis, we are thinking in terms of the role of the Church, the human, historical embodiment of the divine and eternal Christ; consequently, we are oriented in the direction of human problems and human needs, but we chart our course by the unchanging counsels of Almighty God.

"Let this one principle be understood by all, from the outset: the basis of our deliberations on every social question is theological rather than sociological. To begin with humanistic theses is to predestine ourselves to a relativism that will produce no lasting good; but to stand upon the inmovable foundation of our apprehension of God in Jesus Christ will eventually bring all human action under the light of eternal truth and will subject all human action to the test of eternal justice, while at the same time showing a propensity for grace that causes the uninitiated world to marvel. With this principle firmly fixed in our consciousness, we proceed to the question: What is the role of the Church in the troubled areas of this life?

"It is the first responsibility of the Church to proclaim the undiluted truth of God, with a voice of conviction and authority, and not to echo the confused and meaningless sounds that are made by selfish people whose cries bespeak only their personal reactions of joy and pain with the rise and fall of their personal fortunes. This responsibility is centered particularly in the spokesman of the Church, who must at the same time be deaf to the voices that clamor and shout their unreasoning hatreds, and keenly sensitive to the faintest whisper of the still small voice of God that so often makes itself heard in the feeble cries of those who have for many years borne their burdens in sullen but uncomplaining silence.

"Let not Christian people be deceived. by the fallacy of the democratic mind, for when we have polled public opinion we are no nearer to the essential truth than when we first began. The voice of the people is not the voice of God, and every attempt of man to equate the two has resulted in disaster because national catastrophe is the natural consequence of national idolatry.

"What "everybody thinks" is of no consequence except to those people who make their living conducting public opinion polls. But what God says to a man in the loneliness of his soul when he stands like Elijah on the wind swept heights of the mountain of God; or like Moses is transfixed by the awful reality of the burning Presence of God; or like Isaiah he has the very covering of his soul stripped away by the vision of the Lord enthroned above the altar whence the live coals are lifted to purge the lips of men; or like Amos the shepherd prophet, his blood chilled by the roaring of the lion, discerning in that sound the portent of his nation's imminent fall; or like Saul of Tarsus falling blinded and prostrate on the desert sands on the road to Damascus, and rising from that ordeal to bring a world empire to the feet of the Christ who accosted him there; or yet like Jesus himself standing in the waters of the Jordan and hearing a voice out of heaven confirming him in his mission to proclaim the advent of the Kingdom of God, a voice which was to continue to ring in his ears until he completed his mission on a cross; what God says to the listening ear of his obedient servant is of ultimate and absolute significance for all men.

"When, in the days of Noah, none except that faithful one believed the Word that came from God, public opinion was of no avail to stem the rising flood. that swept away the unbelieving populace. When, in the declining years of Judah's national life, God spoke through the prophet Jeremiah, the counsel of that godly man was ignored and he was thrown into a dungeon, but the Word could not be silenced and the rising tide of war swept the nation into destruction. Whether anyone believes the Word or not has no effect on the Word itself. It is the task of the Church, and particularly her spokesman, to proclaim the Word of truth; though all the world reject that Word, the Word remains inviolate, for the will of God is not dependent upon the consent and agreement of men.

"It is the further responsibility of the Church to apply the truth which she proclaims, in the spirit of Jesus Christ, to the needs of all men. Up to this point I am confident that all of you have been quite willing to agree with me; from this point forward I rather expect that only those who are more concerned for the truth than for the preservation of their own hallowed traditions will continue to walk with me in the comradeship of agreement. For men commonly hold that so long as the preacher only proclaims the high-sounding and noble idealism, he is truly preaching, but when he begins to apply it where the people live, he has begun to meddle.

"It is also commonly held that the preacher should "preach the gospel" without touching on the burning social and political issues of his day. This is like saying that he should be a champion of truth in the abstract, but never define his truth nor point his finger directly at the sin.

"If the Church is to realize its true destiny, it must permeate secular history with the saving salt of Christian values. It is precisely in the prophetic ministry of the Church, supported by the godliness of her members, that such an impact is made upon the world as to initiate social reforms as well as to mediate personal redemption. That the latter can be achieved when we blithely ignore the former is the great fallacy of modern day ecclesiology. "The Church was framed for the express purpose of interfering with the world," according to Cardinal Newman.

Paul and Silas were accused of turning the world upside down, and to the extent that the accusation was true, the apostles were being true to their calling.

"Now we have before us a social issue that is freighted with meaning. If we have the courage to apply the Word at this point the doors will open up for us to limitless expanses of the abundant life; but if we come to the hour of birth and have not the, strength to bring forth the child, then we shall slip back again into the darkness of the tomb, and men shall speak with a great sadness and a heaviness of soul of the Church that was big with child but could not endure the pangs of her travail. Now the particular issue which I have in mind is that of the abolition of the principle of racial segregation in the public schools in our land, and the admission of every seeker after knowledge and Truth to whatever fount he my believe will best quench his thirst. On this issue there is a great deal of feeling, but there has been very little evidence of clear thinking, and still less evidence of the Christian spirit,, or the mind of Christ, on the part of those who have spoken for the people of this state. Consequently, our eyes have been so blinded by the fire and smoke and heat that we have failed to detect even a gleam of light.

"Let us recognize two guiding principles here. First: that we do not make the Supreme Court's decision the ultimate basis of authority, for we also recognize that black robed judges are human and are not endowed with omniscience. Neither are they capable of translating their pronouncements of justice into acts that are just for all persons affected by them. Eric C. Rust, in his book entitled The Christian Understanding of History, p. 279, has stated that " ... the greater the complexity of our social organization in its attempt to bring social justice, equality and freedom to men, the more can that organization, and the technical developments which make it possible, be used to spread tyranny and destruction among men."

"Thus to raise the flag of rebellion is to invite federal intervention and the enforcement of martial law, in which case justice would be demonized and become tyranny and death.

"The second principle is that of the supreme value of truth - I am not here concerned primarily with the grievances of the Negro people; nor am I concerned primarily with the claims of the white people; nor even the clamor of the human race; but I am concerned to set forth the Truth which must ultimately be the determinant of all human action, whether those who act do so with purely unselfish motives or not, and whether those who benefit from the action are worthy and deserving of the benefits or not. At this point I would remind the Negro people themselves that it was one of their own greatest leaders, George Washington Carver, I believe, who, when he was asked by a younger associate why he took no steps to guarantee that his discoveries in the field of agricultural science should go to the enrichment of his own race rather than permitting them to fall into the hands of the white man, replied: "Young man, I am not concerned primarily with the Negro race; I am not even concerned primarily with the human race; my primary consideration is the discovery and revelation of truth.""

"I would therefore counsel you not to be governed and motivated by selfish, mean, or deliberately troublesome desires. Do not bring upon yourselves the stigma which attaches to those who stir up strife in the assertion of their rights. First make us know that you sincerely desire to learn from your white teachers by your example of devotion to truth and to true men; then it will be easier for you to gain a true acceptance, not only into our classrooms, but into our very hearts.

"I think that if we give serious consideration to the two principles just discussed, we will see that no great harm can be done to us, and nothing of real value to us can be lost by the admission, on a voluntary basis, of children of different races to the same school. Jesus has taught us that when we are compelled to go one mile, we should freely offer to go the second. To carry out the instructions of the Supreme Court is to go the first mile; it is to do what we are being forced to do, but to receive these people into a genuine fellowship of learning is to go the second mile; it is to embody in spirit and concrete action the teaching of Jesus Christ. To refuse to go the second mile is to declare ourselves unchristian; to refuse to go the first mile is to declare our selves unlawful rebels.

"When the apostle Paul returned the runaway slave Onesimus to his former master Philemon he admonished Philemon to receive him again, not as a slave but as a brother in Christ. But we have not been willing to do this; we have accepted the Emancipation Act, but we have refused to enact on our part a Fraternization Act. If this be thought a hard saying, I remind you yet again that you have the choice of being Christian or of retaining your own traditions. But if you will retain your traditions and exalt them to a place of supreme authority, then you make void the Word which says "For there is no distinction between Jew and Greek; the same Lord is Lord of all and bestows his riches on all who call upon him. (Romans 10-12) "There is neither Jew nor Greek there is neither slave nor free, there is neither male nor female; for you are all one in Christ Jesus." (Galatians 3:28)

"Indeed Christ Jesus admonishes us even, to prefer others above ourselves, for true greatness is seen in the willingness to be servant of all.

"If we reject his counsel we have not in us the mind of Christ who, being on equality with God, humbled himself in order that we might be lifted up. This is the real question before us in this issue of segregation: Whether we will seek to preserve our selfish interests, and thereby become of no effect in the redemption of our society, or whether we will empty ourselves, take on the form of a servant, and become the redeeming and transforming force in an unchristian social order. He that seeks to save his life shall lose it, but he that willingly gives up his life for Christ's sake and for the sake of proclaiming the good news in effective terms, shall gain eternal life. If this sort of preaching be meddling, I am proud to stand in the company of a long line of meddlers with Amos on one end and Jesus on the other."

I was coming to the end of my radio address. Nobody had attempted to blow up the building. Nobody had made a pot shot at me through the window. The station manager was standing and watching, and listening intently to me. My voice was becoming tired, my throat dry, my hands a bit sweaty. But I continued.

"It is the final responsibility of the Church to accept the consequences of its action in applying the Truth. But let me voice a warning at this point: the foxes have their dens, and the birds of the air have their nests, but the Son of Man has no place to lay his head. He is despised and rejected of men, and upon him is laid the iniquity of his people. He who has come to seek and save the lost, has also come to offer himself as a ransom for their souls. For though he came to his own people, they knew him not; neither did they receive him. The mission of the Christ is a sacrificial one; there is no other Christ than the Crucified Christ. And if you would identify yourself with this Son of Man, if you would belong to his Church and participate in his saving mission to the world, then you too must be willing to wander unwanted, hated and despised among your own people; you too must be willing to be a sacrifice, a ransom for their souls; you too must be willing to take up your cross of suffering and shame and death, and follow him. These are the occupational hazards of following Christ in a great social upheaval - criticism, misunderstanding, ostracism, imprisonment and death. These are the calculated risks of serving in the ranks of the King whose banner is a cross, and whose crown is plaited thorns.

"If any man thinks that he can effectively proclaim and apply the truth in this crucial hour, and yet retain the favor of self interested men, then let him pay heed to the counsel of the prophet Jeremiah to his private secretary, Baruch: "Do you seek great things for yourself? Seek them not; for I am bringing evil on all flesh, says the Lord; but I will give you your life for a prize of war in all places to which you may go." (Jeremiah 45:5)

"If you would follow the Lord in this crisis, it is highly likely that a sword will sever you from your family and your friends, and even those whom you seek to help will misunderstand and. misinterpret you. But no man having set his hand to the plow, and looking back, is fit for the Kingdom of God, and, in the fullness of time God will vindicate His servants, and future generations will rise up to call you blessed, for they will see that you stood facing your Calvary, and in the Gethsemane of your soul you cried out: What shall I say, Father, deliver me from this hour? No. For this purpose I have come to this hour. Father, glorify Thy name. Then they will know that this was your finest hour, when you refused to fall back into bondage to fear, but cried out with the spirit of sonship, "Abba. Father, Thy will be done."

I closed my radio address with a warning which I am confident was not received gladly by the people who had already decided that I was bad news for the South and would have to go because what I was saying was not acceptable to them.

"But I solemnly warn you that if the Church keeps silent in this crucial hour, then it may as well keep silent for the next twenty years ... until there arises a new generation that knows not that its spiritual mother was slower to recognize social justice than were the secular courts of the land.

"I further forewarn you that if Christians embrace the principle of enforced separateness at this point, they will in a short while discover that the universal Christ has passed them by and left them stranded upon their self-made island with no company but the idols their own hands have fashioned.

"And I warn you finally, that he who has some Truth to teach, but turns away those who would learn because they are of another color, will presently find that the Truth itself has also fled from him."

When I had finished, the station manager James Woodall, again promised me "You can speak on this station any time you want to." The need never arose again. I had said what I had to say. I drove home and found five people waiting for me. The Methodist Minister Frank Gilmore and the young Baptist minister E.A. Cline, were visibly relieved and heartily approving. Miss Susie May Brown and Mrs. Mae White came to the house radiant with JOY and praise. My wife MarthaLee, hugged me with tears in her eyes. Early next morning Claron Wooten called me to tell me that I had been hanged in effigy in the meeting place of the Ku Klux Klan.

So I was hanged in Shellman and they removed my body, buried it in a mound erected on the town's triangle before I had time to offer a prayer in parting, but I remember it at least once each year at Halloween when my neighbors here symbolically hang Guy Fawkes to commemorate his attempt to blow up the British royalty, while I was only hanged for a "nigger lover". Maybe I deserved it. At least I should have expected it. I had been handing out some heavy theology and historically, the Church has burned heretics. Besides, the Editor at the paper in Atlanta had tried to warn me, and some people in Shellman had hinted that bad things can happen to preachers who say things the people don't want to hear, so by the standards of Shellman society, I was fit to be hanged but I still don't think so; I think it was a mean cowardly trick to hang me in the place where I led their sons in the Pledge of Allegiance to the Flag and to the Nation for which it stands, for that was part of the Boy Scout ritual and I was the Scoutmaster selected by the Shellman Lions Club.

But there was an incident in my boyhood, a mean act on my part, for which I needed hanging, or at least an application of Miss Florrie's Board of Education, known as THE ORANGEWOOD PADDLE, and I will relate it here although I am ashamed of it and partly because of that shame I may even refer to it again in the course of this story about Shellman.

I call the story, which begins on the next page because it deserves full space in this chronicle all to itself: A POCKETFUL OF CORN.

A POCKETFUL OF CORN

"Hurry up, Whistle Britches!" The school bus driver, Fred Powers, turned his turtle visage on me and raced the motor with one foot on the accelerator while he shoved the brake pedal in with the other foot. "I hafta wait on you again like this, I'll drive off an' leave you runnin' after me."

I was comin' as fast as I could run I was gasping for the breath to make my excuse. The pile of books under my right arm kept sliding out of place and the bulge in my left front pocket felt more noticeable than a loaded forty five.

"Start Sooner next time Whistle Britches. Or I'll leave you!" The bus driver closed the door with a handle located near the driver's seat. He raised hard, staring eyes to watch in the rear view mirror as I stumbled toward a seat on the boys' side of the big orange school bus. He had dubbed me "Whistle Britches" the first day I wore my new corduroy pants to school. Now he shifted the gears into low with a scraunching, clashing sound which was soon drowned out by the roar of the engine. The school bus moved forward. I had made it by a hair's breadth.

The only vacant seat I could find on the long bench that ran the length of the bus was right beside ACE, the bad boy of the Howard Elementary School, and my own personal nemesis. ACE turned to me with his customary smirk on his face. "Whatcha got in your pocket Whistle Britches?" ACE reached his hand into my left front pocket and said "Feels like a ear of corn. Whatcha gonna do with your pocket fulla corn?"

"Nuthin'" I said because I knew that ACE spelled trouble and I didn't want him to know what I planned to do with the ear of corn. I had brought it to show to Mister D.F. Bruce, who was the County Agricultural Agent. He would be at the school for the 4H club meeting, and he had inspired me to have my own corn patch. Now I wanted to let him see this perfect ear of corn that I was so proud of. It was the biggest and the whitest and the rows of grains were the straightest and every grain was perfect with a little hook at the top to make it painful to shell it with bare hands. So I wanted Mister Bruce to see what a good job I had done with the little corn patch Papa had let me claim and work for myself.

But ACE screwed up his mouth and said "Whatcha gonna do with that ear of corn in your pocket, Whistle Britches?"

I was already upset because I had almost missed the bus in the confusion of getting the ear of corn and all my books and writing tablets together, and then stumbling into the bus under the withering gaze of the hawk faced school bus driver. And then I had to sit by ACE whom I both hated and idolized, and so when he asked me I said "Nuthin'" which meant I didn't want him to know my secret But ACE would not be put off because he saw an opportunity for mischief.

ACE said "shell off a handful of it an' throw it at the niggers when we pass 'em. It'll skeer 'em good and it won't hurt 'em none. Here, lemme show you how to do it."

Then ACE tried to grab the ear of corn but I said "I can shell it for myself I don't need nobody to show me how to do it."

"Well, hurry up. They'll prob'ly be around the next curve. Tha's where we pass 'em ev'ry mornin'."
I was remembering Dump and what Mama had said to me about mis-treating colored people, and I hesitated, but Ace was persistent and he said "Aw, it ain't gonna hurt 'em. They'll prob'ly git as much fun outta it as we will."

I rubbed the ear of corn in my pocket with my thumb and forefinger. The little hooks on the top of the grains were like rubbing my fingers on a potato gridder. But I shelled off a few grains and held them in one hand while I stuffed the ear of corn back in my pocket. A few of the grains fell on the floor, but they rolled under the seat and ACE said "Shoot! Let 'em go. You got a plenty there."

The big orange school bus was rolling along the hard clay road the Chain Gang had built. Corn and cotton fields were on one side and pine woods were on the other side, and Tobesofkee Creek was about a half mile ahead. There would be a jarring of the whole bus as they crossed the Rattlin' Bridge over Tobesofkee Creek. We headed into the curve, and a cloud of dust rolled up behind us as the big tires struck hard dirt again. I held the grains of corn in my closed fist, and turned to watch out the window. The canvas curtains had been rolled up and were held in place by straps to the frame at the top of the long line of windows.

"There they are!" ACE pointed ahead as we came into the curve. "Git ready! There they are!"

"Where?" I said, for although I saw them, I had not fully accepted what I was going to do. I turned my face into the window and leaned out. The wind took my breath away, ruffled my hair which I had plastered down with water before I left home; I could barely hear what ACE was saying because the wind carried his words away, but I knew ACE had said they were there. They were there too, waiting, huddled at the edge of the road, standing out of the way of the big orange school bus that carried the white children to school but did not stop to pick up black children who also went to Bibb County Schools for the Colored.

"There they are!" ACE pointed at the huddled, waiting black faces crowded to the edge of the ditch to avoid the school bus. Black faces, unsmiling, except for the smiles of fear and servility, smiles taught and practised to conceal the frowns of hatred and anger. faces frightened, querulous, anxious, closed, black. Eyes, staring up out of the blackness of the faces. Eyes big and round and wondering and suspicious and resentful of white faces looking out at them from the windows of the speeding school bus. Questioning and not knowing exactly what the question was. Challenging, yet not knowing precisely what the challenge was.

Eyes turning away to look down at the road underfoot to adjust the cloth book satchel slung from sagging shoulders. Eyes blinking away the dust thrown up by the rolling wheels of the big school bus. Black faces turned up watchfully at the white faces in the windows of the school bus. Black faces drawn back in resentment at having to go to school at all. At their Ma pushing them out the door, saying "Now y'all git outta heah an' to school whether you lak it or not, so's y'all doan grow up to be lak yo Pa an' me, not knowin' nuthin, but to pick white fokes cotton an' wash white fokes clo'es. Now you jest hush yo' mouf an' git onto school an' doan lemme heah no mo' outta you 'bout not wantin' to go to school. Now gawn to school Ah tell you."

Angry at their Pa saying "Now y'all heah whut yo Mama done tole you. Now git on outta heah an' doan gimme no back tawk." The black faces stared up into the windows of the passing school bus. Waiting.

"There they are!" ACE said to me and he leaned out the window. "Black nigger! Black Nigger!" ACE shouted.

Then I was on my knees on the seat and leaning out the window, and I thought I shouted "Black nigger! Black nigger!" at the knot of black faces huddled together beside the road. I could not be sure because I could not hear myself. The wind was in my face, and I was flinging the handful of corn at the black faces turned up to me. The black faces were surprised and pained and angry and afraid, and ashamed because they were black and the corn was being hurled into their faces, and the faces in the window of the school bus were shouting "Black nigger! Black nigger!"

ACE laughed. It was not a pleasant laugh. It was a gleeful laugh. Diabolical. I laughed too. But it was a laugh of hysteria. I looked back into the school bus to see if others were laughing. They were, and this gave me some courage, so I laughed a little more easily, but not with my eyes. There were loud peals of laughter and loud squeals of merriment on the school bus, and the school bus driver looked into the rear view mirror to see what was going on. His eyes were hard and unblinking. Reptilian. His mouth was set in a firm straight line, unsmiling beneath a beak of a nose. He said "What's going on back there?"

The little red haired girl sitting opposite me was blushing and tittering. She thrust her face forward at the school bus driver. "Alfie threw corn at the niggers."

Then she ducked her head as if she would hide from the bus driver's hard, unblinking eyes. But she tittered again and looked at the girls seated next to her, and giggled, pointing with one finger at me.

The school bus driver pushed on the brake pedal, and he eased in the clutch pedal. The big bus, swaying slightly, came to a stop in the middle of the road. "What's that?" The bus driver's eyes in the rear view mirror were on the little red haired girl.

"Who?"

Then several of the girls on the seat beside the little red haired girl took up the refrain. Even some of the boys joined in. "Alfie threw corn at the niggers. Alfie done it!"

The boys and girls laughed and pointed their fingers at me. I looked at ACE but there was no help for me there. ACE sneered and looked away. The school bus driver's eyes in the rear view mirror were fixed on me. "Did you do that?" His eyes burned into me; I looked down because I could not bear the school bus driver's eyes. I tried to hide my own eyes by looking down. I did not reply to the school bus driver, but the little red haired girl tittered and giggled.

"He done it all right. I seen 'im when he done it."

She stretched her neck to look more closely at me. "Look! He's still got some of it in his pocket."

Still I did not answer, and the school bus driver said "I'm talkin' to you. Come up here!" I stumbled to the front of the bus, and stood facing the school bus driver, but my eyes were lowered; I would not look at the school bus driver.
"I've got a good notion to put you off the bus right in the middle of 'em." The school bus driver's face was like the face of a turtle, staring into my face, boring into my very soul.

He pulled the lever and opened the door to accentuate the threat. He continued staring at me. "If this happens again, I'll put you off the bus right in the middle of them." Then he slowly closed the door, meshed the gears noisily, raced the engine, and the school bus moved forward.

The black children stood huddled in the road. Waiting. When the bus had stopped, and the door had opened, they had watched, waiting, and when the door closed and the bus moved forward, they waited, watching. And when it had moved away they began to mumble and to talk among themselves, cursing the white children on the school bus because I had thrown the corn into their upturned faces. The school bus moved farther away and gained speed, and it threw up a cloud of dust, and the dust enveloped the black children standing beside the road. Then the tallest of them raised his fist, and he shook his fist at the departing bus. His face was contorted with rage. He shouted an obscenity at the white children on the bus, hurled the obscenity at the school bus he could not ride, hurled the obscenity at the bus which carried the boy who had thrown the corn safely beyond his reach. Cursed the white boys who had jeered "Black nigger! Black nigger!" at them.

Then all the black children standing in the road joined the tallest boy, for they all felt as he did. They joined him in shouting obscenities and shaking their fists. But we on the bus could barely see them shaking their fists because of the cloud of dust, and we could not hear the obscenities because of the roaring of the engine. But inside myself, I saw their faces and heard their curses; also I saw Mama's face and heard her voice, and I was afraid, more afraid of what I had done than of anything else I could remember.

The school bus stopped in front of the Howard Elementary School. And when all the boys and girls had unloaded, the bus driver hopped down from the driver's seat. He was a short, squat man, powerfully built. He was going both bald and grizzled, and his face was seamed and tanned. He watched until all the children were clear of the bus, then he went inside the building. I stood apart from the other children and watched; I knew he had gone to talk with Miss Florrie.

Mister Bruce came for the 4H meeting but I did not show him the ear of corn. I knew he would say "Why Alfie, what happened? This is not a full ear of corn. What happened to the other grains?" And I knew that if he asked me that I would break down and cry.

When school was out, Miss Florrie called me and said "Don't get on the bus. I am taking you home. I have to talk with your Mama and your Papa about what you did on the school bus this morning."

I looked into Miss Florrie's sad grey eyes, and I knew how Mama's big brown eyes would swim with shame when Miss Florrie told her. And how Papa's blue eyes would blaze with anger when he learned that Miss Florrie had to bring me home from school because of what I had done on the bus.

Facing what I am now going to tell you happened in Shellman was never as hard for me as the ride home in Miss Florrie's Dodge.

Facing what I have to tell you about what happened in Shellman and what I said to the people in Shellman may seem like a dose of bad medicine, and so to delay that as long as possible I am going to tell you another story from my boyhood days because my early conflict between Right and Wrong was not a one time affair. I didn't just nibble on the fruit from that Tree of Knowledge; I kept coming back to it and nibbling some more. And after that Major policy Address on the radio, you really need a little relaxation, so I am going to tell you the story of DUMP, which is the first real face to face conflict with a black person. So here it is: The Story of Me, White Lightnin' and DUMP.

I was still a small boy, and the black person, DUMP, was a teen age girl on the brink of womanhood. But there is another character in this story called White Lightnin', and I have to tell you who White Lightnin' was. He was a small white Collie puppy when Mister Charles gave him to me. The reason Mister Charles gave White Lightnin' to me was that every time Mister Charles blew the steam whistle to signal "Dinnertime" for the crew of workers in the field, the puppy would run away from home and come to my house where he found refuge in my arms. On one occasion this occurred at the outset of a Summer Storm, and both White Lightnin' and I found a safe place hiding under the bed.

When the storm was over, I took White Lightnin' back home but Mister Charles insisted that the puppy was now mine because we had slept together and this made it a binding union. I don't remember what had become of Sandy by this time, but White Lightnin' had become MY DOG, MY PROTECTOR, MY PARTNER IN CRIME in the story of DUMP.

So, Dear Reader, I give you respite from the heavy theology of my radio address to the people of the Shellman area on the Dawson station WDWD by telling how this dog tale which is really a story of how I came to know that there was an inherent conflict in the racial views I had received in Mother's Milk, but the conflict would inevitably come out the way it did, with me being hanged for being "a nigger lover."

DUMP

White Lightnin' grew aggressive as he grew bigger. More protective of me. More territorial. He was the guardian of his domain. And the center of his empire, the very seat of power, was the spot just under the door-steps, leading up to the porch. The back door steps. From this vantage point, he could scan all the approaches to the house while remaining half concealed from the view of anyone coming to the door.

If you looked closely, you could see him lying under the steps, his black eyes burning like two coals in the whiteness of his total being. But if you were a stranger, you would not get close enough to look under the steps before White Lightnin' would bolt out, barking and charging and demanding that you stop and wait until somebody from inside the house came out and said it was all right. He recognized Papa as the one having the final word, as well as the first word, but other members of the family would do. Mama would do very well. And I would do in a pinch, but I was better at urging him on than I was at restraining him.

Dump was not a stranger, but she was different from anyone living in the house which White Lightnin' guarded. Dump was black. She was Uncle Seeb's and Aunt Hattie's biggest girl, and she was almost as black as Uncle Seeb. But not quite. For nobody was black as Uncle Seeb. His blackness shone like a rival sun when the sun in the heavens shone on Uncle Seeb's face. He was invisible in the night, but in the daytime, on a bright day, Uncle Seeb's face glistened giving off its own ebony light.

Dump's blackness lacked the peculiar lustre of Uncle Seeb's, but her smooth round cheeks glowed with good health and humor. When she was in a good humor. But Dump's humor could change quickly under provocation. Then the whiteness of her eyes shone out of the blackness of her face in direct contrast to the blackness of White Lightnin's eyes shining out of the whiteness of his body.

When Dump was in a good humor, she laughed and showed a lot of white teeth in contrast to the blackness of her face. She could also show a lot of white teeth when she didn't laugh, for when Dump was angry her lips would peel back in a snarl.

The snarl exposed the teeth as the formidable weapons of that primitive being who became Earth's supreme predator. It was not good to engage in battle with Dump unless you had lots of teeth too. White Lightnin' had them.

White Lightnin' had a mouth full of white teeth which he showed in friendly prominence when he laughed; he showed them in fearsome prominence when he snarled. White Lighnin' laughed when he was lying close to Papa, and sometimes when he was playing with me. He snarled when another dog came around seeking the same privileges he enjoyed in solitary grandeur. White Lightnin' also snarled and showed his teeth at some people. Black people. White Lightnin' was in the parlance of Bibb County, "a white man's dog."

He considered it his duty to bark at all Negroes who came into the yard, whether they came regularly or as complete strangers. If the Negro ignored this early warning, and approached near to the doorsteps, White Lightnin' would snarl and growl, and the heavy hair on his back and shoulders would stand up. He had never bitten anybody, but he had made several people believe that he would bite them if they made the wrong move. Showing his long, sharp pointed and curving canine teeth in the front of his mouth, he could easily convince a timid soul that he was a dangerous dog.

Aunt Hattie was not a timid soul; Aunt Hattie was a hardy soul. She carried a big stick which she would wave threateningly at White Lightnin' and she would say to him in a very convincing tone of voice "You shet yo' mouf, dawg, fo' I knock yo' teef down yo' th'oat."

White Lightnin' was a vigilant watchdog but he was no fool. When Aunt Hattie brandished her big stick, White Lightnin' snarled at her from under the door steps. He showed his teeth to Aunt Hattie but he did not expose them to Aunt Hattie's big stick. He believed that Aunt Hattie was fully capable of knocking his teeth down his throat. She was.

But Dump was not Aunt Hattie. Dump was not carrying a big stick in her hand. She was carrying a clothes hamper on her head. The clothes hamper was not loaded with the weight of Aunt Hattie's stick driven by Aunt Hattie's bony hands. It was full of clothes Aunt Hattie had washed and ironed for Mama because Mama was in a "delicate condition" which means that she was soon going to present the world with a fifth boy. She hoped it would be a girl because of Margaret's untimely death, but that hope was going to be dashed when Joe appeared. So much for Mama at this moment. Back to Dump.

Dump was swinging along, her well formed hips were swaying rhythmically in what she believed to be a provocative, if not a graceful manner. (Mama would have called it disgraceful.) She was humming a tune inside her head. The thoughts inside her head might be called romantic. (Mama would have a different name for them too.) For Dump was at that stage of female development, evidenced by a swelling and rounding of hips, bosom and buttocks, when it is quite natural for a girl's thoughts to be centered on those titillating preliminaries to mating necessary to the continuation and proliferation of the species.
The basket of freshly washed and ironed shirts, pillow cases, and doillies which she balanced on her head was not for Dump a basket of laundry. It was a crown of gold sitting on the head of a young queen. It was a garland of flowers balanced on the head of a young bride advancing to meet a young man, tall, strong and black, who would enfold this dark beauty in his arms and make her his wife.

And I was sitting there on the doorstep. I was not that tall, virile, young black man in Dump's imagination.I was a short little white boy sitting on the door step, holding a biscuit in one hand and pushing a heavy lock of dark brown hair out of my eyes with the other hand. I was not coming forward with a song of love on my lips to meet the African Queen clothed in her glory. I was speaking in conspiratorial tones to White Lightnin' who was crouching under the door step and watching Dump's approach both attentively and apprehensively.

To Dump, who was big and strong and ready to be mated, and being mated, to fulfill her special purpose in life, I was "The Baby."

And since the imaginary wedding must be put off because in reality she had to deliver the hamper of clothes balanced on her head, Dump would settle for the greatest pleasure available to her. Dump would tease me by calling me "The Baby." Then she would watch me pout in angry humiliation. She would laugh at my anger until her sides hurt. And when I was so angry I could not even speak, she would say to me "Whassamatter? De ol' cat done got de Baby's tongue? Wonder whut he gon' do wid it."

Now Dump approached, wearing the clothes hamper crown on her head, and she saw me sitting on the door step, eating a "syrup in the hole", which is exactly described by its name. You hold a biscuit in one hand, and you punch a hole in it with the forefinger of the other hand, and you pour cane syrup into that hole until it is full to overflowing. Then you press the opening together, and you eat it while the whole sticky sweetness drips onto the fingers of both hands, and even runs down your chin. And that is just what I had done and was doing when Dump came swaying and swinging into the yard, and approached the back door steps leading up to the porch, with me sitting on the doorstep, and White Lightnin lying in his guard house under the step.

And seeing me, but not seeing White Lightnin', Dump rolled her great round eyes until the whites of them stood out in stark contrast to the blackness of her face all around them, she said "Whut's the Baby eatin'?. A syrup in de hole?"

I glared back at Dump. I coughed. The bread crumbs were choking me. I swallowed and licked my fingers. I was tempted to give the rest of the biscuit to White Lightnin', but that would be interpreted by Dump as weakness, as shame at being found eating a syrup in the hole. White Lightnin' was not interested in my biscuit now anyway. He was watching Dump. Noting her unusual appearance, wearing a basket of clothes on her head, swinging her shoulders and hips to the tune of the music inside her.

White Lightnin's ears stood up. His hackles rose. He said "Woof!" This "Woof!" was accompanied and reinforced by a low growl which started deep in his chest. It came out as an ominous threat. But Dump was so engrossed in her role as the African Princess about to be wed that she did not even notice White Lightnin's warning.

"Is Mama's Little Baby eatin' a syrup in de hole?" This question erupted into a fit of pleasure, a howl of approval of what she had just said. The basket of clothes on Dump's head tilted, swayed, but balance was soon restored by her agile movements.

My face was a mask of anger. I mumbled through the biscuit crumbs sticking in my throat, sticking to my lips. "You shut up you ol' black nigger!" I licked my lips and pushed the hair out of my eyes with sticky fingers.

"Whut you say?" Dump stood still, her hands on her hips. "Who you callin' a black nigger?" Dump shook her head so vigorously that the basket of clothes teetered; she reached up to steady the load.

My eyes were clouded with tears. I glanced down at White Lightnin'. He looked back at me questioningly. I pushed out my lower lip; I was breathing hard. "Tha's what you are. A black nigger!" Then, in a strangled voice. "I ain't no baby neither." The very air about us was filled with tension.

White Lightnin' had read the tone of our voices and the angry facial expressions. Dump and I were enemies; he was on my side. Not only was Dump black, but she was threatening. He charged out from under the door step and hurled himself toward Dump. Barking, growling and snarling, and making a great show of his canine teeth.

Dump was caught by surprise, and she stepped backward, the clothes basket teetering on her head. She turned her anger on White Lightnin'. "You git back dawg!" She rushed at him. White Lightnin' halted in mid attack, his hind feet braced to retreat if necessary. He barked and growled and snarled viciously, but stayed at a safe distance from Dump whose eyes were searching for some weapon to hit him with. There was nothing in her reach. No big stick such as Hattie carried in her hands. So she advanced on White Lightnin' with the weapons endowed by nature. She kicked out at White Lightnin', aiming for his ribs with her bare black foot. It was a weapon known not only to the Oriental proponents of Karate. In Bibb County it is known as "the swift kick."

White Lightnin' was expecting Dump to try to kick him. He stopped two inches short of her leg reach. So instead of landing a sound blow to White Lightnin's rib cage, Dump kicked empty air, insubstantial space. She lost her own balance. She stumbled, caught herself in time to avoid falling, but not in time to save the hamper of freshly laundered clothes.

The basket teetered wildly on Dump's head. She threw out her arms to balance herself, to save herself from falling. The clothes hamper slid from her head and tumbled to the ground, spilling freshly laundered shirts, pillow cases and doilies. White Lightnin' retreated and established new line of defense closer to me. At that moment Mama, alerted by all the racket in the back yard, appeared on the porch. Her arrival was heralded by the slamming of the screen door behind her.

Beads of sweat were standing on Mama's upper lip. A wisp of hair was falling across her forehead. Her big brown eyes were wide with concern when she saw the shirts, pillow cases, and other recently laundered items of clothing scattered over the ground. "Dump!" Mama scolded. "Just look what you've done! All my clean things in the dirt!" Mama advanced down the steps toward Dump and the spilled laundry, past me on the step, hardly aware of White Lightnin' standing back near me, ears erect, eyes flashing, but quiet.

Dump stood open mouthed but struck dumb by Mama's face. She held her hands like claws to her cheeks. She stared at the spilled laundry. She was unable to move from her tracks. I sat sniggering on the doorstep, holding my biscuit.

White Lightnin' watched Mama. He thought Mama was going to attack Dump, and he was ready to help Mama if a fight ensued. Instead, Mama bent over to pick up the clothes now scattered over the ground. White Lightnin' rushed to help her do that. He grabbed the sleeve of Papa's best shirt and started dragging it back to his hideout/guardpost under the steps. The shirt dragged in the dirt, White Lightnin' grinning as he stepped on the shirt's tail. He trotted away, head held high in pride. The anger of attack had turned to the pleasure of retrieval.

"Lightnin'!" Mama scolded the dog more sharply than she had done to Dump. "You put that down! You hear me?"

Mama advanced on White Lightnin'. She was a far more menacing figure than Dump had been. Mama was the figure of authority. White Lightnin' dropped the shirt and retreated to his place under the doorsteps. Mama stooped over, awkwardly because of her advancing delicate condition. She picked up Papa's shirt and began shaking it and examining it for dirt and damage. This brought White Lightnin' out again because it looked as if it might be a game, but one hard look from Mama sent him back under the doorsteps. She turned on DUMP. "What on earth got into you Dump? Have you lost your mind?!"

Dump was standing silent and sullen; then she came forward to her own defense. "He sicked the dawg on me!" She pointed an accusing finger at me. "Tha's how come me to drop de clo'es." Big tears were forming in Dump's eyes. Tears of anger, but aimed also at fending off Mama's wrath. "I wuz trynta keep at dawg fr'm fr'm bitin' me."

Mama turned her wrath from Dump onto me. I was not fully aware of the danger I faced; I waited in silence. "You sicked the dog on Dump?!" It was both a question demanding confession, and an exclamation expressing disbelief. "You sicked that dog on Dump and caused all this!?" Mama pointed to the clothes scattered now over the back yard.

"He called me a black nigger too!" Dump the defendant had now turned Dump the accuser. Emboldened by the injustice she felt, she attacked with vigor. "Ain't nobody gonna call me no black nigger and, git away wid it. I ain't gonna stan' fer it."

Mama was holding the shirt that White Lightnin' had dragged over
the ground. She marched over to me and held the shirt out in front of
her as if she were going to put me in a strait jacket. "You called Dump
a black nigger?!" Mama expected me to deny the charge, or at least to
break down in tears of remorse, which would in itself be an admission
of guilt.

I didn't do either. I got my own back up and hurled a charge at Dump.
"She called me a baby!" Tears of anger now welled up in my eyes. My
voice choked. But not enough to silence me in my own defense. "I didn't
sic White Lightnin' on 'er She done it herself. Prancin' around with that
basket on her head." Through tears I glared at Dump. "The big black
nigger!"

Mama turned back to Dump with a withering look. She was displeased
with Dump's insolence. "Pick them up." She pointed to the clothes scattered about everwhere. "Take them back to Hattie to do them over. And
when you bring them back here, you call out and let me know you're
coming. And you'd better not have that basket on the top of your head
either."

Dump began gathering up the pillow cases and shirts and other things,
stuffing them back into the basket. All this while she kept muttering
"Ain't nobody gonna call me no black nigger. Not an, git away wid it. Ah
ain't gonna stan' fer it."

Mama watched Dump with stern eyes of disapproval. When she had the
basket tucked under her arm, Dump went off toward home, taking the
path across the cotton field. Stomping and prancing. Then Mama turned
to me. "You come with me, Young Man."

I knew from her face and from being called "Young Man" that I was in
trouble.

Mama grabbed me "by the scruff of my neck" which means she had
bunched up the collar of my shirt so that I could feel the pressure on my
throat, and she dragged me along toward the wash basin on the shelf on

the back porch. I thought White Lightnin' looked alarmed, but he didn't dare interfere, which probably showed that he was a smart dog, at least not a dumb dog when it came to reading the lines of authority. "When I finish washing your mouth out with Octagon soap you'll think twice before calling anybody a black nigger."

I stumbled along in Mama's wake, glancing back and casting a baleful look at Dump's retreating but swaggering figure as she followed the winding path across the cotton field. Seeing what was about to happen, I protested. "I ain't no baby. And I didden sic White Lightnin' on 'er. She's the cause of it all, the big black ..."

"Hush your mouth!" Mama jerked me even harder. White Lightnin' raised his ears, stared at Dump who was now well into the cotton patch, and said "Woof!" Dump glanced nervously, belligerently over her shoulder, and I could tell she was muttering something. I couldn't make it out for certain, but I made a close guess.

Mama poured cold water from the well bucket into the wash basin; she rubbed a hard bar of Octagon soap onto a rough wash cloth. My face was primped up to cry, and I made one final, anguished appeal. "But Mama I heard you an' Papa say it... You made me an' Junior an' James wash the nigger off us when we'd been playin' marbles with 'em ..." My face broke into tears.

Mama laid the bar of Octagon soap back into the dish. She lifted the wash basin and threw the water into the yard. She put her hand to her forehead and closed her eyes. Opened them again and looked down at her swollen belly. Closed them again. In the most prayerful tone I ever heard, Mama said "Lord have mercy!"

There are worse things than being hanged in effigy for a "nigger lover." One of those worse things was looking into my Mama's anguished face.

Chapter Five

Actually, Claron Wooten did not say "meeting place of the Ku Klux Klan." I was probably the only non-member of the Klan who knew about that. Except some of the Boy Scouts. What Claron Wooten said was "the Town Hall." It was a shabby little building that was used for town meetings, the local Boy Scout Troop, and the KKK. The way I learned about the KKK was this; The Boy Scouts were collecting old newspapers for recycling and storing them there. I was shoving things around, trying to make room for the newspapers when I discovered the sheets. "Hey, Mister Buchanan, what are these?" One of the boys yelled. But that was the place for the hanging.

Hanging, even in effigy, is serious business, even though it is symbolic and does not have the same result as the real hanging. It is a threat, a message of what is coming if the one represented in the effigy does not mend his ways. Real hangings are for murderers, rapists and horse thieves. I had been put in bad company, symbolically. And that I did not know who did it added to the threat while it did not reduce the implication of shame. Claron Wooten, while he was not in agreement with my views on the racial issue, was embarrassed by this shameful act. He called the sheriff, W.E. Nichols, who cut it down and disposed of it, losing, I was told, seventy five votes in the next election.

I was disturbed by the hanging; MarthaLee was frightened. Well, maybe I was frightened too, but I was not willing to admit it. I tried to turn it off with a word of good cheer. "Better the effigy than my own neck." But MarthaLee was not buying the humor. Her eyes told me "that's next."

There would be more threats and there would be more action taken against me, to get me to resign the office of pastor of the Baptist Church, to leave town, or what seemed more unthinkable to me, retract what I was saying, change my tune, and stick to preaching that we are all washed in the blood of Jesus and going to heaven because He died for our sins on the cross to gain God's forgiveness. Presumably, His Blood had made us all white, except for the blacks who would just be a separate problem for God to have to solve.

At any rate, I went on preaching what I thought was important, namely, that we are all God's children, black and white, and brothers in Christ Jesus, and we ought to act like brothers, and be willing to learn together in the same class room where it was assured that good Christian teachers were helping both black children and white children to learn what they need to know in order to live together in a free and equal society.

The signs were beginning to show up on the utility poles around town, and the people were showing some unfriendly face when I went downtown, and some were urging me to mend my ways. But the real threat came in a manner I had not expected, and I was not ready for it, and to this day I do not know whether I handled it in the right way, that is to say, I doubt that I responded to it the way Jesus would have done. I only know that I did what came naturally to a man being faced with a grave threat to his life, and, I believed, what represented a threat to the safety and welfare of my wife MarthaLee. Here's what happened.

A man came to me one day to deliver a threat in person. It was not some thing in the mail. It did not come as a telephone call. It was not a symbolic act carried out in the Town Hall/KKK Meeting Place. The man came to me.

I had never seen him before. Obviously he did not attend any one of the three churches I served. He was sunburned and wearing work clothes so I assumed he was a farmer from out in the county. He drove a battered old Chevrolet which he parked in the shade of a pecan tree between the church and the pastor's house. I was out there looking at the nuts on the tree, although it was yet uncertain that I would be around when they ripened. He walked over to me and said "Preacher, I come to tell you something." I could see bad news in his face.

"A buncha fellers gonna come and take you for a ride one night soon." This was certainly something worth driving into town to tell me, but I could not know whether he had come as friend or foe. Had he learned about it and come to warn me? Or had he been sent to put fear into my soul before the event took place? His face was inscrutable.

I was a long time in making a reply. At last I said "How many men are coming?"

"Don't know," he said, still being inscrutable. "Several, I reckon."

Again, I studied his face. "Are you going to be one of them?"

"Don't know. I might be. I might not be." He was beginning to fidgit a little.

I said "If there is going to be more than six of you, you try to be number seven in line."

He studied my face closely and said "You be keerful, Preacher." Then he turned, got back into the old Chevrolet, started the engine, and drove away.

I did not think anymore about the nuts forming on the ends of the branches of the pecan tree. I went back inside the house and I was open-ing the closet where I kept the shotgun. MarthaLee said "It's Summer-time. You're not going hunting?"

I said "I don't have to go anywhere. The hunters are coming here." Then I told her about my visitor. I loaded the shotgun. It was a Remington automatic; it held six shells after I took the plug out. Then I leaned the gun against the wall near the front door. And waited.

They never came. If they had come, I cannot tell you, dear reader, what would have happened. All I know is that I did not intend to be taken for a one way ride into the countryside around Shellman, Georgia. I knew that if I went and came back, I would not be a whole man when I returned. I looked at MarthaLee. She was a beautiful, slender woman with dark hair and big brown eyes. I loved her very much. I did not intend for her to become a widow because I went for a ride in the country with some white men who did not like what I was saying. I did not intend for her to have to live with a eunuch either. The shotgun stood by the door for weeks after that, and I never had to use it because I had already used the threat of it; nobody in the group of men who planned to come for me wanted to be in the first six. They all wanted to be number seven.

I am grateful that the men did not come. Grateful that I was not taken for a ride and grateful that I did not have to kill six men to keep from being taken for a ride. I am a bit claustrophobic, and I realize that even if I had survived the shootout I would have had to live in a very small jail cell for a long time.

Then the pressure began to build for the vote.

I became pastor of the Shellman Baptist Church, and incidentally owner of a cat named Romulus, because the members of the congregation voted for me. I could be stripped of that office, although I might be left with the cat, by a vote against me. That is the way Baptists do it because they don't have bishops.

The opposition had been convinced of one thing by my radio address: I did not intend to stop talking about the issue. The hanging had convinced them that I would not be intimidated into leaving. And the threat to take me for a ride had convinced them that I would fight back. So only one avenue was left open: to vote me out. And the vote was set for June 27, 1954.

Those who wanted me to leave were very busy lining up the vote against me. They were strengthened in this effort by the economic factor. Money. Farmers out in the county told the merchants in town that if they did not get rid of that preacher they would go to other towns to buy what they needed. They also told the cotton gin operator and the peanut dryer that they would take their cotton and peanuts to other towns unless they would get rid of me. Why people who were not members of the churches I served, and did not even live in Shellman, were so adamant about getting me to leave may seem like a mystery, but it is very clear in terms of money. They used cheap Negro labor to raise their crops, and they could foresee that a change in the educational system would mean that the Negroes would be better educated and "a nigger who is educated is uppity." So they must be kept in their place by maintaining the social order in which the white man is superior and the black man's inferiority will guarantee his continued servitude.

"Vote that nigger lovin' preacher out if you can't git him to go no other way."

Those who supported me were getting ready for the vote too. They were enlisting all who would "stand by their preacher." But mainly they were giving personal moral support to me and MarthaLee. Miss Susie May Brown and Mrs. Mae White and the Landfords and the Thompsons and the Arnolds were at our house daily with words of support and encouragement. We had become very important persons to them.

I was gearing up for the vote too. The forces at work against me were making me more determined to stand by my guns I was urged by my critics to "stop harping on the subject," but there was no other subject for me to harp on. The opposition would not let me forget that on June 27, their intention was to give me my walking papers, and when I went down town to shop or to pick up my mail at the post office, they would refuse to speak to me. I began to prepare my sermon for Sunday morning, June 27. I was not certain that I would need one for the evening hour because it appeared that I would be swept out of office. But the sermon. Yes, the sermon would be called THE WALLS OF THE CHURCH. The very structure itself seemed to be crumbling, but I prepared to speak on the Walls of the Church. Most of that sermon, was lost in the house fire I told you about, but there was a brand snatched from the burning, and here it is:

"Let us remember that the Church is composed of twice born men, and it is the second birth - the spiritual birth as a son of God - not the first birth as a child of men that counts for something. For it is in this experience that we become heirs of the grace of God, joint heirs with Jesus Christ of the heavenly glory. If the Church can point to ten such men, who can say with Paul "I count all other things as refuse for the sake of Christ" then the Church is strong and rich, and no man needs to worry about the welfare of the Church. But though she can point to ten thousand men who think alike, if their thinking reveals

that they are motivated by factors other than their peculiar relationship to Jesus Christ, for instance economic factors, social pressure, personal pride or ambition, then it is evident that the Church is suffering from the malady of an unregenerate nature. If the Church's judgment on spiritual matters is determined by the threats of outsiders to stop trading with church members, then we no longer have here a Church of the Living God, but a tool that is manipulated by the Almighty Dollar.

"If such a thing can come to pass in this church, then it has already slipped from its foundation which is Jesus Christ, and its walls have already begun to crumble, and those who live in it are in great peril, for the Church has become the temple of Dagon, and Christ Jesus Himself will be the Samson Agonistes to bring down its pillars. You cannot worship both God and mammon; unless there is repentance in the house of the Lord, and a return to our first love, the Lord will come and remove our lampstand from its place."

Now I was ready to deal with the ultimate issue here: whether I was free to speak the message I was being accused of harping on.

"It is with us no longer a question of whether we hold the same opinions on a question of social, political and religious significance; it is rather a question of whether God's servant is to speak as he feels compelled of God to speak, or whether he must take his cue from those who pay his salary. If I am God's man, then I am your pastor. If I am your man, then I am a hireling in God's sight. Now, if there is a misunderstanding at this point, it is not due, as some of you think, to what you refer to as a "mistake in judgment" on my part, but rather to a mistake which you made three years ago when you called a pastor, not a hireling."

Claron Wooten was Chairman of the Deacons and he swapped places with me in the pulpit when I had finished my sermon on the Walls of the Church. Standing up there and appearing a bit self conscious because of the unpleasant nature of the task, he announced that the church was in conference to handle business. He did not have to say what the business was; everybody knew it was to fire the preacher. One of the leaders of the opposition stood and made the motion to terminate my position as pastor of the church. He did not say what the ground was for the proposed action; again, it was not necessary because everybody knew it was because of my outspoken position of the race issue. I had planned to make a brief statement in my own defense anyway, or demand that the reason be stated clearly, when a miracle happened in church.

Or the totally unexpected occurred, or God - or maybe it was a Goddess - intervened. For Mrs. Mae White rose to her full five feet in height and began to speak. Her action, that is, her speaking, would not have had the approval of the Apostle Paul who wrote all those letters to the churches telling them how to do the business of being churches. But I don't think even the great Apostle Paul could have stopped Mae White. She was a very determined little white haired lady; she wore a hearing aid, and her voice was noticeably affected by her deafness, but what she had to say stood that church on its ear.

She began by telling the church what a good pastor I had been for the past three years, and how fortunate the church was to have me in that role. She listed my merits and achievements and good qualities, and said that I am a good and faithful pastor to a sinful flock that didn't deserve what they had in me. She listed some of the more damning sins of some of the leading members of the church, especially the deacons who were so eager to get rid of me.

She told some of the things about them that had escaped my attention in the three years of my ministry, and which I am sure they hoped had not been noticed by the other members of the church. So I was as surprised to learn how good I was as I was to learn what a rotten bunch of sinners I had been preaching to. Evidently, she knew their darker secrets and revealed my hidden virtues, things that made it worthwhile for me to face the image in my mirror when I shaved in the mornings, not to mention the possibility that MarthaLee really had a prize in me and she could thank her lucky stars that she was not hitched to Manry Stewart or some lesser light among the deacons and leaders of the church.

When she reached her peroration, she asked "How is it that you feel competent to judge the shepherd of this flock in the matter of his discharge of his duty in speaking a message which God has commanded him to speak?"

As Mae White settled back into her pew, there was a different atmosphere in the sanctuary from that which had prevailed in the earlier part of the hour when men's tempers were flaring and their contempt for the pastor was evident. A few other persons made some brief statements, the discussion ended, and the ballots were handed out to all the members. Then Manry Stewart said he wanted to attach a rider to the original motion, that whatever decision the vote revealed, everybody would pull together

The ballots were marked Go and Stay. The members were instructed to tear the ballots and drop the part indicating their wish into the collection plate. It was when the ushers collected the ballots and counted them that the miracle of Mae White became known. The Stay ballots numbered sixty six and the Go votes were thirty seven. The church had sustained me.
Now the irony of Manry Stewart's rider became evident. He had expected the vote to go against me, and he hoped the church would now be united in its opposition to me. It went the other way, and his feelings showed in his face. And it was not difficult for me to see that he did not

intend to go along with the people who had voted for me to Stay. But now was a time for celebration of victory.

As MarthaLee and I left the church building, Mae White and Susie May Brown and the Landfords and the Thompsons and other supporters walked with us to the house A good group of us went together for lunch in Dawson, and nobody in the restaurant there refused to serve us. In fact, we were such a happy, victorious lot of people that the restaurant people thought we must be celebrating a birthday. They were right. We were celebrating the triumph of Good over Evil, of Life over Death, of God over the Devil. And for that day at least we would not even let bad thoughts enter our minds. I announced that MarthaLee and I were going on a vacation. We would go to Louisville, Kentucky and stay in an apartment on the campus of the Seminary there. I would do some reading and writing in the library, we would walk in Cherokee Park the way we had done as students when that was the only form of recreation we could afford. And we would recharge our spiritual batteries, so that when we came back to Shellman, we could pick up the work there and go forward with hope and confidence.

It didn't turn out quite that way, but it was just as well that we were away because all the bad things would have happened anyway, even if we had stayed at home. And it gave Romulus an opportunity to get acquainted with Mama. For we left him with her while we were in Louisville, and he used up one or two of his seven lives while he was there.

CHAPTER SIX

Those were halcyon days following the favorable vote. I really did feel a surge of confidence. I had won. The majority of the church members were on my side. For all that I had said about the lonely prophet on the mountain a Baptist church is still a democracy. The majority rules. I was marching at the head of an army of the Lord, and Mae White and Susie May Brown were my two lieutenants. With these two I could whip the devil any old day. But the opposition was going to show me some surprises. And by some strange twist of fate, Romulus was involved.

Jimmy Nix was my next door neighbor. He was a pleasant young man with wife and small children. He taught agriculture at the local high school. Or he was the county farm agent, or both. He was an influential member of the farming community, and he was important in the school system. He also kept a pack of bird dogs. I have no objection to bird dogs. But bird dogs and cats don't mix well. So when Jimmy Nix let his dogs out for a little exercise, they headed for my back yard and a bit of sport with my cat. Romulus was sunning himself on the back porch when they came, and he immediately saw that he was in a precarious position. His solution to the problem stood close at hand though. A big pecan tree.

Romulus ran up the tree and settled into a safe crotch, then began calling to me for help. I went out and drove the dogs away and began calling to Romulus. But Romulus did not know how to get down. Or he pretended not to know. This called for a man with an advanced degree. At last I hooked a coal scuttle onto a long fishing pole and raised it up to Romulus. He gratefully climbed into the coal scuttle, I lifted him down, he dashed inside the house where he rubbed against MarthaLee's ankle to say that all was forgiven between the two of them. For a day or two, he was a very decent sort of cat before reverting to normal. He would not make any more trouble with neighbors until the incident of Zack Crittenden's dog, but that can wait, because I must first deal with Jimmy Nix.

Even though I was relatively young in the ministry - people would comment that I was young in appearance, and I was to learn that Jesus and I were about the same age when we got into trouble - I was often confronted with religious or theological questions, but never before had anyone posed one like Jimmy Nix did. His small children were enrolled in the Sunday School and, I assumed, performing at an acceptable level because Mrs. Gladys Wooten made certain that the little ones got the necessary care and instruction. But Jimmy came to me with a troubled face, and he said "Do you think it is a sin for me to let my children attend the Sunday School, since you and I don't agree on this racial issue?"

I had to run quickly over everything I had been taught in the seminary, and I found nothing that would be of help to me in answering such a question. What puzzled me most about it was that Jimmy Nix actually appeared to be serious about it. So I tried to give him a serious answer. I said "I think you could do no better in Shellman than keep your children enrolled in the Sunday School here where they will be taught that Jesus loves the little children of the world, especially the little black and white ones."

This did not seem to make Jimmy Nix happy, and I am not certain that it helped to relieve his sense of wrongdoing, but I think it helped him to resolve the issue of what to do about me the next time my tenure as pastor came to a vote before the church. He would definitely be with Manry Stewart on that.

Manry proposed to secede from the Union. He said he felt so strongly about the matter of racial mixing in the schools that he planned to organize and lead a militia group to oppose the unjust imposition of federal power by secession. He jokingly asked me if I would join his militia. I had turned down a commission of First Lieutenant in the Air Force to come as pastor to Shellman, and I wanted to say that I didn't see any hope of doing better in his outfit, but instead I gave him a serious answer. I reminded him that secession had already been tried and after four years of bloody warfare, had failed. I added "In our Civil War most of the Southerners were self employed, but the situation is different now. Here you are, a farmer and a mail carrier. You draw subsidies and a salary from the federal government. How can you talk about secession?" But Manry was probably about as sincere about giving up his job of mail carrier as he was about all pulling together after the vote was taken on me and it didn't turn out the way he expected it to do.

Manry did not take my lesson in American history with the grace befitting a Baptist deacon who delivered the mail for Uncle Sam and raised fine hogs on a farm just outside the city limits of Shellman. But it was George Robinette who pushed me near to the limits. George was married; he had small children, and he was operating a sawmill which employed a team of Negro workers. One of his children, a boy about eight years old, had a very threatening disease which manifested itself in the strange behavior of rocking back, and forth continually and uncontrollably. This was a very disturbing situation, and I could see that it would be a very big problem for the boy when he enrolled for school in the fall. I had gone to George's home to visit the boy and to try to be a comforting factor in the boy's parents' lives. While I was talking with the boy's mother George came into the room and confronted me with a display of anger.

George pushed right up into my face and demanded "do you still think it's all right for my children to attend school with niggers?"

I looked at the little boy rocking back and forth on the bed I looked at the anxious and embarrassed mother standing beside the child. I looked at George's angry face. I said "George, I don't believe going to school with black children is the biggest problem you are facing with this boy. I believe you have a much bigger concern than that with him."

George's anger boiled over. He was approaching violence. He said "Leave my house ... by the back door, like a nigger."

I left, even by the back door because George was standing between me and the front door. When I arrived at home the telephone was ringing. MarthaLee answered it, listened for a moment, and handed it to me. "It's for you. It's Mabel Robinette. She sounds upset."

George's wife had called to apologize for her husband's behavior toward me in their home. There were tears in her voice. When I hung up, I turned to my wife and told her what had happened. She said "Well, folks here have been saying you are trying to be a prophet. Now I will make a prophecy."

I could see the Irish humor in her dark brown eyes. I said "Speak, for your mate is listening."

"I prophesy," she intoned, the humor now becoming a twinkle, "that George Robinette will be sleeping on the couch for a while."

Later, it was told to me that a black woman in the community who had heard about the incident, said "I ain't sho' I wants mah chillun to go to school with Mister George's. I'se skeered some of it might rub off on 'em."

So the days and nights passed, filled with both anxiety and hope, for the opposition was building up, and our few close friends were drawing closer to us, forming a ring of love and concern about us. I began to feel that I knew how it must have been with the early church, a few close friends surrounded by an alien and hostile world. We prepared for the vacation trip though, and we went by way of Macon, to visit with Mama, and to leave Romulus with her.

It was enmity at first sight. Mama looked on Romulus with a jaundiced eye, and Romulus knew he was persona non grata, or an unwelcome cat. He sensed that we were leaving him there. He climbed the curtains in Mama's best room, hung there, glaring back balefully at all of us. Mama banished him to the garden and examined her curtains to assess the damage. "I'll put food and water out there for him," she said. "He can catch mice too." Mama was convinced that God has a purpose for every creature, and that the purpose for a cat is to catch mice.

Mama did not share my racial views, but only she and God were permitted to speak a word of criticism of me. She had taught me to show a "proper respect for darkies" but not to erase the line between us. She would keep Romulus for me while MarthaLee and I were off to Louisville, but she was convinced that I had ruined my chances at success in the ministry by getting involved in "the nigger question" when all that is required is that "we treat them right and let them stay in their place." As we drove toward Louisville, I remembered and told MarthaLee the story about Aunt Hattie.

THAT DOG OUGHTTA BE WHUPPED

If it seems to the reader that I was the friend of all dogs and all dogs loved me and fought loyally for me, that is a misconception. Some dogs saw me as the enemy, and these dogs I did not love and cherish. There was the case of the hound who belonged to Uncle Seeb and Aunt Hattie. I do not even have a name for this dog, which may have Freudian implications, but I have a story about him, which is really a story about Aunt Hattie, and I will recount this story here, for what it is worth in the account of my discovery of the world about me when I was a little boy growing up on the farm that lay just across the cotton patch from Uncle Seeb's and Aunt Hattie's house. The story is called THAT DOG OUGHTTA BE WHUPPED, and you will very soon understand why I have given it that title.

"Git back! Git back!" I cringed, trembled, and cowered before the big black dog, fearing that the bristling beast would charge right into my face, and not daring to turn and run because the dog would surely overtake me in two bounds, and be upon my back and legs, and bring me down. Better to have the menacing hound in front of me, facing me, where I could at least see him, even if I could not face him down. "Git back! Git back! I tell you! Git back!"

But the dog did not get back. Instead it charged at me, barking, growling, and snapping its teeth, and spreading its toes apart as its feet dug into the ground by the sheer force of its stiff legged charge. He was now so close I could feel his hot breath, see the saliva dripping from his hackles, see the hairs standing like bristles on his neck, see the eyes flashing in the excitement of the chase and in the elation of having cornered his quarry. For I was indeed at bay. I did not dare move out of my tracks. It is doubtful that my feet would have moved even if I had given them the command to do so.

All I could do was swing the bucket between myself and the dog, pendulum fashion. The bucket, now only half full of water intended for Papa who was plowing the corn field on the back side of the farm, was all that stood, or rather swung, between me and the black dog, a mixed breed of hound of indeterminate ancestry. And the dog was getting splashed or splattered by the water as I swung the bucket at him because I had nothing else to swing,

Oddly enough, this bothered the hound and me about equally for different reasons.

It disturbed me to lose the water because Mama had warned "Now hurry and take this to your Papa while it's still cold, but don't spill a drop of it." But the water splashing out did serve to keep the dog from making actual physical contact with me because some of the water splashed on him. And each time this occurred, the dog would flinch and jump aside as if the cold water might actually hurt him, although on a purely rational basis, the water must have felt good even to a dog on a hot summer day.

But a dog that will dive into the icy waters of a lake to retrieve a stick thrown by his master, does not like to have a tea cup full of water thrown on him.

And so while my little bucket of water might have seemed a flimsy defense against the snarling dog, it was all I had, and as the hound came charging right up into my face, breathing his hot breath on me and making a terrible racket, I swung the bucket, and water flew out of it in all directions, and the dog jerked back onto his haunches, and it seemed that his hind legs could not get out of the way of his front legs, and he left long claw marks on the bare ground of the field road that ran past Aunt Hattie's house as he dodged the wildly swinging bucket.

Charging forward again in that interval when I was trying to regain my balance after swinging the bucket violently, the dog's hind feet would then seem to run over its front feet in a frenzy to get at me. The dog kept up this attack, barking, snarling, growling and scratching up the ground as he charged and drew back just out of range of the bucket loaded with cold water sloshing out. I continued shouting at the dog. I was not even sure just what the words were that I shouted. Probably I repeated the same words over and over "Git back! Git back!" And my cries were as much a call for help from outside as they were verbal missiles hurled at my attacker. But it seemed that the big black mongrel would not give up his attack, but would press and harry me until I could not longer even swing the bucket and stand my ground in the face of the bared teeth and curling lips.

Then there was another sound, a voice calling to the dog, directed at the dog, commanding the dog's attention, demanding that the dog stop what he was doing. I could not tell what this new voice was saying, what the words were, for my mind was fastened upon the attacking dog, but I knew that the voice was loud and shrill and high pitched, and I could see that the voice penetrated the dog's consciousness, and that the dog knew and recognized the voice, realized that the voice was scolding him for what he was doing, knew the voice was commanding him to stop what he was doing. And in fact the dog had already begun to lessen the intensity of his attack on me when the command was accompanied by and reinforced by a terrible sensation of pain covering the major portion of the dog's body, particularly his back and hind quarters which were turned toward the house as the dog faced me. And the attack on the dog came, not from my water bucket and its contents, but from the rear, from the quarter left unguarded in his head long attack on me.

The pain which the black dog felt streaking over his exposed body came from a brush broom.

A brush broom is a bundle of small bushes or sprouts tied together with a string and comprising a large number of individual stems and twigs which altogether make up a very effective instrument for sweeping the bare dirt yard surrounding a house in the country. When the brush broom was new, the twigs and stems were all covered with fresh green leaves, making the brush broom soft and pliable. And if it were brought down on a dog's back in this condition, it might produce a severe fright, but not much harm. But as the broom aged, and with use, the leaves dropped off or were worn off, and the stems and twigs became bare and stiff and brittle, then the whole bundle could be wielded as effectively as a weapon as it had once served as an instrument of cleaning and neatness.

In this case the brush broom, leafless and brittle, was being used as a weapon in the gnarled hands of Aunt Hattie, who now brought it down on the dog's back with both force and vehemence; it was indeed an effective weapon. The dog, caught by surprise, since his whole attention was centered upon his attack on me, and the necessity for dodging my water bucket and is contents, was not sufficiently distracted by the familiar voice of Aunt Hattie, suddenly felt a thousand stings on his skin. He whirled, snarling, teeth bared to meet this attack from the rear, but just in time he recognized his owner, whose authority he respected and whose anger he feared second only to that of Uncle Seeb.

Uncle Seeb usually wielded a stick of stove wood to enforce his authority. The dog, now seeing Aunt Hattie, brush broom in hand raised for a second blow, changed his angry snarl to a pitiable whine, a yelp, a plea for mercy, and a complaint that he was only doing his assigned duty of guarding the house and its immediate environs against the intrusion of strangers, the current stranger being me.

Then scratching off with all four feet competing for the title of fastest of them all, and in a vain attempt to dodge a second blow of the brush broom which Aunt Hattie was already bringing down on his head and shoulders, the dog tucked his tail in a vain attempt to cover those parts which Nature has given to perpetuate the species, the dog now fled from Aunt Hattie's voice and her brush broom.

"You git under the house, dawg! Git on! Git!" The dog obeyed, and when he had got under the house, he turned, looked back on the battlefield from which he had fled, having had the glory of conquest snatched from his teeth by the blows of a worn and brittle brush broom, and transformed by Aunt Hattie's shrill voice into ignominious and shameful retreat he now crouched, ears alert. He started to bark again, but this soon turned into a mournful howl, and he turned, ears drooping, and went farther under the house where he routed out the hens that were dusting themselves in the shade, and he lay down and licked the wounds inflicted by Aunt Hattie's brush broom.

Then Aunt Hattie turned to me, all reassurance and comfort and solicitation. Her sharp eyes readily saw that I had not been bitten, mauled or even scratched. Only frightened out of my wits. And possibly out of the next two weeks of growth. She then set about to repair the damage done by the dog to my ego, my psyche, my self image. And if possible, to avert any retaliation that might come as a result of my report of the incident to my Papa, whose anger was a thing not to be taken lightly. For when it was hot, it was likely to scorch everything nearby; even as it cooled, it tended to harden into acts of vengeance which bordered on the cruel and unforgiving in their execution.

Papa was known to deal harshly with marauding packs of dogs that attacked and damaged his livestock. On one occasion he came upon dogs attacking a yearling calf in the back pasture. He waded in among them with a stick, kicking and clubbing them until they gave up the attack and fled. The calf was not dead, but it was badly injured, and he had to butcher it immediately to cut his losses. Papa recognized the dogs and he knew who their owners were. Negroes mostly, for they had the hungriest dogs.

Next morning, with the calf hanging in the smoke house, and Papa's anger unabated. he called to me to get into the old Dodge with him. Mama tried to persuade him to leave me at home, but Papa said I was old enough to learn what happens to cattle-killing dogs. We drove to the houses where the dogs belonged. Papa told his story. He had the owners to call their dogs out. He identified them, and shot them between the eyes with his .38 Smith & Wesson, leaving them for the owners to bury, drag off, or dispose of as seemed fitting for dogs shot for killing calves.

When we returned home, Mama said, "I hope there won't be any trouble."

"There won't be no trouble," Papa replied. "I have done took care of the trouble."

Mama bit her underlip and said "But the Sheriff ..."

Papa snorted. "That bootlegger turned Sheriff!? He won't make no trouble."

Whether the story ever reached the Sheriff's ears is unknown; it had reached Aunt Hattie's. She consoled me by saying "Ef that ol' dawg ever open his mouf when you passin' mah house Ah frail the daylights outta 'im an' Ah specs Seeb take a sticka stovewood to 'im when Ah tells im 'bout it. Now don' you ever be skeered of nuthin' roun' Aunt Hattie's house."

Aunt Hattie was a natural born psychologist, or one trained in the School of Experience and Hard Knocks. She not only foresaw that I would tell Papa; she also foresaw the inevitable demise of the dog if Papa decided he was a threat to my safety. This would result in fewer rabbits and possums to go into the big iron pot on the back of the cookstove. For without the dog, Seeb was but half a hunter.

Aunt Hattie, being better than just a piddling psychologist, but one worthy to be at the head of her class, said to me "Now you be sho' to tell yo' Papa jest 'xac'ly whut happened, and you git yo' Mama to 'xamine you close all over, an' ef she find even a scratch on you lef' by my dawg, you tell yo' Papa to come an' shoot 'im, an' Ah drag 'im out fr'm under mah house wher' he hidin' so yo' Papa can shoot 'im." For Aunt Hattie knew that telling Papa this was the surest way to safeguard the dog's life and protect the cookpot from the curse of emptiness.

When I found Papa plowing corn on the back side of the farm, I ran to Papa, crying and sobbing, for even though Aunt Hattie had dried my tears on her apron, and given a teacake to eat, when I saw Papa, the tears sprang anew into my eyes.

I flung myself on Papa, saying "Papa that mean ol' dog oughtta be shot!" I begged him to let me have his gun."I'll shoot 'im myself!" But Papa, both amused and pleased by my grit, had me to tell the story in great detail. Then he said that he thought the cold water and brush broom treatment might have cured the hound of his bad habits and that we might give him another chance.

"Lettin' you take the pistol to 'im might create more problems than it's solved. You might skeer Aunt Hattie clean outta her wits if she seen you comin' with that thirty eight in your hand, and on toppa it all, she'd think I'd done lost my mind for lettin' you have it."

I had watched Papa tilt the nearly empty bucket up and drain the last drop of water into his thirsty throat. Still unsatisfied, he pushed the empty bucket away and seemed to be thinking of more water, but my mind was still on the dog. "Papa" I said, "If Sandy was with me, I bet he would have whupped that ol' mean black dog. Wouldn't he?"

"I reckon he would, if he was with you."

"Papa, where has Sandy gone to?"

"God knows Son. He could be clear on the other side of the county. How long's he been gone now? Two days?"

Mama said he might be gone for a week, but she wouldn't say why he left. "Papa, how come Sandy ran off?"

"I reckon he's gone a courtin'. Son. Dogs do that. When a girl dog is in the heat, all the boy dogs in the county go a courtin' er."

"What's the heat, Papa?"

"The heat's when a girl dog decides she wants to be a mama and have a whole litter of new puppies. That's how come all the boy dogs show up and ev'ry one of 'em wantin' to be the papa of all them new puppies."

"Will Sandy be the papa, Papa?"

"I reckon he might. He's a strong fighter. But I reckon the mama dog may have somethin' to say about it too."

"Papa, how come Aunt Hattie's ol' black dog didn't go a courtin'?"

"I don't know the answer to that, Son. There are some things about a dog that a man jest can't figger out." Papa started to make a cigarette, and as he was pouring the Bull Durham into the little paper, his eyes twinkled and he said "I reckon maybe Sandy warned him to stay home this time."

"I wish Sandy'd come on back home and whup that ol' mean black hound. Papa, will Sandy bring the new puppies home with 'im?"

"I reckon not. Son. It'd be a little early for that. And the ol' mammy dog is awful possessive about her puppies, once she gits 'em." Papa was lighting his cigarette now. He drew the smoke in, and exhaled. "But after the frailin' Aunt Hattie give that black dog of hers I don't reckon he needs another whuppin' on toppa it whenever Sandy gits back home."

Papa finished his cigarette and said "I'll just unhitch ol' Kate an' we'll go to the house early. I'm still thirsty. And I reckon Kate would like a cool drink too." He was looping the trace chains over the hames, and tying up the plow lines. "Tell you what, Son. I'll set you up here on ol' Kate's back an' you can ride her to the barn. And when we go back past Aunt Hattie's house, if that black dog runs out at us, he can't reach you up there. And if he does come close, I'll haul off and kick the daylights outta 'im. And that'll learn 'im a lesson he won't soon forgit."

I was so pleased with this arrangement that I did not even mind about Kate being sweaty and all lathered from pulling the plow. I thought Mama might say "Lordy Mercy! Now just look at the seat of your over-alls! I'll have to wash them now." But I was too proud to let that bother me.

The procession, with me on Kate and Papa walking alongside, approached Aunt Hattie's house. The trace chains were jangling; leather straps were flapping against Kate's lathered haunches; the black dog barked once from under the house, and then he was silent; didn't even show his face, but it was enough to let Aunt Hattie know, and she came out of the house onto the porch. She yelled at the dog in a high pitched, shrill voice. "You shet yo' mouf' Dawg, or Ah take mah bresh broom to you ag'in."

Then Aunt Hattie called out to me "Doan you worry none 'bout thet ol' black dawg, Alfie. When Seeb come home fr'm the fiel' he take a sticka stove wood to 'im an' I bet he doan never bother you ag'in." She turned to Papa and said "Jes' lookit Alfie settin' up on 'at mule lak a little man!"

In such grandeur did I pass Aunt Hattie's house. And Papa said "Well Son. I reckon you won't have no more trouble outta that dog. I think you learned him a lesson. You and Aunt Hattie together. I reckon he won't fergit anytime soon."

I smiled back at Papa, because I was smiling inside myself, and I clutched Kate's bridle reins in my little hands. "Aw Shucks!" I said. "I ain't even skeered of that ol' dog no more. Come up, Kate!

****

And now while we are reckoning, I reckon that is enough for me to tell you about my adventures as a very small boy, and the influence of Aunt Hattie on me, for the present, so I will take you back to Shellman, and tell you about being "hanged for a nigger lover" because that is what this story is about. But I feel that it might not have happened the way it did if Papa had not taken Sunshine in and then had not taken him on the Snipe Hunt.

It might not have happened that way if it had not been for my encounter with Dump on her way to her royal wedding.

If Mama had not sent us to take a bath because we had been playing "winnants" on Sunday morning, before she would let us come to the dinner table, I might have grown up differently and consequently, acted differently when the Supreme Court handed down the Brown vs. the School Board decision.

And if Papa had just paid Aunt Hattie the fifty cents he owed her instead of sending me to tell her to go to the devil, how much differently I might have felt about everything.

If Junior had not landed the clod on Aunt Hattie's roof, I might have been spared that little bit of guilt that moved me to do the right thing.

And certainly if I had not thrown the corn in the faces of the black children standing on the edge of the ditch from our big orange school bus loaded with white children, I would not have been haunted by that memory, and required to pay for that sin.

Aunt Hattie, armed with a brush broom and natural psychology had her profound effect on me.

But here is another story about Aunt Hattie that I will tell you in order that you may understand my upbringing under her influence. The story of my hanging in Shellman can wait; we don't have to fear that it will go away.

GO TO THE DEVIL FOR FIFTY CENTS

Mama said to Papa "It won't be long now. Less than a month. Thank the Lord!"

"The way he's a kickin' an' jumpin' about it'll surprise me if he stays in there another week." Papa's face showed both concern and pride.

Mama smiled sadly. "I hope this one is a girl ... like Margaret."

Papa's face was closed now; he was quiet, thinking about Margaret. After a while Mama squeezed his hand, as if to say I didn't mean to bring up Margaret. She had squeezed his hand because she needed his strength. "I am so heavy on my feet. And so tired." Mama's big brown eyes had dark circles around them. "I can't get through the day without rest."

"Well, lay down an' rest. I'll lay here beside you."

"There's all the work ..."

"Let the younguns do the housework. 'Ol Aunt Hattie can do the washin' an ironin'."

"She does. And then sends it here by that Dump. That worries me. Dump teases Alfie. But Hattie brought them herself yesterday."

"Then let ol' Aunt Hattie bring 'em all the time, if you don't want Dump around."

"It still costs money." Mama's voice was tired, bordered on nagging. "It's fifty cents every time she does them."

They were drifting off to sleep in the middle of the day. Then there was a loud rapping on the steps at the back of the house. I heard it and ran to see who it was. White Lightnin' barked loudly but he didn't charge out from under the steps because it was a big heavy stick that was rapping on the step.

"I'se come to collect f'r washin' an ironin', Alfie. You run an' tell yo' Papa."

Aunt Hattie stood at the base of the steps that led up to the back porch. Her withered frame was draped in thin cotton dress that came well below her knobby knees, and reached almost to the top of her shoes. old broken work shoes. Tied together shoe strings served for shoe laces. The dress was faded so that it was impossible to tell what its original color was.

Aunt Hattie's black face was deeply lined. Her forehead was high and shiny. Her eyes watery, Her mouth toothless. Gnarled hands, with pink palms, grasped the "dew stick" which she used for knocking the wetness from the weeds and cotton stalks alongside the path that led across the cotton patch. The "dew stick" was also used for driving off barking dogs. White Lightnin' was well acquainted with Aunt Hattie's "dew stick", and he remained under the steps, barking.

"You tell yo' Papa I'se heah, Alfie. Tell 'im it's fi'ty cents he owes me f'r washin' an ironin'."

"Papa's takin' a nap, Aunt Hattie." I sat down on the step and reached through to pat White Lightnin' on the head. "I don't know if I oughtta bother 'im." I did know that Papa did not like to be bothered when he was taking a nap. "He don't like for nobody to bother 'im." A lesson I had learned painfully.

"Well, you see is yo' Papa wake yit, Alfie. Hit's near time he be goin' back to the fiel' anyway. An' Ah done walked over heah to c'llect what he owes me. I done brought nem clo'es yestiddy, an' he wan't heah when Ah come to bring 'em."

I peeped into the room where Mama and Papa lay on the bed. Papa was awake because he had heard the loud rapping on the doorstep. But I was right about Papa's mood. He was not ready to get up, and he didn't want to be bothered.

"Ol' Aunt Hattie's here, Papa." I poked my head fearfully into the door-way and waited for Papa's response.

"What does she want now?" Papa did not sound encouraging, and I became certain I had made a mistake by calling him.

"She said she wants her fifty cents for washin' and ironin'. She said that's what she's come for."

"You tell ol' Aunt Hattie to go to the devil." I had been right about Papa's mood. I hadn't expected the response to be quite this bad. Papa put his hands behind his head on the pillow, and he looked up at the ceiling where two or three houseflies were defying the laws of gravity by standing upside down on the ceiling. Papa watched flies while he considered Aunt Hattie's request for the fifty cents he owed her for washing and ironing.

"Yess'r." I stared at Papa for a moment to see whether he would amend what he had said. He didn't. Then I turned and darted from the doorway. "I'll tell 'er what you said."

"You shouldn't have done that." Mama said. "It's wrong." Papa watched the flies on the ceiling, and didn't reply.

I ran to the top of the steps. Aunt Hattie looked to see if I had the money in my hand; she saw that I did not. "Papa said to tell you to go to the devil, Aunt Hattie." I wanted to get it said before my courage failed me, but when it came out I felt very bad and afraid. I had never before been the bearer of a profane message. Never, on my own, had I dared to tell anyone to go to the devil. Not even Junior. And I had been angry enough at Junior to do it, but fear and better judgment had prevailed. The words were the moral equivalent of telling somebody to go to hell and although Junior had goaded me at times, I was afraid to say it.

Afraid Junior would beat me for it. Afraid that if I told Mama or Papa Junior had beaten me, then I would have to tell why. But now Papa had told me to say it to Aunt Hattie and I had said it.

I said inside my head "Papa told me to; it must be all right." But from my gut came the response that it was not all right. My head told me that white people can say those things to niggers that niggers can't say to white people. But my gut told me otherwise, and Aunt Hattie's response confirmed what my gut said. Aunt Hattie looked at me with angry sparks in her watery eyes. She worked her wrinkled lips over her toothless gums. She gripped the stick in her hands until the veins stood out on the backs of her hands. Then she spoke. "Alfie, I' se shamed of you. I never spected to heah sech words fr'm you. An' you jest a little chile. Whut yo' Papa done put you up to, Chile?"

Then Aunt Hattie spat in the dust at the base of the steps that led up to the porch where I was standing. She whirled around and hobbled off, gripping the stick in her gnarled old hands, and striking the ground with the stick each time she took a step in the broken work shoes with the broken and tied up strings for laces. As she walked, the shoes still stood apart at the tops and exposed her thin and wrinkled ankles.

White Lightnin' ran out from under the steps when Aunt Hattie turned to go, and he barked at her because he recognized the anger in her voice. But she waved her stick threateningly at the dog, and she said "You git under the house, dawg, 'fo Ah learn you a lesson you won't fergit!" White Lightnin' kept his distance and continued barking, but in a rather subdued voice. Aunt Hattie went on striking the ground with her stick, and muttering "Shame! Shame! An' him jest a chile. Ah never spected."

I felt the shame. I went away to my little hiding place under the scuppernong arbor where the vines hid me from view. There I played, though half heartedly with the little toy truck that Willie had whittled out of a block of wood, then nailed bottle caps on for wheels. Willie was my oldest brother and I idolized him. But while I played with this primitive toy, I watched Aunt Hattie crossing the cotton patch, and entering the unpainted wooden shack where she lived. I sat there in my hiding place, and when Papa came out of the house to get ready to go back to his work in the fields, I stayed very still and quiet, for I was ashamed. Ashamed of what Papa had done, and even more ashamed of myself.

Papa brought Kate the mule from the barn; he put the harness on her, and then he turned to Mama who was standing on the porch, watching him, "Well, I'm going to the field." It sounded like such a needless thing to say, and Mama made no reply. Papa said "Where is Alfie? What's he doin'?"

Papa finished buckling the harness on Kate, and he turned again toward Mama as if he would say something more, or he expected her to say something, and she said "You shouldn't have done it. It was wrong." Then Mama turned to go slowly back into the house.

Papa gave an angry tug at the knot he was tying in the hame string, and he said loudly enough for me to hear it in my hiding place "a damn' nigger'll worry a man to death about money." Then he jerked at the line fastened to Kate's bridle. "Come up Kate." He walked away, following the mule, putting his feet down hard and whistling the way I had learned that he whistled when he knew he had done something that Mama disapproved of and he didn't feel good about it.

As Mama was going back into the house, I heard her say as if she were just talking to herself, or maybe to the Lord: "He ought not to have told Alfie to say that to her. It wasn't right."

The next day Mama told Papa that she was out of kerosene, and Papa had noticed that his little sack of Bull Durham was so nearly empty there was no use to pull the string to hold it together at the top, so Papa called me and said "You run and get the kerosene can. We'll hafta go to the store and get some."

He started the engine of the old Dodge, and I climbed into the front seat beside him, but I was quiet because I saw Mama walking out toward the car. She stood beside the window on Papa's side, and she said very firmly to Papa "You better stop and see Aunt Hattie and pay her. You know that wasn't right what you did, and it's a sin for you to go and buy tobacco for yourself when you owe Aunt Hattie for washing and ironing and doing the work for me that I'm not able to do for myself."

Papa didn't say anything in reply, and I could sense that the issue was sharp between them. Then Papa put the Dodge in gear and drove out of the yard.

We pulled out of the sandy driveway and into the road that had been scraped by the Chain Gang; we approached Aunt Hattie's house; we could see Aunt Hattie standing out by the road. She was leaning on the mailbox with the lettering on it that ran down to squiggles at the bottom of the letters. But when she saw Papa's old Dodge coming she stood up straight and waved an old rag to hail Papa and let him know she wanted him to stop.

Papa began whistling as he slowed down and I looked up at Papa's face because I knew what his whistling meant, and then we pulled up to Aunt Hattie and I could see she hadn't waved us down to wish us a happy birthday. But Papa put on his best face and said "Mornin' Aunt Hattie. You want somethin'?"

Aunt Hattie's frown told me that the question was not needed. "Ah wants mah fi'ty cents what you owes me f'r washin' an' ironin'." She stepped closer to the car and said "An' Ah wants to know how you specs me ter c'llect it where you sent word by Alfie here fer me to go."

Papa hadn't said anything in his own defense yet and he was fumblin' the pockets of his overalls. Aunt Hattie went on. "You specs me ter c'llect whut you owes me frum de devil?"

Now Papa's fingers had located what he was searching for, and he reached out the open window of the old Dodge toward Aunt Hattie's gnarled hand with the pink palm. Aunt Hattie reached for the coin in Papa's hand, but she was not done with her reprimand. "Ah'm plum s'prised at you sendin' a word lak dat to me when Ah ain't done nuthin' to make you mad at me but wash an' iron yo' clo'es."

Papa turned to me and said "Did you tell Aunt Hattie to go to the devil, Son?"

My face was drawn with pain; my lips trembled; the salty tears stung my eyeballs. "You told me to say it." Now I faced Papa with the shame and the anger boiling up inside me. "You told me to tell Aunt Hattie to go to the devil. You told me to say it, Papa."

"Well, damn it all, you don't hafta ..." Papa was about to say that I didn't have to say everything I was told, but he knew that would not do, because he demanded obedience in all things, so he sputtered "You oughtta knowed better!" But there was more anger than strength in what he said. He held out the fifty cent piece to Aunt Hattie. She took it, still looking reprovingly at Papa.

Her final shot was "An' him jes' a chile. Alfie jes' a chile."

Papa put the old Dodge in gear. The gears scraunched and clashed. The Dodge lurched forward. Pulled away from Aunt Hattie's mailbox. And Aunt Hattie clutching the fifty cent piece. Papa threw his head back so far an observer might have thought he was driving from the back seat. He whistled in a manner that said he had now put the worst behind him, but it told me he was not happy about it and maybe not satisfied with himself.

Well, while we are on the subject of Aunt Hattie, here is another story in which I do not come out as the hero in shining white armor.

A CLOD ON THE ROOF

When I was "jest a chile" I had three older brothers. I mentioned Willie who was my role model and hero and protector. Then there was Junior; he was two years older than I was, so we were always in competition, and the only time I ever won was when we had that ripe tomato battle in the garden and I mistakenly picked up a broken brick which was about the same color as a tomato but it had a different effect when I hurled it at Junior's head. James was two years older than Junior, and I didn't have a chance in battle with James, unless Willie, whom we all called Tillman because Gran'ma was called Willie, came to my rescue.

James and Junior sometimes teamed up on me because I was "jest a chile" and they got me into trouble with Aunt Hattie when they hatched up a piece of mischief in the plum bushes that bordered the cotton patch between our house and Aunt Hattie's. "How far do you think it is?" Junior asked James as we crouched in the plum bushes and looked at Aunt Hattie's house.

"Farther than you can th'ow a clod." James replied to taunt Junior because Junior prided himself on both the distance and the accuracy of his throwing arm.

"You wanta bet?" Junior measured the distance with his eye as he studied the unpainted weatherboard house with the rusty tin roof on the edge of the cotton patch. "I betcha I can lob one right on top of it."

It was just a two room shanty. Two rooms and a kitchen set apart and joined by a dog run, a sort of outdoor walkway made of pine boards. A brick chimney stood above the roof of the main part of the house. A terra cotta liner with a cap on it jutted through the roof of the kitchen and marked the location of the wood burning stove used for cooking. A thin wisp of smoke came out of the stove pipe, indicating that Aunt Hattie was cooking dinner. The window sash on the side of the kitchen facing the thicket of plum bushes was weathered to match the grey weather boards. One pane was broken out of the window. Aunt Hattie had patched the hole with cardboard to keep out the wind and the rain.

I said "You better not!" For I was alarmed by the expression on Junior's face. "Uncle Seeb'll come out here an' ..."

"Shucks! Seeb ain't even in there." Junior scoffed at my fear. "Ain't nothin' he can do about it even if is in there. I ain't skeered of no ol' nigger." Junior picked up a clod of hard red clay. The clod was about the size of a baseball. He rubbed at the rough edges with his fingers, and some of the dirt crumbled off leaving a red stain on Junior's hands. He parted the wild plum bushes with his left hand, holding the clod in his right. He could see more clearly now, but the bushes still formed a canopy overhead. It would be difficult to see the boys unless their movement drew attention to them.

"Well, why don't you go ahead and th'ow it?" James grinned as he urged Junior on. "Lemme see you drop it down the stovepipe. Go ahead. If you ain't skeered of ol' Aunt Hattie."

James' gibe was moving Junior to overcome both fear and his better judgment. "I can't see too good in these bushes," Junior complained. "I can't raise my arm up high enough to throw it."

"Well, git out there where you can see. If you ain't skeered you'll be seen out in the open. Git on out there."

Junior's face reddened. He pushed toward the edge of the plum thicket. "If I can just git my arm up."

James stood under the plum bushes, grinning. I said "You better not do it, Junior. If Papa finds out..."

"Yeah! Who's gonna tell 'im?" James punched me on the arm. "You gonna tell 'im? Papa ain't gonna know nothin' unless you tell 'im."

I crouched lower under the plum bushes. "I hope you git caught. I hope Uncle Seeb ketches you. It'll serve you right." At that moment I hated my brothers. They were going to get me in big trouble; I was too little to oppose them.

"Shut up an' stay outta my way. I can't see what I'm doin' with you in my way." Junior pushed closer to the edge of the cotton patch. When he reached the clear space he stood up, hurled the clod and dived back into the plum bushes. "Ouch!" he yelped as a thorn hung in his shirt sleeve and scratched his arm.

The clod sailed in an arc over the cotton patch while three pairs of eyes watched its flight. It landed heavily on the tin roof just above the kitchen, and crumbled on impact. A stream of red dirt moved slowly down the steeply pitched roof.

"Bull's eye!" James exclaimed. The crumbled dirt gathered speed and cascaded past the window, and fell to the ground.

"Lordy mercy!" Aunt Hattie was in the kitchen. She stood still. "Whut was that?" She started toward the kitchen door.

Then she saw the red dirt falling past the window to the ground. She stared out through the window, her own face concealed by the cardboard covering the space where the window pane had been broken out. She couldn't see anyone but the tops of the plum bushes were moving. "Somebody in dem bushes!" Aunt Hattie said.

She stood motionless, watching. The bushes were moving. The high cheek bones of her face glistened with sweat, and her lips moved without forming words. Only a muttering of anger and frustration. Then, "Some triflin' younguns in dem bushes th'owin clods."

Junior and James giggled under the bushes. My eyes were big with fright. "You're gonna git it if Papa finds out!" I hoped Papa would find it out.

"Ha!" Junior snorted. "How's he gonna find out? Ain't nobody even in there. If there was somebody would come to the door."

"Here, th'ow another one, Junior." James pushed a big red clod toward Junior. "This'll bring 'em out if there's anybody in there."

"We better be gitten outta here!" I warned. "That is what we better be doin'."

"Well you just git out, Scaredy Cat." Junior was feeling cocky now.

I started to move toward the open cotton patch. "Don't git out where somebody'll see you." James grabbed my arm to restrain me. Then, turning to Junior, "Here, take this clod. It's got little rocks in it. When it lands on the roof they'll think the world's comin' to an end."

Junior took the clod from James and stood up in the edge of the cotton patch He drew his arm back to make the pitch. The door to Aunt Hattie's kitchen flew open. She came charging out with a stick of stovewood in her hand."Whut y'all up to? Settin' out in nem plumbushes an th'owin' clods on folkses houses. Jes' wait twell Ah gits mah han's on y'all."

Aunt Hattie's voice was charged with anger. She was coming across the cotton patch two rows at a tine, and waving the sick of stovewood over head. "Bless God! Jes'stan' where y'all is twell Ah gits mah han's on y'all."

Junior stood for a moment, frozen between the windup and the pitch. His mouth fell open. His fingers relaxed. He dropped the clod and. took to his heels without uttering a word.

James was close behind him. "Run!" he called to both Junior and me. "Y'all run!"

I was already doing what he was urging me to do. I was running for my life, but falling behind my bigger brothers, and yelling "Wait for me! Wait for me!" They looked back but they did not slow down. I was desperate.

Aunt Hattie ran out of steam and stopped running. But she stood, waving the stick and yelling at us. "Y'all jest wait twell Ah tells yo' Papa whut you done. Y'all gonna git it f'r sho' when yo' Papa know bout whut you done. An' Bless God Ah be watchin' when he whups y'all."

The pre-vision of justice being meted out Papa style brought a sweet foretaste to Aunt Hattie's mouth. Her anger subsided. She began to shake with laughter. "Jes' lookit nem white younguns run! Bless God! Ah b'lieve Alfie gonna ketch up on Junior an' James if his little short legs doan give plum out on 'im. Bless God!"

And now after this diversion into the boyhood stories, we can go back to Shellman, which had become a very intense place. MarthaLee and I welcomed the retreat from battle and the hope of a little rest in Louisville.

With memories of early childhood training in race relations ringing in my head, we drove on to Louisville, where we were received with wonder by the people who had never experienced what had happened to us in Shellman. We settled into an apartment on campus, thinking Rest and Recreation. Then the bad news began to arrive in the mail.

But not yet. There was time for reverie, for talking with old friends, men who had been my teachers. We were now on a first name calling basis since I now held the same degrees they did. Time for students who were amazed at what had happened to me and wondering what would happen to them when they went out to proclaim the Word. Time for walks in Cherokee Park, remembering that this was the only form of recreation we could afford when we were students. Yes, students. I had spent six years at the seminary, and MarthaLee had studied at the University of Louisville, getting her degree and qualification to teach in public schools. I had even done a summer's study in German language there, in the hope of being able to read the German theologians in their own language. But most summers I spent mowing the grass on the Seminary grounds and painting the latrines in the men's dormitory and hauling off garbage when there was no opportunity for me to preach in summer revivals in country churches in Kentucky.

I had talked with a New York publisher about rewriting my doctoral thesis in a more popular vein, but I was determined not to lose the academic impact of it. It was called THE DAY OF THE LORD: A STUDY IN JUDGMENT AND REDEMPTION. I said to the publisher "I would like to write something worth while that people will read."

He studied my face. "Which? Something worth while? Or something people will read?"

Now, with three years of experience under my belt, and a new insight to both Judgment and redemption, I was going to try for both because my venture in writing to the editor of the Atlanta Journal/Constitution had convinced me that it was possible to write something worth while that people would read. They might not like it. They might hang me for it. But they would read it if it touched their lives at sensitive points. So I dug into the job in the Seminary Library, and before I had finished the first chapter of my book I got mail from home in Shellman.

Miss Susie May Brown informed me in her letter that there was a rumor going about Shellman that the Brooksville and Friendship churches were planning to take action against me. "A rumor is a precursor of bad news," I said to MarthaLee. The next day an official letter arrived from the Brooksville church.

Benevolence, Georgia
July 12,1954

Dear Brother:

After much thought and consideration of your views and expressions on segregation or the non segregation of the 'White and Black races, we, the Brooksville Baptist Church, met in called conference the night of June 30,1954 so that each member might express his or her opinion by ballot for or against your pastorate of the church. Twenty one (21) votes were cast; nineteen (19) against and two (2) for.

Therefore, believing as we do that it would be detrimental to the welfare of our church should you remain as its pastor, we regretfully and respectfully ask for your resignation.

Sincerely,
Eddie E. Arnold, Deacon
W. I Arnold, Deacon

We studied this missive soberly, and I said "It is a good time for us to take a walk in Cherokee Park." The park lies adjacent to the Seminary grounds. As we walked, we thought of Bob and Kay Culpepper who used to have breakfast with us in the park in our student days. Now they were missionaries in Japan. "His people back in South Georgia must be proud of him," I said. "Taking the gospel to people of another race on the other side of the world."

MarthaLee's response was to grip my hand tighter. She said "Sometimes I wonder if it would not have been better if you had gone into the chaplaincy." I was beginning to wonder the same thing.

A few days later, a letter came from the Friendship Church:

Shellman, Georgia
July 20,1954

Dear Brother Buchanan:

The Friendship Baptist Church in conference last night, July 19,1954, voted to end your services to the church as pastor effective as of the date of the conference. For your information the vote was 31 to 6 with 2 abstaining from voting.

Respectfully,
R.B. Martin, Moderator

I lost interest in the rewriting of THE DAY OF THE LORD: A STUDY IN JUDGMENT AND REDEMPTION. I felt that the Day of the Lord had come. At least the judgment part of it. "I guess this calls for another walk in Cherokee Park." She seemed a bit enigmatic about it, but what else was there to do? What else could happen?

There was a letter from Claron Wooten. He said that the School Board in Shellman was going to ask MarthaLee to resign her teaching position. "I have bought a little time for her though," he said, "by urging the School Board members to wait a few days." He explained that this was to give MarthaLee time to offer her resignation without being asked for it "because in this way she could save face."

MarthaLee had a face worth saving, but not that way. It was a classic wild Irish Rose face that didn't need any help. And she had the fighting Irish spirit to go with her face. She was a Gillis from Soperton, Georgia, and her family name was just a different spelling of the Irish Gilley flower, renowned for its delicate beauty. I had met her during World War Two when both of us were handling sensitive powders for loading the fuses for the bombs that would sink the navy of the Japanese Empire in the Pacific ocean. Now we knew what was coming. We waited; even walks in the park didn't help much. But she made no response until the letter came from the School Superintendent.

July 10,1954

Dear Mrs. Buchanan:

The trustees of the Shellman School have concurred in the opinion that it would be the better thing for the Shellman Schools if you would submit your resignation as a teacher for the coming year. The trustees, with the knowledge and consent of the County Board of Education, have requested me to write and ask for your resignation. It is also the desire of the board to keep down any publicity on the matter.

Please give the above matter your very earliest attention.

Yours very truly,
J.D. Shepard, Superintendent

The Superintendent had made a mistake. The Trustees of the Shellman School had made a mistake. And the County Board of Education had made a mistake. The mistake was that they had underestimated MarthaLee. She was not going to grant their desire to keep down publicity. She was, in fact, going to give it just the sort of publicity that their action deserved. I could have told them if they had asked me that it would not work with MarthaLee. But they did not ask me. I was in fact, the reason they were asking for her resignation. So, together we wrote a reply to J.D. Shepard, MarthaLee signed it, and called his bluff.

Mr. J.D. Shepard, Superintendent
Randolph County Schools
Cuthbert, Georgia

Dear Mr. Shepard:
I will not resign. However, in view of the expressed desire of the trustees of the Shellman School, and the request forwarded through you, it has become imperative that the grounds of this request be plainly stated. Moreover, any action that is taken to invalidate the existing contract will have to be initiated by those parties interested in my removal, and the responsibility therefore must be borne by them.

Sincerely,
Martha Lee Buchanan

Nobody involved wanted to make a public statement that a good teacher of the Second Grade of the Shellman Elementary School was being fired because her husband was saying that people ought to accept the ruling of the Supreme Court of the United States on Racial Segregation in Public Schools. They were racists but they were not stupid. We heard nothing more about resignation from Mr. Shepard.

But by this time our vacation was spoiled. The "retreat" had now been turned into an "attack". We said goodbye to old friends, two of whom deserve special mention here: Jim Coker and Ed Straney. Jim was completing his doctoral studies in Louisville; both he and Ed were serving churches in Columbus, Georgia. Both of them had made strong statements on the racial issue. Neither of them had been fired. Perhaps it was because they had not written letters to the editor of the Atlanta papers.

So we packed our bags and drove home. We stopped at Mama's house near Macon, to retrieve Romulus. He heard my voice when I greeted Mama. He came bounding out of the garden, leaped into my arms, cast a baleful glance backward at Mama who reciprocated his feelings, and rode home happily with us. He dug his claws into the back rest of the front seat of the Ford, and held on. Mama reaffirmed her love for us, Romulus forgave us, we went home with a premonition of bad things yet to come. The bad things were not long delayed in coming.

It was at about the time when we had reached the lowest ebb, and it seemed there was no real hope of staying in Shellman, certainly no chance of achieving a resolution of the crisis, that MarthaLee turned her big brown eyes on me and said "Why did you go into the ministry anyway? I've never heard you say there was a vision or a voice from heaven, or any great event in your life that caused you to make that decision. I do know you were young at the time, probably too young to know any better. But why did you have to be a preacher and try to change the world and get us into all this trouble?

"You could have done something else, and we could have lived normal lives like other people do. Instead, here we are with most of the people wanting us to leave, and we have no place to go."

I couldn't put my finger on it myself. Certainly no Damascus Road experience. But I was always certain that I would be a preacher. At least, ever since I got over the childish fancy of being a Greyhound bus driver. And I was in one of my story telling moods, when I sometimes find the truth hidden under a clod of Georgia red clay, and I said "maybe it was because of the cyclone shelter, if you have to find something supernatural, although there is nothing more natural than the weather, and a cyclone is just part of the weather."

"But what has the cyclone shelter to do with it? I never even heard you mention a cyclone shelter, and I certainly was never in one."

"Well, it was Papa's idea to build the cyclone shelter, or as Gran'ma put it, dig a big hole in the ground, and fix it up to protect us from the cyclones that were predicted to hit our region of Middle Georgia. We all pitched in with the digging and the building of the cyclone shelter, although I was so little most of what I did was get in the way of the others. We finished it just in time."

"Just in time for what?"

"The cyclone. We all saw the funnel cloud moving toward us and we ran, Gran'ma leading the way, Mama and Papa, we four boys, and Sandy the ever present dog. We got in and pulled down the lid just as the cyclone hit. The rain came with it and we were standing ankle deep in water when we heard, felt something crash onto the top of the shelter, and when we tried to get out we couldn't because of the weight. We were trapped, but when the storm was over Mister Charles came with an axe and chopped away, saying, "Looks like the cyclone took the roof off that ol' hay barn and dumped it right on toppa your cyclone shelter."

"All the time we were in there, Gran'ma kept saying "Lord God! Buried alive in this hole in the ground! And me without my snuff! I'd a heap ruther be blowed away than be buried alive!"

"But Mister Charles hacked away until we were able to get out. We looked all around and saw the house was still standing, and this set Gran'ma off again on the folly of going into a hole in the ground to escape a cyclone.

"It was all very exciting, but it was what followed the cyclone that has a real bearing on the fix we are in now, because that was when Uncle Seeb introduced me to Ol' Needmo'."

"I never heard of Ol' Needmo'. Who is that?"

"You probably experienced him under a different name. Anyway, it was in the context of our discussion of Ol' Needmo' that Uncle Seeb brought me around to telling about my call to preach. I reckon I'd had the notion for some time, maybe ever since I gave up the hope of becoming a Greyhound Bus Driver, but I hadn't made it public."

"Are you telling me that Ol' Needmo' called you to preach? And got us into this mess? That's like saying the Devil made you do it."

"Not exactly. I reckon I could have gone into the Air Force Chaplaincy and I wouldn't have got hanged."

"No. But they would have put you on KP or had you picking up cigarette butts, for not following orders. But go ahead and tell me about Ol' Needmo'. I'll listen."

OL' NEEDMO'

Daybreak on the day after the cyclone! The sun rose like a great ball of fire, which I guess is what it really is, on a world reborn in that short midsummer night while I slept and dreamed of being trapped in the cyclone shelter. Papa was up before daylight, and when Papa was up nobody else got any sleep. He was eager to get out and see the effects of the storm. Papa always had to walk in great long strides all over the farm after a big rain. Or even a small shower. He had to see how much the corn and cotton had grown, and what damage had been done. He had to see the good and the bad and weigh the one against the other.

"I wanta see what it's tore up and what it's growed up." But when he thought I had got my eyes open, he said "I wonder about Seeb and Hattie. They didn't have no cyclone shelter to run into, and I wonder if the cyclone done any damage at their house."

My eyes grew large with the expectation of finding out what had happened, and I said "I could go and see, Papa."

Papa said "I'd like to know, but I don't have time to go myself. You run and ask your Mama." I had already learned that if I asked Papa he would say "go ask your Mama," but if I asked Mama she would say "run and ask your Papa." So I was caught, and I said "it'll be all right with Mama." Then Papa said "you run and ask her anyway. Then you run over there and check up on them two. But don't stay too long because your Mama will git worried and hafta send for you."

I started to run, then hesitated, and Papa read the fear in my mind and on my face, so he said "Sandy can go with you to keep that ol' black dog of Seeb's offa you."

That removed the last obstacle to my heroic errand of mercy, and with Sandy racing ahead of me and spoiling for a fight, I set off across the cotton patch for a visit with Uncle Seeb and Aunt Hattie. And as it turned out, with Destiny.

Destiny was waiting for me in the persons of Uncle Seeb and Aunt Hattie.

I found Uncle Seeb sitting on a cane bottom, straight back Chair tilted against the porch wall. He was admiring the glorious sunrise. Uncle Seeb was a ponderous man with an impressive belly that balanced on the chair when it was tilted back against the wall. His neck was thick, and the skin gathered in folds there, and the sweat ran down most of the time when it was hot; it was hot most of the time in summer. In Bibb County it was hot at daybreak with the sun coming up like a great ball of fire in the sky.

Uncle Seeb's face shone like the sun itself, but it was like a black shining sun, like ebony. Papa said "I don't reckon there's another face in Bibb County that's blacker'n Seeb's. And Papa ought to know because he was acquainted with the people of color in Bibb County. Black, yellow, brown, and just pale. But he favored the ones that were black because Papa didn't approve of mixing, and when he saw a yellow face, or a pale one with frizzy reddish hair, he would say "There's been a white man in the wrong bed somewhere." You could tell that Papa didn't approve. Papa approved of Seeb though, the blackest man in the county.

It was not necessary to say that a black man might have been in a white woman's bed because he would have been lynched.
Uncle Seeb smiled when he saw me coming, and he displayed an impressive array of ivory in his mouth, matching the whiteness in his eyes, which made the blackness of his face shine even brighter by contrast. Uncle

Seeb had a mouthful of white teeth, but he had one tooth that was not white; it was gold.

Uncle Seeb's gold tooth caught and held my eye whenever he smiled, which was whenever he looked at me. Once had stared wonderingly at the great black face with its toothy smile, and I had said "Uncle Seeb, how come you got one yellow tooth?"

Then Uncle Seeb said "Lawd, Alfie, now you talkin' bout my gold tooth?"

I nodded solemnly and said "How come you got one gold tooth?"

He smiled again and said "Now you done ast 'bout somethin' goes way back befo' you wuz bawn, an' befo'Ah wuz bawn ag'in."

My wonderment grew, and he said "Befo' mah Lawd tole me to give up mah bad ways an' go preach His Name."

Six days in the week Uncle Seeb was a cotton and corn tenant farmer, but on Sundays he was a preacher. Six days in the week he labored in the fields, but one day a week he labored in the Lord's vineyard. Six days he was black Seeb, the blackest in Bibb County, but on that one day he was The Reverend. And when he stood in the pulpit of the Shiloh Baptist Church, dressed in his black suit, and when he opened his black leatherette bound Bible, then his black face Shone with the fire of the Lord. "Befo' Ah give up mah bad ways an I become a preacher."
"What bad ways did you hafta give up when you become a preacher, Uncle Seeb? What bad ways?"

"Fightin', Alfie." Uncle Seeb was reflective. I waited to hear about the fighting.

"Ah wuz bad 'bout fightin' in my younger days. An' there wuz this pretty little gal. She wuz a high yaller, an' Ah thought she wuz the prettiest gal Ah ever seen. But Ah ain't the onliest one think she pretty. Other young fellers think it too. So we got inta a big fight over that pretty little yaller gal, an' Ah los' mah tooth, an' thas how come Ah got one gold tooth."

"Did it grow back gold, Uncle Seeb? Did it grow back thataway?"

"Lawd no, Alfie. Hit cost me a bale a cotton, this gol' tooth did. No, Alfie, hit didn't grow back lak they do f'r you 'cause I done got too big an' old f'r that when Ah got to fightin' an' loss mah tooth. This gol' tooth, hit cost me a bale a cotton."

He displayed the gold tooth for my admiration by flashing a big smile at me.

"Ah ain't proud of how Ah come to have it, but now Ah got it Ah ain't shamed to show it." I could see that he was proud of the gold tooth, and I wished that I could have a gold tooth to replace the one that was getting loose and Papa was teasing me to let him pull it.

I sat on the doorstep to think about what Uncle Seeb had said, and I forgot that I had come to see if the cyclone had done any damage. Sandy was standing on the ground near the steps; he was growling, and his bristles were up just to let Uncle Seeb's old black hound know that he had better stay under the house, The hound barked some and even growled a little, but the growl ended up sounding more like a whine, and he backed farther under the house. I was just sitting quietly thinking about things. Then I remembered the cyclone. "That was some storm we had, wasn't it, Uncle Seeb? We all run in the cyclone shelter when it hit."

"Sho' nuff!" Uncle Seeb had been able to see from a distance that the old hay barn was missing its roof, but that was all he had seen until he saw Mama and Papa and all the rest of us coming away from the storm shelter. He had counted us as we came out, even Sandy, and he had said to Aunt Hattie "Thank de Lawd evvybody safe 'cept the ol' hay barn whut done los' hits cap."

Now he flashed a great white and gold smile at me. "Ol' Massa, when he go on a rampage He sho' tear up Jack. When 'at bolta lightnin' hit Ah said to Hattie, Ol' Massa sho' th'owin' a fit. Ef you done ennything bad lately you better be prayin." Then he laughed to let me know' that he was joking about Aunt Hattie being the one who needed to pray, but Aunt Hattie appeared in the kitchen doorway at that moment. She had a little pan of bread scraps in her hand, and she frowned at Uncle Seeb.

"Lawd have mercy! You oughtta be 'shamed of yo'self, Rev'ren, sayin' a thing lak whut you jes' said in fronta Alfie an' him jest a chile."

She pitched the bread scraps out into the yard. Eight or ten chickens came running to get them. Some Barred Rocks called domineckers, Rhode Island Reds. Some mixed, all hungry. One old Dominecker who had been moulting and hadn't yet replaced all the feathers she had lost, came over to me, looked up at me with her head cocked to one side, and pecked my little toe nail. "Shoo!" I kicked at her and drew my feet up under me. I turned to Aunt Hattie and said "That ol' hen thinks my toe nail is a grain of corn."

Then Aunt Hattie noticed that I was sitting on the wet doorstep, and she said "law me Alfie! You settin' on nem wet do'teps an' Ah bet you done got yo' seata yo' britches wet." She lifted me up and felt the seat of my short pants and said "Sho' nuff! You soppin' wet an' yo' Mama goan th'ow a fit an' Ah be one to hafta wash an' iron 'em too. Lemme git you a cheer to set in."

"Aw, I don't mind a little wet, Aunt Hattie. It ain't gonna hurt me. You shoulda seen the water in the cyclone shelter yesterday."

"Ah bet, an' now Ah heah you got trapped in that ol' hole befo' hit was all over. Still ain't no cause f'r you to set on a wet do'step at mah house an' yo' Mama think Ah doan know how to treat you when you come to visit."

Aunt Hattie went back into the house to get a chair for me, and a fly landed on my bare knee. I slapped at the fly, missed; the fly lifted into the air and settled on the other bare knee. The Dominecker hen came back to have another close look at my toe. I said "Uncle Seeb. How come you don't screen in your porch? You could screen it in an' then nothin' couldn't git in to bother you."

I didn't mention the flies and chickens by name because Mama had told me not to say things that might hurt Aunt Hattie's and Uncle Seeb's feelings. So I just said "Nothing couldn't git in to bother you if you had a screened in porch."

But Uncle Seeb's great belly shook with laughter when I asked, and his black face shone like it had been polished, and his teeth flashed white and gold, and he said "How come? On accounta Ol'Needmo', Alfie. Tha's how come. On accounta Needmo'."

I stared in wonderment at Uncle Seeb then, and I said "Who is Ol' Needmo' Uncle Seeb?"

"You ain't never hear tell of Ol' Needmo', Alfie? Lawd! I 'llowed yo' Mama an yo' Papa done tole you 'bout ol' Needmo'. Jess about evvybody know 'bout Ol' Needmo'."

My amazement deepened. I had never heard of Ol' Needmo'. Gran'ma had told me about the Booger Man, and Mama had explained to me that the Booger Man is the old devil who gets people who are bad, which is why they sometimes called him the Bad Man. This alone sufficiently frightened me to keep me from going out alone in the dark. Once I had awakened from a bad dream; the Bad Man was chasing me with a pitchfork. I was sleeping with Junior at the time, and I cried out, but Junior said "Aw shut up and quit jerkin' the covers." But Ol' Needmo'? Maybe he was the one who had made Uncle Seeb bad about fighting when he was young and interested in that pretty "yaller gal". So I looked solemnly and fearfully into Uncle Seeb's face. "Who's Ol' Needmo' Uncle Seeb. Tell me who he is."

Then Uncle Seeb said "Needm' flour to make biskits to feed hungry younguns. Needm' clo'es f'r wintertime comin' on. Needmo' shoes f'r all our bare feet. Needmo' 'bout evvything. So ain't no chance of buildin' no screen porch, Alfie, on accounta Ol' Needmo'."

Aunt Hattie came back with a chair like the one Uncle Seeb had, and she said "Heah Alfie, you set on a cheer now an' Ah hope you stay long anuff f'r yo' britches to dry 'cause Ah sho' doan want you to go home an' yo' Mama see you been settin' on mah wet do'steps."

I said "Aw, it don't matter, Aunt Hattie. I don't mind if I git wet in hot weather. It don't matter. I don't mind."

It was hot weather and Uncle Seeb's BVD's were already wet with sweat from his enormous body. Once I had asked him "How come you wear your Winter underwears in the summertime? Ain't they hot?"

I myself pulled off everything Mama would let me pull off in hot weather. The first thing in the Spring was to get rid of my shoes. Go barefoot. That was like putting wings on my feet. Then I wanted to shed my underwear. Then my shirt. My back and shoulders would get sunburned, and the skin would peel off. Mama would say "Lord Alfie! You've blistered again! If you don't wear a shirt when you're out in the sun you'll burn up. Just look at you!"

I would say "But I want to get brown."

Then Mama would say "Be thankful you're white." And even at that tender age I didn't need to be told what that meant. Papa had already told me the reason I couldn't drink coffee and must drink buttermilk instead.

"Drinkin' coffee will turn a growin' boy black." I was older when I realized that coffee costs money; we produced our own buttermilk.

But when I asked Uncle Seeb about wearing his heavy knitted BVD's in the summertime, his answer surprised me. "Naw, Alfie. Onst they gits wet with sweat hit's jest lak bein' wrapped in a cool wet blanket. The mo' Ah sweats the cooler Ah gits, inside my underwears."

But now I was sitting on the straight back cane bottom chair Aunt Hattie had brought for me, and my feet wouldn't touch the floor. So I hooked them behind one of the rungs of the chair. I thought that would hide them from the old Dominecker hen. Then Uncle Seeb's face became very serious, and he said to me "Alfie, whut you goan be when you grows up?"

He didn't say anything about the silken hairs on my arms that Papa had seen as an indication that I would grow up to be a successful pig raiser. He didn't ask what I was going to do. He just asked "Whut you goan BE when you grows up?" Then he leaned back against the wall, with the front feet of his chair raised off the floor, and his big belly balancing him. And he waited, watching me. Smiling now, but serious, like he really wanted to know.

I sat there frowning because of the memories. I remembered riding with Papa to Mister Robb's, and Mister Robb pulling those hairs and saying I'd be a pig raiser. I remembered Uncle Babe doing the same thing and cackling with glee when I winced at the pain. I thought about Tex on the Chain Gang, and the dump truck which had replaced the Greyhound Bus in my ambitions. I sucked in my breath and looked fearfully at Uncle Seeb because I was guarding my secret.

Uncle Seeb was studying that frown on my. face, and he said "But you doan hafta tell me ef you don't wants to. Ah jest ast, an' ef hit's yo' secret, an' you doan wanta tell nobody 'bout it, you doan hafta tell nobody. Hit's jest yo' secret an' hit doan b'long to nobody else."

I started to say something. I was going to say I didn't mind Uncle Seeb knowing but I didn't want anybody else to know. Uncle Seeb stopped me though. "Sho' now you got a secret an' you got a right to keep yo' secret, an' you doan hafta tell me lessen you wants me to know."

Then because of what Uncle Seeb had said, that I didn't have to tell him, I knew I wanted to tell him. I wanted to share my secret with Uncle Seeb. Aunt Hattie was standing in the doorway, watching and listening. She was holding the little pan again, with some more bread scraps, and she stood very still and quiet because she saw that this was a very serious conversation going on between me and Uncle Seeb, and she didn't want to interrupt it. I saw Aunt Hattie standing there, and I knew it was all right for Aunt Hattie to know too.

I looked at Uncle Seeb and I looked at Aunt Hattie, and I looked down at my bare feet which I had taken down from the chair rung so I could study them while I was making up my mind what to say to Uncle Seeb and Aunt Hattie. Then I just blurted it out, but in a subdued voice too. "I'm gonna be a preacher when I grow up. Like you."

Just like that, solemn like. And Uncle Seeb brought the two front legs of his chair down on the pine boards like twin pistol shots."Lawd God!" he said.

"A PREACHER! You heah whut Alfie say, ol' woman? He goan be a preacher when he grow up!" Seeb's great black shining face was radiant. "Lawd done lay His Han' on Alfie! He goan be a preacher!"

Then Aunt Hattie's face was wreathed in smiles too, and she seemed about to hug me, but Uncle Seeb gave her a restraining glance, and he said "Now you done heah whut Alfie say but doan you go blabbin' it to nobody. He done tole us but ef he want ennybody else to know, he tell it hisse'f. But ain't nobody in mah house goin' 'bout the neighborhood blabbin' it."

"Sho' Ah know. When Alfie want ever'body to know, he tell it hisse'f." Aunt Hattie's face beamed though, and she walked quickly to the edge of the porch and tossed the bread scraps into the yard. Her eyes focused on a young rooster, less than half grown. He was standing fearfully at the edge of the flock of chickens, and she said to the young rooster "YOU git in 'ere 'an git yo' share, chicken, cause yo' goin' inta the ministry one a these days soon. Alfie goan be a preacher an' he goan start pracisin' up on you."

She slapped her knee with the empty pan, and shouted "Praise God! We gonna have us a chicken dinner heah soon as Ah ketch 'at young rooster an'wring his neck. Nen we see how Alfie perfawn on a chicken leg!"

I ducked my head in embarrassment, and hopped down from the chair. Well, maybe it was more self-consciousness than embarrassment. Anyway, I called to Sandy and said "I reckon I better go home now. Papa said for me not to stay too long and git Mama worried and hafta send Junior for me."

I ran down the steps, scattering the squawking hens. Sandy barked, gave the hound under the house a threatening glance, and then ran alongside me. He seemed to know something wonderful had happened there, and he was part of it.

"Awright Alfie, we proud you come to visit us. You tell yo' Mama I wash them britches when she pull 'em offa you."

She wrapped her gnarled old hand with the pink palms in her apron, and her eyes followed me as I started to run for home. "Law me! Gonna be a preacher when he grow up! An Ah gonna fry 'im a chicken to start off on!"

Uncle Seeb stood up, straightening his back slowly because of the lumbago, and he called to me "You hurry back to see us, Alfie an' we tawk some mo' 'bout things. 'Portant things." Then, as I raced away, Sandy running beside me like a herald of the Coming of the Lord, Uncle Seeb called out again. "Bye, Alfie, you come back an' we whup Ol' Needmo' one a these days. Praise God! Gonna be a preacher when he grow up!"

======================

MarthaLee smiled that little Irish smile that had first caught my eye when we both were loading the fuses for the bombs and shells that blasted the Japanese Navy out of the Pacific Ocean. The smile, unlike our nights on the line in World War Two, was a fleeting one. Her mind went back, to the predicament we were in at Shellman because of my public position on the racial issue. But she switched that off with one part of her mind, and said "You mentioned Uncle Babe. I never got to know your kinfolks, but I assume Uncle Babe was white."

"Very much so. Uncle Babe was my mother's brother, and his view on the racial situation was typical of the white farmer who had black men to plow and pick their cotton."

"So did you spend much time with Uncle Babe? And did he influence your mind?"

"Not much time, but it didn't take Uncle Babe long to make his impression on me. That's another story though, and it deserves a title of its own: CAUGHT!"

CAUGHT

It was late Summertime when Mama said to Papa "We need to go to Babe's and bring the children's Gran'ma home with us." It seemed to me that almost everything good happened in the Summertime, with the exception of Christmas. But then Summertime allows for more things to happen because the days are longer and we could run outdoors where most of the good things were happening. Anyway, the best thing that could happen would be to bring Gran'ma because she made the best tea cakes in the world. Or at least the best in Georgia, certainly the best in Bibb County.

Gran'ma was at Uncle Babes's because he was Mama's brother. Gran'ma was Papa's Mama but it never occurred to me that she was anybody but my Gran'ma. I knew that Uncle Babe was not Papa's brother; it was easy for anybody to see that.

Mama felt that she needed to visit her brother because His wife had died and left all those motherless children, but she was going to bring Gran'ma home with us even though Uncle Babe's children were motherless because it was only fair for Gran'ma to spend half the year with us, even if Babe's children were left to be brought up by the hair of their heads. Mama was provoked because Babe had not remarried, so that his children would have a suitable mother to bring them up. I don't think it had occurred to Mama that Uncle Babe might have some difficulty getting a suitable woman to marry him and bring up his children.

So on Sunday we got ready to go. Mama said there wouldn't be room in the car for everybody, so she left Margaret in charge at home, and she and Papa took me with them in the Dodge to Uncle Babe's in Spalding County near Griffin, sixty miles away.

"We will take the baby with us," Mama said to Margaret. "Willie (that's Tillman, the oldest boy) can help you if the other boys get rowdy." James and Junior did sometimes get rowdy. But Willie could quickly put an end to their rowdiness in ways that they would remember until they felt the impulse to be rowdy again.

Margaret said "Don't worry about us, Mama. We'll be all right." Then she hugged me and told me to be a big boy, which was what I wanted to be anyway, Margaret knew.

"How much farther is it to Uncle Babe's house, Papa?" I was hot and tired. Beads of sweat stood on my flushed cheeks. My query was a whining complaint that has been heard millions of times by the parents of small children traveling together. It was one that Mama and Papa had heard umpteen times since they left home shortly after sunup on that bright September morn. "How much farther is it?"

The sixty mile drive to Uncle Babe's house was brighter in prospect than it was on the road. For the road was dusty and deeply rutted where the rains of late Summer had washed the red clay away into the ditches alongside, and then had carried it away to the nearest creek which had taken it to the next largest creek, and eventually to the Ocmulgee River which was no longer the clear and shining water that had inspired the Indians to give it that name before the white man came with his plows and his cotton, to turn it red like a river of blood.

But the roads between our house and Uncle Babe's, the roads winding between cotton fields and cut over pines, these roads were rough. Papa said it was like driving on a washboard. "Shake a man's false teeth out if he drives more than fifteen miles an hour!" But it was Mama's duty to visit her brother and his children, and her reward was to bring Gran'ma home with her to help with her own children.

"The poor motherless things are being brought up by the hair of their heads," Mama repeated to justify the toils of the road. "They're growing up there with no mother to guide them, and there's no telling what could happen to them." Mama stopped just short of indicting Uncle Babe for failing to provide satisfactory moral and religious training and an admirable example for Aggie and Mutt. The two older boys, Henry and Bob, were beyond paternal rule, but Mama felt he was not doing right by Aggie and Lloyd whom we all called Mutt, the one cast out upon a world full of mortal dangers, a motherless babe, to be brought up by the hair of his head, and Aggie could not be expected to take the place of a mother.

The motherlessness of my cousins who lived sixty miles away had not yet become a matter of real concern for me. I had concerns of my own that were more pressing. "I'm thirsty!" I announced as the old Dodge struck a very deep rut in the road.

"Just hold your horses," Papa advised me. "We'll soon be at the watering trough."

I swallowed the saliva in my throat, and added with a note of greater urgency "I've got to pee too!"

"Well now, that may be harder to hold," Papa conceded. "But I reckon we will come to a clump of plum bushes alongside the road any time now. You just keep your eyes peeled for a good place to stop, and we will take keer of that half of your needs."

"I don't want nobody to see me." I didn't peel my eyes, but I did rub them with my fists because tears of fatigue were forming behind my eyeballs. Rubbing made my eyes worse, but I rubbed them anyway because they felt worse.

"I don't think we'll hafta worry about that. We ain't met a car in the last half hour, and there didn't nobody come by the whole while I was fixin' the flat back a ways." Then Papa spotted a clump of bushes up ahead.

He pressed the brake pedal and the Dodge swayed and swerved onto the rough shoulder of the road. "You just hop out and run behind them bushes, and take keer of your bizness. Your Mama and I will sit here and see that nobody looks at you while you do it."

I hesitated. I squirmed. I held myself. Papa said "Don't tell me you've already done it."

"I'm skeered to go by myself. You go with me, Papa."

"I might see you." Papa pretended mild shock at this idea.

"Oh, go on with the child." Mama was impatient. "He might get on a snake."

Mention of the snake aroused new fears on my part and new complications for Papa. But I agreed to go to the secluded spot behind the plum bushes, after Papa agreed to carry me, and then to stand there with me to protect me from snakes. Also to shield me from view of passing motorists; nobody passed, but Papa had to shield me anyway.

When we came back to the car, unseen and unbitten by snakes, Papa said to me "Now you crawl into the back seat, and lay down an' sleep 'till we git to your uncle Babe's house." But I insisted that I was not sleepy, and I also insisted on sitting in Mama's lap for the rest of the way.

"Well, brush your hair out of your eyes," Mama chided me, and then she brushed my hair out of my eyes. "I don't know how you can see where you're going with your hair hanging down over your eyes that way."

Papa looked down at me. My eyes were already beginning to close. "It might cover his eyes, but he never misses nothin' that moves and very little that sets still. I reckon he can see right through it like a Airedale."

I frowned at these remarks but I was too sleepy to protest. I was soon sleeping but I was aware of the conversation going on overhead. Mama was still worrying about her brother Babe, whose real name I later learned was Henry, and that was where I had got my own first name. Mama went on. "I just hope Babe got my letter telling him we were coming. I mailed it on Tuesday and this is Sunday. If the mail didn't run before he got off to town yesterday, he wouldn't have it in time to shop for what he needs. You know how he is about wanting to put a big dinner on the table for company."

"From the looks of 'im I know how he is about puttin' a big dinner on the table whenever the table is, set." Papa knew he had put his foot in his mouth with this statement, but the temptation was too great for him. "I reckon if Babe has ever set down to a empty table it wasn't no dinner table."

"It runs in the family, Mama said defensively. "Being stout, I mean. All the men in my family work hard in the fields and they have to eat hearty."

Papa had some more thoughts on the men in Mama's family, and why they were all stout, but we had arrived. Uncle Babe's house loomed straight ahead. We wheeled into the yard, and faced Uncle Babe's rambling weatherboard farmhouse with a porch around two sides of it. Papa did not want to be in the middle of an argument with Mama about her family when we alighted from the Dodge. Certainly not an argument which he could see he was foreordained to lose. So he stowed the rest of his thoughts in the back of his mind, and brought the Dodge to a halt in the shade of a big oak tree not far from the porch which ran along the East side of the house. Uncle Babe was sitting on the porch, waiting for his sister, and my Papa, and any of the younguns they might have brought with them.

Uncle Babe's beefy red face broke into broad smiles when Mama and Papa and I arrived. He heaved himself from his chair, and lurched toward the porch steps. He was hitching up his khaki trousers and pulling at

his suspenders as he walked. When he had it all in place, he let the suspenders fly back, and they smacked against his blue chambray shirt. As
a small concession to comfort, he had left the top button on his trousers
standing open. A large V was formed at that point where the top of his
trousers met his rather impressive belly, and it was obvious that the belly
would win out over the trousers in any contest.

Walking in quick, short steps toward his arriving guests, he stopped and
stood at the top of the steps to greet us. In his movement he had given the
impression of being pushed forward by his short, thick legs, and now that
he had come to a halt, it seemed that he might become overbalanced and
tilt forward and be pulled downward by the weight of his belly. But he
balanced himself at the top of the steps, smiling broadly, and holding out
both hands to receive Mama and Papa at the same time. Then he hugged
Mama and patted her on the back, and he shook Papa's hand, wringing it
as if he were trying to twist it off his arm. Papa locked his elbow to keep
that from happening. Mama always said that her brother Babe had a firm
handgrip, and Papa agreed, wincing at the thought.

I was hanging back and rubbing the sleep from my eyes. Mama turned
quickly as if she had just remembered my presence, and she said in an
undertone "Now you go up and hug your Uncle Babe's neck. You hear?"
Uncle Babe's booming voice and Papa's hearty response drowned out
what Mama was saying, but I knew what was expected of me anyway,
and I frowned, drew back, and then hid behind Mama's skirts. I looked
down at the ground and mumbled some indistinct words of opposition
to Mama's instructions that I show Uncle Babe how glad I was to see him
and what a rare privilege it was to be there in his home.

"What did you say?" Mama pulled me around in front of her, and pushed
me toward Uncle Babe, but I clung stubbornly to her skirts. "Here. Wipe
your nose!" Mama said, doing it for me with a handkerchief which she
had got by unclasping her big pocketbook, digging briefly in its contents,
then snapping it together again. To cover for my lack of enthusiasm,
Mama returned to embrace her brother again, and this time, having dis-
charged his responsibilities to Papa, Uncle Babe concentrated on Mama;
he crushed her in a bear hug. Mama was big enough though that Uncle

Babe's short arms soon lost their purchase on her, and he looked about for someone smaller to hug. His eyes fell on me.

"Here Boy! Come over here an' give your Uncle Babe a big hug!" I hung back and clung to Mama, but Uncle Babe reached out and got hold on my arm, and pulled me to him. Then he noticed the long downy hairs growing on my plump little arm. He exclaimed "God A'Mighty! This boy's got more hair on his arms than I've got on my head!" He jerked playfully at the hairs. "Sure sign he'll make a cracker jack hawg raiser when he grows up." He squinted up at Papa, and said "Why don't you just give this boy to me? I'll make a real farmer outta 'im. Ain't no sense in you keepin' 'im down there in a one-mule operation in Bibb County."

I pulled back from Uncle Babe who had now turned his attention to Papa because he wanted to see what effect his words would have on Papa. Papa's response was to haul out his little sack of Bull Durham, and begin the complicated process of getting ready to smoke. Mutt and Aggie appeared at this time, and attention shifted to them. So it was not necessary for Papa to defend his little one-mule farming operation in Bibb County.

Mutt was older and bigger than I was, and AGGIE was older and bigger than Mutt. They both exuded health and happiness. Their tanned, smiling faces revealed none of the pitiable aspects conjured up by Mama's description of them as poor motherless waifs. It was evident that Gran'ma had been doing a good job of compensating for Uncle Babe's shortcomings in that area. If they were being brought up by the hair of their heads, they had a plenty of it to provide a handhold, and it was still growing. Mutt's forelock needed pushing back as much as mine did, and he did this from time to time with a wide sweeping motion of his hand.

Aggie had tried, but with little success, to put curls into her heavy brown locks, and now as she ran to hug Mama, whom she called Aunt Josie, she swung her head and sent her hair flying over her right shoulder. It didn't stay over her shoulder, so she flung it again. "My! How you two have grown!" Mama exclaimed "And you've both got the family build."

This assurance of their genetic integrity caused a momentary clouding of Aggie's face. But it pleased Mutt.

Mutt was so pleased to learn that he looked like the family that he did handsprings on the ground. This unnerved Mama. She was inclined to frown on "showing off" on the part of youngsters, but she had not finished with her appraisal.

"I do believe you're going to be a big man like your Daddy. And strong too."

This caused Mutt to feel the necessity of showing me just how big and strong he was. "Come on, Alfie," Mutt said to me, seeing that I was so little that I might never grow up to take my place among the giants of the family. "I'll show you the airplane I built."

The model airplane had ben whittled from a block. of wood. The wings were attached with glue. And the propeller was fastened with a small nail, so that it would whirl when Mutt ran with it into the wind. Mutt demonstrated this by running into the wind, with the airplane held aloft in his hand while his lips made a sound approximating that made by an airplane becoming airborne.

"I could make it fly by itself if I wanted to," Mutt said confidently to me.

I stood open mouthed, waiting for Mutt to perform this miracle of flight, but he disappointed me. "But I ain't figgered out how to make it land once it gits goin' good, and I'm skeered it will fly all the way to China, and I don't wanta lose it." I had no idea how far China was, but I was sure it was too far for Mutt to go to recover the runaway airplane, and I didn't blame Mutt for not wanting to risk the loss of such a valuable aircraft.

Even though Mutt did not make his wooden airplane fly, I was so impressed that I said "When I go back home I'll ask Willie to build me one. I bet Willie can build one that will fly." I was going to say that Willie would even figure out how to make it land in the cow pasture instead of flying all the way to China But Mutt did not show any enthusiasm for the idea that Willie could build a better airplane than the one he had built. So I held my peace and waited for the next revelation.

"Come on," Mutt said. "I'll show you the battlefield." I followed him eagerly.

Gran'ma had told me about the war when ol' Sherman had come "to set the niggers free" and I wondered where the battle took place, but Mutt's battlefield looked just like a corn field to me, and it might have done so to any casual observer, but Mutt explained. "We had a big dove shoot here last week, and it sounded like a young war."

The ground was littered with empty shell casings because Uncle Babe had invited his friends and neighbors over for the dove shoot after the birds had gathered in large numbers because they had been enticed by the generous outpourings of chicken feed in carefully chosen spots over the field, these places being advantageous to the shooters. I picked up some of the empty shell casings and was about to put them in my pocket, but Mutt saved me just in time. "You better be keerful and not put one in that's still loaded. A nigger done that and it blowed his leg off. But a nigger don't know no better."

I mistrusted my own ability to tell which ones were still loaded, and which ones were truly empty; I dropped them all back onto the ground of the battlefield.

I was even more impressed with Mutt's ability to produce and survive a war than I was with his creative genius in building an airplane with a block of wood.

I didn't want to leave the battlefield until I learned whether Robert E. Lee won the battle, but Mutt had more to show me. "Come on and I'll show you the mule barn and the hawg pens. So I had to leave the battlefield without learning who won, but my mind was made up to get Willie to build me an airplane that would both take off and land, So we were off to the mule barn. I didn't actually get to see the mules. Just the mule barn. The mules had been turned loose to graze in the pasture because it was Sunday. I had to settle for looking at the empty stalls, and I had to take Mutt's word for it that there was a mule for each stall, of which there were many. They stood in an endless row along each side of the mule barn. I tried to count them, but I lost count when I got half way down the other side.

No matter. I learned about Uncle Babe's humanitarianism in letting the mules go to pasture on Sunday, and about his kindness which extended to people too. "The mules and the niggers both git Sunday off from work," Mutt said, but he pointed out the risk involved in being so lenient. "But you got to break 'em both in again on Monday mornin' 'cause a mule and a nigger both'll fergit ever thing he knows from Sattidy noon 'till sunup on Monday."

This wisdom of mules and people of color was probably second hand, but it made me aware of the hard lot of a farmer big enough to own and work so many mules and people of color.

I was on the point of the decision that Uncle Babe must be the biggest and the richest farmer in the state of Georgia, although I was not sure that Georgia was bigger than Bibb County and the County where Uncle Babe lived. I knew that Papa had said Georgia was bigger than Bibb County, but seeing that Uncle Babe's operation was so big gave me second thoughts. I was going to ask Mutt but before I could get the question out of my mouth, he was showing me the hogs in the fattening pen.

The hogs were so impressive I couldn't think about them and the mules at the same time. Uncle Babe's problem of training his workers with short memories was beyond me anyway. So we looked at the hogs. They were already so big and fat they had difficulty getting up from the muddy, smelly "wallow" where they were reclining when Mutt and I came to look at them. But when Mutt poked them with a long stick which seemed to be kept close for that purpose, and said "Sooee" at them, they grunted and raised themselves up and waddled over to the trough to eat some more corn. They didn't act hungry though, the way Papa's pigs at home did whenever he threw a few ears of corn to them.

There was barely enough room for the hogs to walk more than six or eight steps in any direction, so walking was not as important to Uncle Babe's purpose in penning them up as eating was. The trough was full of corn, and Mutt explained to me that the idea was to get the hogs as fat as possible and as heavy as possible before cold weather.

"Soon as it gits cold anuff we'll have a big hawg killin'." Mutt spoke as one learned in the history of this practice to one who was ignorant of it. "Last winter we had one weighed over six hunderd pounds." He didn't attempt the Math problem of figuring out how much sausage, hams and lard this turned out, but he described this as "a heap of ev'rything good". I could see that these fat hogs would turn out "a heap of lard." But I didn't have time to think much about it because Uncle Babe called to us from his place on the porch.

"Dinner's ready!" Uncle Babe called in a voice that we could hear above the grunting of the hogs who were being fattened for the kill but seemed unaware of the fate that awaited them, come cold weather. "Mutt!" Uncle Babe made his message more personal now. "You boys come on heah an' wash up an' git ready to eat."

When we got to the house, the first person I saw was Gran'ma. She had been "seein' to the dinner" when we arrived and Mama was being hugged, and before she could make her way out to the porch, I was off to see the wonderful world of Mutt, and so I had missed the main person I had come to see: Gran'ma.

Gran'ma threw her arms about me, hugging and kissing me. "Lord God, Chile! How my baby has grown! A body wouldn't know you. You've growed so!" But Gran'ma did know me in spite of all my growth. Maybe it was because I was still the littlest one there.

I didn't mind Gran'ma hugging and kissing me. In fact, it felt good, but I wished she wouldn't call me her baby in front of Mutt who was standing there grinning. Still, Gran'ma did make the best teacakes in the world, and for that it was all right for her to call me her baby. "Gran'ma," I said, thinking of teacakes and muffins, "You are goin' home with us, ain't you?"

"Lord God Chile! I aim to !" Gran'ma started hugging me again, looking back over her shoulder to see if Aggie was doing all right with the dinner things. "I reckon these younguns here can do without me for a while." She noted with satisfaction that Aunt Hettie, the black woman Uncle Babe had hired to help with the dinner, was lifting the biscuits out of the oven, and she added "I reckon I've learned Aggie about all she needs to know about cookin'. Leastwise, she can practise up on Babe an' Mutt 'till she ketches her a man of her own."

"Aw, Gran'ma! You know I'm not interested in gettin' married yet."

"I know you ain't interested in nuthin' else," Gran'ma responded to Aggie's disclaimer. She worked her toothless gums to better position the Brewton's snuff on the back of her tongue. "But I reckon Mutt can do little light jobs like bringin' in the stovewood an' help out thataway, an' they'll git along somehow."

Mutt had been at least five feet tall when he was flying his airplane to China; he had even grown some more when he was fighting his young war in the corn field; now he shrank several inches when Gran'ma said he would be able to do little light jobs like bringing in the stove wood. My appetite improved at the sight of Gran'ma, and I was able to put the hogs in the fattening pen out of my mind when I saw what a good job Gran'ma had done teaching Aggie how to cook.

Papa bragged on Aggie and said he hadn't eaten anything so good since he left home that morning. The truth is he hadn't eaten anything at all since breakfast.

Aggie blushed and said "Aunt Het ought to get all the credit. If it wasn't for her, ev'rything would be a mess."

Aunt Het smiled, wiped her face with the apron. It was impossible to tell if she was wiping sweat or tears of gratitude for Aggie's words. She said "Miss Aggie, she jes' talkin." But it was obvious she liked to hear this kind of talk. "Heah's mo' biskits right outta the oven. Doan y'all want mo' biskits?"

Papa said "I'll take another one, Aunt Het." He opened the hot biscuit and laid a slab of butter inside it, then went on bragging on Aggie. "You're gettin' pretty enough the boys will be hangin' around here like flies on the syrup pitcher. Babe'll lose his cook before he knows what's goin' on. Then he'll hafta depend on ol' Aunt Het here all the time."

Mama thought she ought to put a stop to that kind of talk because it might go to Aggie's head, so she said "Pretty is as Pretty does." If Mama had known about all the things Mutt had been telling me, she would have warned him of the twin evils of boasting about what you do have and lying about what you don't have. But Mutt was safe for the moment because she hadn't yet heard what Mutt had told me. Besides, Uncle Babe had been watching me, and he had decided that I was not doing justice to the feast that had been prepared in my honor, and he thought this called for some encouragement on his part.

"Eat, Boy!" Uncle Babe admonished me. "You ain't never gonna grow up and amount to nuthin' if you don't eat." I had been warned earlier by Mama not to take seconds until everybody else had. And here was Uncle Babe holding out a drumstick to me and saying "Eat, Boy!" And Gran'ma hadn't got half way through her first and wasn't anywhere near the second because it was hard for Gran'ma to eat without any teeth. So I was caught between Mama's warning and Uncle Babe's urging.

Uncle Babe turned to Mama and said "You ain't feedin' that boy anuff at home. Tha's why he ain't no bigger'n he is now. Then when he goes some place where they got food, he don't know how to eat. Now you jest leave 'im here with me and I'll fatten 'im up so you won't know 'im when you come for 'im."

I had a mental image of myself standing in the fattening pen like the hogs Mutt had shown me. I wondered if Uncle Babe would make me eat so much I would weigh more than six hundred pounds. Mutt smirked at me, and I felt tears springing behind my eyeballs and stinging them. Aggie saw both my discomfort and Mutt's pleasure. She rapped Mutt on the head sharply with her tea spoon. "That'll do outta you, Mutt!" she warned. "I know you've been tellin' Alfie a pack of lies, and you've prob'ly got 'im too skeered to eat." She rapped Mutt again for good measure because he laughed the first time.

Aggie looked at Mama for some sign of approval of her disciplinary measures. Mutt ducked his head. The rapping hurt, but he laughed uncontrollably in an attempt to hide the fact that he felt the pain.

Mama pursed her lips, and looked disapprovingly at Mutt. "Lying's a sin," Mama said, assuming that Aggie was close enough to Mutt to know what he'd been doing. A warning wouldn't hurt even if Aggie was wrong about Mutt's disregard for the truth. It might serve as a preventive measure in case he was tempted to play fast and loose with the truth in the future. "You'll never get to heaven telling lies," Mama added as a special incentive.

What with an airplane capable of flying to China, a corn field where a war had been fought recently, a mule barn with empty stalls due to his Pa's leniency, and a pig pen full of fattening hogs, it is highly unlikely that Mutt had been greatly concerned about the eternal destiny of his soul.

Uncle Babe was still holding out the drumstick to me, and when Mama had finished lecturing Mutt about lying, Uncle Babe said to me "Eat, Boy! I don't want nobody gittin' up from my table hungry." Mama gave me the nod; I took the drumstick; Gran'ma still hadn't finished her first. I felt that Uncle Babe had made me an offer I couldn't turn down, and I would find a way to make it up to Gran'ma once we got her home with us.

When dinner was over, Uncle Babe's table had lost its attractiveness. Dinner plates with scraps of food and chicken bones on them do not provide the sort of setting conducive to conversation, which was what Uncle Babe now deemed most desirable. He said "Let's all go set a spell in the shade, an' cool off while our dinner settles." Then he pushed his chair back from the table as a signal that he was leading the way.

Mama said that she would stay and help Aggie with the dishes, but Uncle Babe stopped her. "She don't need you to help. She's got ol' Aunt Hetty to help 'er in the kitchen. You come all this way to visit. Now set down an' rest before you hafta start out ag'in to milk the cows on your little one mule farm."

Mama ignored her brother's remark about our small farm, but she said she didn't feel right about leaving Aggie in the kitchen, because she hardly ever got a chance to talk with her anyway. What Mama was hoping for was a chance to talk with Aggie because of what had been said at the dinner table about her drawing admirers like flies to the syrup pitcher. But Uncle Babe was aggravated by Mama's intransigence when he had made a good suggestion. He said "Then let ol' Het do it all, an' Aggie can come an' set with us. Aggie don't hafta stay in the kitchen. Let ol' Het do it all. Tha's what a nigger's for."

Aggie was embarrassed for Aunt Hettie's sake, and Mama made motions at Babe in an attempt to shush him up, but he was only antagonized by this, and he said "Tha's what I'm payin' 'er for. God knows she totes off anuff vittles inside that baggy dress she's wearin' to feed her whole crowd for a week. Come on an' set down. You didn't come all the way up here jest to tell me what to do with my niggers, I hope."

Mama pursed her lips and became silent, which meant that she was put out with Babe, but she realized that to say more would only make matters worse, and result in more humiliation for Aunt Hetty. Now she was even more concerned though about the way the children were being brought up because Babe was not setting a good example for them to follow.

Gran'ma intervened at this point. "You go an' set with 'em, Aggie." She pushed Aggie toward the door, and took the bowl Aggie was holding in her hands, "I'll stay with Het. Me an' her can take keer of things in here. I'll have the next six months to jaw with them."

When Aggie was gone Gran'ma turned to Aunt Hetty, and said "Now Het, you jest don't pay no mind to what Babe said. He has jest got to blow off steam because he's got somebody to hear 'im, and he don't mean nuthin' by it."

Aunt Het said "Yas'm," and started rubbing a bar of Octagon soap in hot water to get some suds. "Ah knows, but Ah'd ruther he not tawk thataway."

Mama accepted the truce, but in her own mind she was saying that while she thought the colored should stay in their place, Aunt Het had given no cause for Babe to abuse her that way, and even though he was her brother, the Lord would surely visit judgment upon him. Apparently, the Lord had something like that in mind, but He was going to let Babe bring it on himself, which he proceeded to do shortly after we were all seated comfortably in the shade of the big oak tree.

Uncle Babe had dragged two straight backed cane bottom chairs off the porch and into the shade of the oak tree. He said to Mama "I got a cheer for you too."

Turning and addressing himself to Papa, Uncle Babe said "You can git you one an' bring it out here." When he was settled under the oak tree where a slight breeze was moving the leaves overhead, he unfastened the second button on his khaki trousers, enlarging the V. He blew out a great sigh of relief, and said, again to Papa "It's been a hot, dry summer here. But we're about done pickin' cotton and started pickin' a little corn. Finish up when the weather turns cool."

Papa was rolling a cigarette from his little bag of Bull Durham, and licking the paper to make it stick. He hadn't got around to making a response to Uncle Babe's comment on the weather, and the progress of the harvest. Mama was starting to fan herself with a recent issue of the Market Bulletin, a paper sent free to farmers by the Georgia Department of Agriculture. She was still considering a reprimand couched in terms of Babe's responsibility to teach his children to show respect for their elders, even if they are colored. Uncle Babe, equally unconcerned about Papa's little farming operation back in Bibb County, and Mama's concern for righteousness, looked all about him, and his eyes fell upon me. I was standing between him and Mama. Uncle Babe laid a heavy, freckled hand on my head, and studied me critically. I looked up into his face, and smiled weakly.

"Now Boy," Uncle Babe said to me. "When your Mama an' your Papa start to go home this evenin' you jest stay right here with me." Then he displayed what he considered a winning smile. "I'll make a real hawg raiser outta you, Boy."

To emphasize his point, Uncle Babe pinched my arm where the soft, blond hairs shone prophetically in the sunlight filtering through the leafy branches of the big oak tree,

I jerked my arm away. "I don't wanta stay with you!" My eyes were about on a level with Uncle Babe's because I was standing and he was seated, leaning back, on his chair I'm goin' home with Mama an' Papa when they go." My arm was stinging where Uncle Babe had pinched and then twisted the hairs. I could feel tears spring into my eyes, and I looked down at the ground to conceal the tears from Uncle Babe.

Mutt was watching and enjoying my discomfort, and probably thinking of ways he could increase it if I stayed. But he knew his Pa well enough to suspect rather strongly that he was teasing, and had no intention of taking on the responsibility of another little boy on the same day he's losing his chief helper, Gran'ma. So Mutt just watched and grinned. Uncle Babe, who had been tilting his chair back on two legs and balancing himself in this position, now let the front legs of the chair down, and leaned forward.

"You don't wanta stay with me!?" He acted as though. he had made an offer that nobody in his right mind could turn down. And I had turned it down! I drew away from him and stood closer to Mama.

Uncle Babe turned to Papa, who by now had his handmade cigarette going well and he said to him "Now what about that? You promised to give
me that boy, and now are you gonna give him to me or not?"

I turned to Mama, my eyes pleading. Mama smiled back at me, reassur-
ing. Papa blew out a puff of smoke, and said "What about it, Son? You
wanta be Uncle Babe's boy?"

I looked first at Papa, and then back at Mama, like a cornered cat. Then I
whirled about and faced Papa. My voice was choking in my throat. "No!
I don't wanta be Uncle Babe's boy! I just wanta be YOUR boy!" My body
trembled with emotion.

Mama laid the Market Bulletin down. She turned her eyes darkly on
her brother. But Uncle Babe avoided Mama's eyes; he looked at Papa and
at me. "You better jest give that boy to me an' be done with it." He was
fumbling in his pocket for something, but having difficulty reaching it.
"I ain't got no little boy no more. Mutt's about growed up."

Mutt gained several inches in stature when he heard his remark. He
smirked at me; I was getting littler, but not less determined to hold my
ground. "Winter's comin' on," Uncle Babe wheedled, "and I need a boy
to sleep with me an' keep my feet warm at night."

Papa inhaled and let the smoke out through his nostrils. He turned to
me. "Son, wouldn't you like to stay with Uncle Babe and keep his feet
warm at night? I reckon he could tell you stories the way I do."

"I don't want Uncle Babe to tell me stories! I just want YOU to tell me
stories! I WANTA GO HOME!"

"Well, I see we ain't gittin' nowhere thisaway," Uncle Babe had found
what he was fishing for in his pockets. He drew out a plug of Brown
Mule. Then, leaning and straining in the other direction, he drew out
his pocketknife. He cut a plug and put it in his mouth, closed the knife,
put it back into his pocket. Relaxed.

Mama's eyes were starting to spark fire. "That's enough now, Babe," she warned. "Enough!"

Uncle Babe ignored Mama. He put the package of Brown's Mule back into his shirt pocket, worked the plug in his mouth down with yellowed teeth, then he said to me "I reckon I'll jest hafta ketch you an' tie you up with a plow line, an' make you stay here with me."

Again Mama said warningly "Babe!" But Babe kept his eyes on me. I was backing away from him. I said defiantly "You can't ketch me 'cause you're too fat to run fast."

Uncle Babe's body jerked forward on the chair. His face grew redder and beefier than ever. "Too fat, am I!?" He lurched forward out of the chair, catapulting his heavy body toward me. I stood paralyzed by fear and surprise at Uncle Babe's mobility.

"I'll show you who's too fat to run!" He kicked over the chair as he rose; he stumbled in his first few steps; then he righted himself and got both feet under him again. My paralysis melted away, and I ran for my life. My short legs moved like pistons. But Uncle Babe moved even faster. Hurtling across the ground he soon closed the gap between him and me. Catching me up in a bear hug, Uncle Babe exulted "I gotcha!" Then blowing for breath, "Now ... who's.... too fat... to run?"

"Turn me loose!" I screamed, striking out at Uncle Babe with tiny balled fists. "Lemme go! Lemme go I say!"

Uncle Babe's arms pinioned me so that I could do nothing but scream and kick. But he was already in trouble beyond his own awareness. For while he was trying to get hold of my kicking feet, and to quiet my screaming, he was puffing and blowing as if he were on the verge of apoplexy. Then he felt a very firm hand take hold upon his collar; he twisted his beet red face around, and he was staring into Mama's blazing eyes.

"That's enough, Babe!" Mama's face was so close that all Uncle Babe could see was her eyes. "Put the child down and leave him alone!" He released me. I twisted violently away and ran off a short distance, then stopped to watch the contest between Mama and Uncle Babe. It was going against Uncle Babe. His eyes were bulging and his breath was coming stertorously. He opened his mouth to say something, but no sound came forth. Mama said "That's enough of this foolishness. You'll have a heart attack!"

Mama's concern for her brother was short lived though. "You've scared the child nearly to death." She turned away from him and approached me. "Come here!" I ran to Mama and she took me in her arms. "Now you know your Mama and Papa wouldn't leave you here." I didn't know it. "Stop crying and be a big boy, so Uncle Babe will know you're not afraid." I didn't care what Uncle Babe knew.

My screams had brought Gran'ma on the run from the kitchen; Aunt Het was close behind her. "Lord God, Het!" Gran'ma laid aside the dish that was in her hands. "Somethin's happenin' to the Baby!" She rushed out onto the porch to see me struggling in Uncle Babe's arm. "Babe!" she yelled in a high pitched voice. "You turn my Baby aloose!"

Babe had not heard her. Or if he had, he gave no evidence of it. Gran'ma started down the steps, putting one foot down and then the other onto the same step, and holding her arms out to balance herself. "You hear me, Babe? Lord God, Het! What's he doin' to my Baby!?"

Before Gran'ma could reach the struggling pair, her Baby was safe in his Mama's arms, and Uncle Babe was heaving and coughing; his eyes were bulging; his cheeks were swelling; and he was first red, then white in the face. Mama looked at him and said "Lord have mercy! You're having a heart attack!"

But Uncle Babe wheezed and heaved until he finally got his breath back. He said "I'm awright. I jest swallered my chaw of 'backy is all." Then he wheezed and coughed some more, and it seemed that he would be all right, but at the sound of his voice, my fears were renewed.

"I wanta go home!" I wailed. "I wanta go home! Now!"

Papa moved restlessly on his chair. He got up and began moving about. "I guess we better git started," he announced. "It'll be sundown there before we know it. I don't wanta be out on the road after dark." He turned to me and said "You run an' he'p your Gran'ma git her things together." I turned, and seeing Gran'ma so close, I got her skirts in one hand and held onto Mama's with the other.

Uncle Babe was breathing a little more regularly now; he wiped his forehead with a sweat rag that he had drawn from his hip pocket. He looked at Papa, wheezed again, and said "You better jest spend the night with us."

Papa knew that this impractical suggestion was only a concession to society's convention of politeness, and he said "Thank you, but we better hit the road. The ol' cows hafta be milked on Sundays same as weekdays."

Uncle Babe was feeling a little better about things. Even in his distress he had issued the invitation to stay. And fortunately it had been declined. He turned back to me; I was clinging to both Mama and Gran'ma. "Ain't you gonna hug ol' Uncle Babe's neck before you go?" He gave me a gap toothed smile, but it was a bit pale around the edges because of the chaw of 'backy he had swallowed.

"NO I ain't!" I clung even more tightly to Mama's skirt and to Gran'ma. "I wanta go home! I wanta go home! Now!"

Aunt Het was still standing on the porch, wringing her hands in her apron. "Lawd be praised! He done punish Mister Babe for what he done. Mebbe he doan mean no harm but he sho' oughtta be shamed! Lawd have mercy! Lawd done punish 'im though. Lawd be praised!"

CHAPTER SEVEN

We returned to Shellman to find that the people who were loyal to us were even more loyal than when the vote was being taken. They came to the house to talk and they had us in their homes to talk. It is very important to have someone to talk with when the going is rough. But that was only half of the story. The Opposition had been talking with one another and they had come up with a plan, a campaign, a slogan: Why don't you resign? Every way I turned, I ran into the question: Why don't you resign?

The two forces within the church had pulled apart since the vote, in denial of Manry Stewart's pledge to pull together. The ones who were unhappy about the way the vote went, quit coming to church to hear what I had to say from the pulpit. But they had something to say to me when we met in town. They said "We will never come back to church as long as you are pastor here." This was a very serious matter, for a pastor to lose a large part of his congregation. They knew this, and they drew the logical conclusion, and put it to me in the form of the question: "Why don't you resign?"

I did not resign, even though they had stopped coming to church, so they came at me from a different direction. "You are making it hard on yourself by staying here. You could go on somewhere else and be much happier." Someone has recently written a book in which he tells the story about the woman who was brought to Jesus to get his judgment on her, and when he invited the one who was sinless to cast the first stone, they all dropped their rocks and Jesus said "Neither do I condemn you. Go, and sin no more." The gospel story ends there, but the modern writer has had the woman say to Jesus "Go where?"

Now that I think about it, I wish I had asked that question, for I really don't know where I could go in the middle of such a fight. God had sent me to Shellman. To go AWOL did not seem to me to be an honorable way to end my mission there. So while the appeal to self pity seemed at first glance to be an attractive one, if I had resigned, any place I went, I would have to say "Well, they suggested that I resign, leave Shellman." Now, what am I to do? Besides, there were my two stalwart lieutenants, Mae White and Susie May Brown, and the others who had voted STAY. Now MarthaLee and I needed them, and they needed us. Maybe that's what I should have said when my opponents asked "Why don't you resign?" But there is a word somewhere about casting pearls before swine.

Then there was the town. Shellman. If I did not care enough about myself to resign, then I ought to care about the town of Shellman which had never before in its history suffered such disgrace as I had brought upon it. "You are getting the town of Shellman a lot of adverse publicity. That hanging. It's being spread in every newspaper and on every radio in the country." Now that was really bad. I had come to a town that had more college graduates and alcoholics than any other town of its size in the state of Georgia, and look what I had done to its reputation by getting myself hanged and almost fired, and the picture of that grave with the poetic epitaph. Add to this the public disgrace of having my wife asked to resign her teacher's position because of her husband's views on race. In early times school teachers were run off by unruly boys, and others were fired for scandalous behavior, and still others, God forbid, because they just could not teach, and maybe because they did not know anything to teach. But to be asked to resign because her husband was a "nigger lover". And then she demanded that the School Board show cause publicly. It was just too much. "WHY DON'T YOU RESIGN?"

Besides, they had tried to make it easy for me to leave with dignity rather than in disgrace. "You were given the vote of confidence so that you could save face by resigning instead of being fired." And I thought I was given the vote of confidence because Mrs. Mae White had opened some eyes and made them see the judgment and the glory of God. Now I look into the mirror and see a face, the same old face I have been stuck with all my life. And still I had not the decency to resign, but continued to show my face in public. "Why don't you resign?"

There is a limit to human patience, though. And since these gentle tactics of people who were concerned for me and my wife did not work, they would just have to turn down the screws, and let out the big secret: That I was a communist spy operating in their midst, a very dangerous fellow to have infiltrating the life of this quiet little town, and the FBI was investigating me, and would soon reveal to the world just what I was doing in Shellman. Senator Joseph McCarthy was riding high in Washington, D.C. at the time, and I had verbally thumbed my nose at him a time or two. He had not yet called me before his committee, but J. Edgar Hoover would surely take care of me when he had all the goods on me.

In fact, the FBI was involved in what was happening in Shellman, and I was the reason, for I had contacted the FBI for an investigation into the hanging in the Town Hall. I asked the FBI agent to find out who was responsible for the hanging, but if the FBI ever came up with any incriminating evidence, it was not made known to me. Perhaps it is still hidden in their files along with their story of the killing of Martin Luther King. I had been accused of influencing the nine old men on the Supreme Court; now I was to be held responsible for the collapse of Democracy in America. And I was the fellow who was as humble as Moses. "But why don't you resign?" With this sort of press, why should I resign?

Money. When all rational arguments fail, money will do the trick. Manry Stewart said I didn't need my salary because the NAACP was paying me to stir up trouble in Shellman; the church cut my salary in half. Fortunately, MarthaLee's salary continued because the School Board had second thoughts about firing her without cause. We continued to eat, although I did not get a second invitation to pick peas in J.O.E. Jackson's pea patch after the Friendship church, where he was a member in good standing, fired me. I never learned who the six members there were who voted for me. But I did not resign and there was an interesting thing that happened as a result.

My persistence in staying on in Shellman brought out the sleeping poets who might never have broken into print if I had gone away quietly. In addition to the poetic epitaph on my grave, there were signboards nailed to utility poles. One was at the main intersection in town. It was about four feet square, of heavy material, and done, quite appropriately in black and white. It read:

Old Rev. Chocolate Drop Kid
He talk loud and long.
He tells us with the white folk
That's where we belong
He says to the white schools we must go
But I hear them gentle voices Singing Old Black Joe.

Romance

I had become a legend in my time at the tender age of thirty three. Now I am past eighty as I write these memoirs. Back then I didn't expect to last so long. But such fame is a powerful incentive to keep on living after some people wish that I would have the decency to resign, even if I didn't die by hanging.

The muse continued sitting on the local poet's shoulder. The next verse to appear included a couple of my friends. I am not certain of their feeling about their literary immortality.

Buchanan calls the signal
Claron rings the bell
D. K. blows the whistle
And all Shellman goes to hell.

Claron Wooten was the man who met me on that Saturday evening when I arrived in Shellman three years earlier. He grew weary in his support of me when the fight was extended. D.K. Bynum was my friend to the last, in his heart, and only decided in the end that I should be put out of my misery some way. Now their names are enshrined with mine.

One final attempt was made by Julian Gill to get me to resign. Julian Gill was a druggist, a Methodist, and something of a clown. It was he who, in the local Lions Club, made that brilliant suggestion about finances. The treasurer had read his report, said that there were several outstanding bills to be paid and no money to pay them. Julian Gill made the motion that the treasurer be authorized to pay them; the motion carried. Now Julian Gill suggested that I resign because I was insane. There is another story about Julian Gill which I am saving to beef up a spot in the story where it will need a bit of color.

Now, fifty years later, I am able to look back on these events with some humor, and to write about them with a degree of irony, but at the time they were very serious, and I was deeply concerned for my safety, and for my wife's welfare, and for the future of the people who were standing by us in this crucial hour. I tried to reach some sort of reconciliation with my opponents, but it didn't work. On one occasion a young man who was working on the top of a utility pole in town touched the wrong wire and was knocked unconscious to the ground. I helped to get him into the ambulance operated by Leonard Spann. We rushed the man to the hospital in Cuthbert. He died in spite of all that could be done. And as I and Leonard Spann were returning in the empty ambulance to Shellman, I said to him "we have worked together today to try to save a man's life. Why can't we work together in the church to bring the message of God's love to the people of Shellman?"

He answered in terms both clear and final. "Because we don't agree on the niggers."

I had planned to tell you this point about some members of the clergy who were not in agreement with me on the "nigger question" but instead I will tell you about Zack Crittenden because that mean cat Romulus has come back into the story and. demands my attention. Zack Crittenden was a Methodist; he operated a farm machinery store in Shellman. That is, he owned it and was always sitting in a rocking chair out front when I passed on my way to the Post Office downtown. Zack was known as something of a wit, and when I had been in town only a few days he inquired about my recreational interests. He said "Preacher, do you hunt and fish?"

I replied that I like to hunt but had never taken up the sport of fishing. He then asked if I knew what a half wit is. I thought that I had met some people who worked hard at qualifying, but I saw that he wanted to answer his own question, so I said "What is a half wit?"

Zack said "A half wit is a man who likes to hunt but don't fish."

Then Zack asked me if I would like to know what a nit wit is, and I declined to fall into this trap, and went on to the Post Office.

After the trouble about race broke out in Shellman, Zack stopped me again on my walk to town and gave me a lesson in theology. I had at that time completed all the requirements for being called a Doctor of Theology, but I was always interested in hearing anything new that other people had learned about God, and Zack, like the good priest in Chaucer's Canterbury Tales, would gladly both learn and teach, so I allowed Zack, to teach me what he had learned about God. "God," Zack told me, "never intended for white men to work; that's what He made niggers for."

Now, patient reader, in case you have forgotten that I started to tell you about Romulus' re-entry to the story, I will tell you now that Zack Crittenden had a dog. The dog was a Pointer, which is a breed of bird dog favored by Southerners over Setters, because while Setters have long hair that collects Cockle Burs, Pointers are short haired, and are not so much bothered with Cockle Burs in their coats. Zack's old Pointer bird dog was white with brown spots and he will remain nameless here because I never knew by what name Zack called him, but the important thing is that Nameless was very devoted to Zack. Each morning when Zack drove downtown Nameless would follow, taking the short cut through an alley that ran past the Baptist pastor's home. He would arrive at the farm implement store, lie there until Zack drove home for lunch, run past my house again to Zack's house, and when Zack returned to work, or rather to the store, Nameless would again go down the alley, trotting with his hind end slewed out of line in the fashion that is popular with dogs that are not in a hurry to get where they are going.

Romulus, who had not forgotten his traumatic experience with Jimmy Nix's bird dogs, now transferred all of his hostility to Nameless, and he planned his revenge, an act which was possible for him because Nameless was only one dog, while Jimmy Nix's dogs were many. So Romulus found a place under the Forsythia bush by the alley, where he could be concealed from view while he could watch the approach of Nameless. On the day which may be termed the canine equivalent of The Day of the Lord, Romulus was ready when Nameless was returning to the shop after eating a meager lunch at home. Meager, I say, because Nameless was rather raw boned which indicated he was not very well fed, but it may be that Zack had fitted this into his theology and concluded that God intended for dog's to be underfed to make better hunters of them.

That is beside the point. The point is that when Nameless reached that place in the alley directly opposite the Forsythia bush, Romulus was ready for him. He leaped out, landed squarely on Nameless' back, sank the claws of all four feet into such flesh as Nameless had covering his bones, and held on while Nameless, howling with pain and terror, fled toward Zack Crittenden's place of business. Romulus, satisfied that the score had been settled, dropped off before Zack saw him, and returned to his place on the back porch and licked himself contentedly.

The reader of this chronicle of my involvement in the racial issue may wonder why it is that I have chosen to bring cats and dogs into the story. The truth of the matter is that I love cats and dogs. I now have a little dog, an Alaskan Spitz who has been with me for fifteen years. Her name is Taffy. She likes people but views every other dog as an interloper upon her territory. Taffy is absolutely loyal to me. Unlike the heroic dogs of both history and fiction who fight to the death to defend their human masters, Taffy expects me to go to any extreme to protect her. I believe she sees me as her god, and expects me to be ever present and provide for her every need, and respond to her pleadings, very much as we expect God to reward us for our having chosen Him as our champion in the lists of this life.

I also have a cat now who is the present day equal of Romulus of Shellman days. This cat is a big yellow Manx who considers that the absence of the useless tail found on most cats is a mark of distinction. He too is loyal to me, and displays his affection by leaping onto my lap if I sit down, and onto my chest if I lie down. Finding the perch tenuous, he is not averse to sinking his claws into cloth or flesh to avoid losing this contact with me.

So much for Taffy and Max. I would be very lonely without them, and I suspect that a case of loneliness might have brought on the idea for God to create Man. Certainly the world has never ceased to be an interesting place, maybe the most interesting spot in the universe, for God. This brings me back to Zack Crittenden. In addition to teaching me about the three dimensional aspect of the mind of man, and the two dimensional aspect of theology as it applies to white and black people, Zack was a very interesting character, and no other Methodist in Shellman stands out more significantly than Zack in my memory, and in my attempts to understand who I am in terms of my boyhood experiences. For when I was a very little boy growing up in walking distance of Macon, Georgia, walking distance being however far you wanted to go when no other means of transportation was available than your two feet, Jack Nyan played a role similar to that which Zack Crittenden did in my Shellman years. I mentioned him to my wife in connection with the hobnail boot prints on his door, dating from the Civil War, but I believe that he merits a whole story in its proper setting, so I am going to tell you now the story I call DAMYANKEES.

DAMYANKEES

September came. The Howard Elementary School on a rise near the Methodist Church, opened its doors to the children in grades one through seven. I found a new friend. His name was Foster. And Foster had a scooter. Not at school, but at home. And he lived only a short distance from me. But the scooter was to become vehicle in which I would ride to a new experience of Southern history.

What is a scooter? A scooter is a flat board with four wheels and an upright steering mechanism of a crude nature, but fairly adequate for a board with four wheels. The board is about eighteen inches long, and six inches wide. It is big enough for a small boy to get both feet on it by placing one foot in front of the other.

The wheels on a scooter are small, about the size of wheels on roller skates. But with ball bearings, they will easily carry a small boy's weight at a rapid clip. On a hard, smooth surface.

The scooter is propelled by foot power. You put one foot on the board, and the other foot on the ground. Then you run on one foot, pushing against the ground with that one foot until the scooter is in motion. Then you lift the motive foot to rest on the board, and ride along, rewarded for your efforts.

If it is a smooth hard surface, and downgrade, you can ride a long way. What seems like a long way to a small boy. A boy small enough to enjoy riding on a scooter. I was growing, but I was still small enough to enjoy riding on a scooter.

Even though it was early September, the days were a little longer than the nights Even though the Howard Elementary School was open, there was still time in the long late afternoons to ride a scooter. And to feed the chickens. And to drive the cows home for milking between sundown and dark. You could still ride a scooter, if you had a smooth hard surface for the four small wheels to roll on.

I had all the necessary elements except, the scooter and the smooth hard surface.

So I came and looked into Mama's face, and said "Mama, can I go and play with Foster?" Mama was pressing freshly churned butter into the cedar mold with the wheat sheaf on it, and I waited for her answer while she pressed the butter. The bowl of butter sat in a larger bowl of ice to keep it cool and firm enough to work. Mama was standing; she was tired; and it was not the best time to ask.

"Where?" Mama pressed the butter firmly into the mold. She added a little to round off a half pound cake, pushed the handle of the removable bottom with the heel of her hand. She dumped the round cake of butter, wheat sheaf up, onto a small sheet of waxed paper. "Where are you and Foster going to play?"

"At Foster's Uncle Jock's house. Can I go, Mama? Can I? Foster's got a scooter, an' he said I can ride on it. At his Uncle Jock's house. Can I go, Mama?"

"Why at Foster's Uncle Jock's house?" Mama laid the butter mold aside. She folded the waxed paper about the cake of butter. She was careful to get all the edges straight. "I don't see why Foster can't just bring the scooter here."

"Aw Mama. You know the scooter wheels won't roll in the dirt. Foster's Uncle Jock's got a paved walk to ride on." We had a dirt yard that turned to mud when it rained, and to dust when it was dry, and was rough and ridgy in between rainy spells and dry spells. It was necessary to take the scooter a place where we could find a hard, smooth surface. That was at Foster's Uncle Jock's house.

Mama had reservations about letting me go to Foster's Uncle Jock's house to ride on Foster's scooter. "Did Foster's Uncle Jock invite you?" Mama believed firmly in going only where she was invited. She tucked and folded the paper under the cake of butter, then put it on the scales to make sure that it weighed a half pound. It did, and a fraction over. "Or did Foster's Aunt Julia invite you to come?"

"Foster said it's all right with his Aunt Julia. He said he ast her if we could and she said it was all right." That was a bit weak, but I believed it was the general substance of what Foster had said.

Mama started pressing more soft butter into the mold. She was deliberating on the question, and I was watching her face closely, anxiously, for some indication of consent. She deliberated a long time. Then she set the butter down and said "Well, when you get there you ask Foster's Aunt Julia if it's all right." My face brightened. "And don't stay till you've worn your welcome out. You be home before sundown to feed the chickens, and to drive the cows to the barn for your Papa."

I started to run to the door with my license for pleasure. She stopped. "Wait a minute! If Miss Julia offers you cookies, don't take but one." I started again to run. She stopped me again. "And mind your manners." I knew that meant to speak when I was spoken to, and to say "Please" and "Thank you."

We stood in the driveway at Uncle Jock's, looking up at the big white two story ante bellum house. It had tall white columns on the front portico. Boxwood shrubs grew along the paved walk where Foster and I intended to ride the scooter.

Uncle Jock's walkway was really paved with bricks, and the surface was neither smooth nor even. But it was better for the scooter wheels than the dirt under the chinaberry trees in my yard. The white paint on the tall columns was peeling. The green paint on the window shutters was flaking off, exposing white spots underneath, but the house where I lived had not been painted in my memory. A few bricks were missing from the top of the chimney on the South end, but it was a grand old house. It had been painted at one time. The later addition to it was even built of bricks, and they had been painted to match. They too were peeling. I had never lived in a house like Foster's Uncle Jock's.

Uncle Jock's old Buick stood proudly in the driveway under a giant pecan tree. In the Spring the tree dropped blossoms on it. In September it dropped leaves and nuts. All of this was brushed off when Uncle Jock and Aunt Julia prepared to drive to church in the Buick on Sundays.

Aunt Julia and Uncle Jock were sitting in the little sun room. Aunt Julia was crocheting an afghan in a geometric pattern that looked like it might be a radiating star. She was a tall, spare woman, with a patrician face and grey eyes behind small rimless glasses. She hugged Foster, and spoke with kindness, but restraint, to me. It was enough to meet Mama's requirement, not more than enough.

Uncle Jock was reading The Macon Telegraph. It covered national and world events in a concise manner, events in Macon and Bibb County in depth and detail. He was a big, heavy man. His large head was topped by a heavy thatch of yellowish white hair. It had been red in his youth - Uncle Jock liked to brag of his Irish ancestry - and it now contrasted with a perpetually red face which took on a purplish hue whenever Uncle Jock became excercised over some issue. At times, if there was not a current issue at hand, he would dredge up some unpleasant memory of injustice done to him.

He could get purple over what President Herbert Hoover and his Republican administration had done to the country. He could get even purpler over what Abraham Lincoln had done to the South. He would become apoplectic at the mention of General William Tecumseh Sherman's March through Georgia. And at what Sherman had done to the very house in which Uncle Jock and Aunt Julia now received me and Foster.

He received us with an affable grunt, but it meant that we were welcome, and it took the place of a standing and verbal reception. Uncle Jock was old enough to sit anyway. Foster told me he guessed his Uncle Jock was in his seventies and maybe even in his eighties. It was too hard for me to guess his age.

Uncle Jock had a lame leg. It did not keep him from getting around, but it did serve as an excuse for a mostly sedentary life. Not that he required an excuse.

Uncle Jock had remarked more than once, and publicly, that "God put niggers here to do the runnin', an' white men to tell the niggers when and where to run." This bit of theology had never been tested against the normal measuring sticks, but it was not seriously questioned by Uncle Jock's contemporaries in the white community. Anyway, because Uncle Jock was in his seventies, or maybe even his eighties, it was not required of him that he stand when two small boys, one of them his nephew, and the other me, entered his house.

He was lame. But the real purpose which his lameness served was justification for the gold headed cane. Any man, even with two good legs, might be excused from carrying Uncle Jock's weight about with him on long walks, without help, and especially that "any man" were in his eighties, or even in his seventies. The gold headed cane was Uncle Jock's help in walking. It also took on the character of a weapon when Uncle Jock gripped it's gold head and stabbed the floor with the other end of the cane to vent his wrath on the DAMYANKEES who had never ceased in seventy years of oppressive and vengeful actions, to visit affliction upon the genteel Southern folk.

Physical defects call for explanation though, and Uncle Jock explained his lameness and his dependency upon the cane. "You boys'll hafta excuse my not gittin' up to make you welcome. I was throwed from a horse years ago. It was when I was a young feller breakin' in a colt to the saddle. An' my leg ain't been the same since. Now with the rheumatiz and all, I don't git about much ... But mind you, I ain't complainin' about my injury; there was many a brave Southern boy who lost a leg or a arm goin' ag'in the damyankees in The War."

The War was The Civil War, the War Between The States. The Confederacy against the Union. The intervention of the World War had not made a very deep impression on Uncle Jock. He tapped his cane on the floor, and he was Moses, and his cane was the rod that became a serpent when it was cast before Pharaoh, whose spiritual descendant was Abraham Lincoln, who would not heed the Word of the Lord to "let my people go." It was the rod that divided the waters as a sign of God's approval of the Southern way of life as opposed to the wicked way of the North.

"Now you boys jest set down over there, and Miss Julia'll git you a glass of lemonade. You look hot enough to ketch afire from ridin' that blamed scooter up and down the walk."

The "Miss Julia" was to let me know what to call her. "Aunt" was used if a woman was really your aunt by kinship, or by small boys when address-ing elderly colored women who were servants of the family. Nobody had any trouble in making the distinction, so nobody had any trouble with double use of the term. But Foster and I had been "ridin' that blamed scooter", and we required some refreshment which Miss Julia would provide after we sat down.

We had ridden the scooter first, then gone inside to make our presence known, though it was no secret from the moment the metal wheels hit the brick walkway. But by this reversal of the normal procedures, it was less likely that I would discover that I was not wanted until the best of the visit was over. And I had done very well with the scooter, for a nov-ice. I had had only two bad spills, and had skinned only one knee. Now I was facing Foster's Uncle Jock, who would be Mister Jock to me, and who gripped his gold headed cane and said to me and Foster "Set down! Set down!"

Then Foster's Aunt Julia produced lemonade, and teacakes to go with it, and she urged me to take two teacakes in violation of Mama's instruc-tions. And I did because Foster did, and she urged me, and I wanted them, could have eaten a half dozen for starters, and I hoped Mama would not ask me about it when I would have to give my report of the visit. I knew for a certainty that if I lied about it, Mama would know I was lying, and if I persisted in my lie, she would say "I will ask Miss Julia the next time I see her at church." To be found a liar "at church" would intensify the punishment that awaits all liars and gluttons.

"Tell the boys about the time the Yankees came." Since Uncle Jock had already mentioned the "Damyankees", Aunt Julia thought it would be good to introduce Foster and me, especially me, to some local history dating back to the Civil War. "Show them General Sherman's bootprints on the door."

Uncle Jock was willing. For this exercise he was willing even to get to his feet. But he thought we boys were not yet sufficiently fortified for the lesson

"Give them boys more teacakes. They ain't had near enough to eat." He moved toward the door. "It ain't right to see nobody hungry. Unless he's a damyankee. Even a nigger deserves to be fed if he'll work." Uncle Jock was studying the door as if he were trying to decide where to begin on it. He turned back to me and Foster. "And growin' boys more'n anybody else."

Miss Julia said in an undertone to me, "You know we were right in the path of General Sherman's army, and he made his headquarters here in this house. He and his army were here for nearly three days." Miss Julia's explanation was made up of both bitterness and pride. Bitterness that this proud old house had been occupied, violated, by the hated foe. Pride that this old house, filled even now with bitterness for the days of The War, had borne its part in the South's suffering under the heel of the conqueror, and it had not been conquered.

The conqueror's heel had left its mark though "Them's ol' Sherman's bootprints, Boy. You're lookin' at his bootprints!"

Foster's Uncle Jock addressed himself directly to me. One must assume that Foster had heard the story before. It was part of the family's proud legacy. "He was wearin' cavalry boots with nails in the soles and heels. When he come up on the porch, an' seen that the door was locked, he jest hauled off an' kicked it in. There's the print of his boot on it to this day."

Uncle Jock stood now, using his cane for a pointer. He did not need it for support. The immensity of the event he was recalling gave him strength. He had pulled the great oaken door inward, and he tapped it with his cane, pointing to some scuff marks and what appeared to me to be nail prints in the lower panel of the door. "There's his mark right there where he left it. He jest hauled off an' kicked it in. Kicked in the front door to this house!"

"But...but...Mister Jock!" I was staring at the door. I was deeply moved by the tale of Sherman, but my question caught Uncle Jock by surprise. "What did your Papa do when ol' Sherman come an' kicked the door in?" I was thinking of my own Papa who would be standing in the doorway with his .38 calibre Smith & Wesson blazing, as he had done in front of the old failing down shack in the Burl Green Woods when the moonshiners led me and Junior out, preparing to drown us in the Tobesofkee Creek. "Did ol' Sherman kill your Papa?"

Uncle Jock readily overcame his surprise at my question. "My Papa was away in The War, Boy. A fightin' the damyankees. Jest like ev'ry other brave red blooded Southerner. Wasn't nobody at home but me an' my Mama an' the niggers. We was outnumbered, Boy! Outnumbered and outgunned! All the white men was in the Southern Army. Wasn't nobody left at home but the women an' the chillun. An' the niggers, of course. We was all alone an' the damyankees at the door. All alone an' the damyankees a kickin' the door down. An' me jest a boy at the time."

I could see the boy and his mother cringing before Sherman and his whole Union Army. "But what did you do, Mister Jock? Did the Yankees git you an' your Mama an' carry you off?"

"Well, like I said before, I was jest a boy at the time. Not hardly big anuff to put a gun to my shoulder. I wasn't no bigger 'n you, an' not as big as Foster there." Foster and I glanced at one another to compare sizes. He was bigger. "An' when we come back here to the house, my Mama an' me, ev'ry hawg on the place had been butchered an' et by the damyankees. I reckon that's one time they got a belly full of hawg meat."

I had been lost some where in this narrative. Uncle Jock had left me terror stricken at the door, facing the armed horsemen of General Sherman and a whole Union Army. And nobody to oppose them by force of arms.

And now Uncle Jock was coming back to the house to find the hogs eaten by the Yankee soldiers. I stared up into Uncle Jock's purplish face.

"But Mister Jock! They didn't ketch you then? You outrun the ol' Yankees?" I was holding a mental image of my own hiding place in the chimney base under the house where I had hidden as an even littler boy to avoid capture by the gypsies. "Did you runaway an' hide from ol' Sherman an' the Yankees when they come to the door? Did you an' your Mama run away an' hide?"

Uncle Jock stabbed the floor with his gold headed cane, and he stared at the bootmarks on the door. "Before they got to the house, Boy." And with this memory Uncle Jock was no longer standing here with me and Foster. He was in that far off world and time. He was part of the terrible ebb and flow of Southern history. He was back there. "We got word that Sherman was a'comin He was a killin' and a burnin' ev'ry thing in his path. We knowed he was headed for this place, an' we drove all the horses an' the cows into the woods to keep them scalawags from stealin' them all."

My mouth stood open; my eyes were fixed on Uncle Jock as he resurrected that picture of flight. "We had a nigger a ridin' ev'ry horse, 'cept the ones me my Mama was a ridin'. And a nigger a leadin' ev'ry cow outta the barn lot. But we couldn't do nuthin' with the blamed hawgs. Can't lead nor drive a blamed hawg. Jest had to ride off an' leave 'em to the damyankees. An' then, when me an' my Mama come back, an' all the niggers that was with us, that was after Sherman had gone, them damyankees had et ev'ry hawg on the place. Jest butchered an' et ev'ry one of 'em."

Aunt Julia broke into Uncle Jock's tale, and I turned my gaze on her. "Chickens too!" Aunt Julia said. "They caught and killed every chicken on the place. The geese and the turkeys too. There wasn't a fowl left alive in Sherman's path."

Now Aunt Julia was standing too, looking through the open door at the wide expanse of lawn. She spoke with offended indignation. "They let their horses graze on the lawn too." She paused, and a smile of satisfaction crept into her stern, patrician features. "But they didn't get the silver." A triumphal smile wreathed her face.

"The silver?" I thought she must be talking about the hoard of money. "But I thought .... I mean Gran'ma said they had confed'rate money. Was Confed'rate money Silver?"

Gran'ma had indeed shown me some Confederate paper money, even some script printed by the State of Georgia. And I, comparing the nickels and pennies I had saved with the amounts printed on the paper money, thought people must have been rich back then. Now I was thoroughly confused, because Gran'ma had said "Lord God, Child, It ain't worth the paper it's printed on. You might as well tear a page out of the Sears & Roebuck catalog an' try to spend it."

Miss Julia straightened me out on the matter of silver. "Silverware, Alfie." She explained. "Knives and forks and spoons for the table. But when they heard Sherman was coming, they wrapped the silverware in tablecloth, tied it up and lowered it into the well."

Uncle Jock saw that Miss Julia's story had topped his own. He punched the floor a time or two with his gold headed cane, started to return to his Morris chair in the living room, but he didn't go more than three steps. Miss Julia was not done with her story about silver, and he knew he couldn't walk away until she had finished. She went on with her story. "Then after Sherman and his army of scalawags and scavengers had gone, they lowered a darkie on a rope into the well to haul the silver up again."

My face, so intent on Miss Julia's account of heroism, relaxed now. I was relieved that the silver had been saved from ol' Sherman's greedy, plundering hands. But oh how I wished that I might be the boy on the end of the rope, for I assumed it was a little boy, a little black boy like Sunshine, who played that daring role, being lowered into the dark and dank depths of the well to recover the silver.

Miss Julia, encouraged by my facial expression, continued her story, but on a less thrilling note. "That silver is right here in this house right now!"

Her face now showed faint, softening lines of romanticism. "Mister Jock's mother gave it to us for a wedding present when we were married." Now her face was that of a saint raised to beatification in the days of Joan of Arc. "General Sherman and his men drew water out of the well to drink and to water their horses, and they never knew the silver was there." A smirk now marred the beatified countenance.

I believed then that the South must have won The War after all. According to the books I had read from the library in the Howard Elementary School, Generals Robert E. Lee and Stonewall Jackson had won all the battles, even though they were outnumbered and outgunned. So with this story of Southern heroism, it was possible to discount the verdict of history.

Uncle Jock's face had now returned to its normal red color. It had lost the purplish hue of rage under the refining influence of Aunt Julia's story of the silver, and how it was saved from Sherman's grasping and greedy hands. And now the silver was back in the house where it belonged, Uncle Jock returned to the main story. "Damyankees prob'ly et with their hands anyhow." He stared angrily at the door, and I could see the purplish hue returning. "Damyankees didn't need no fine silverware to gobble up a rasher of hawg meat."

I looked out through the open nail scarred door, and saw that the sun was about to set in the Western sky over my house. "I better go now," I said. "Mama said for me to be home before sundown. I hafta help Papa with the cows and ev'rything." I didn't mention feeding the chickens and closing up the hen house. That sort of work would not sound nearly so grown up as helping Papa with the cows. I started through the doorway, looking again for the print of Sherman's boot. I felt I was now a part of history, of the South's brave struggle against the damyankees who had outnumbered and outgunned the brave boys in grey, but had never conquered their spirit. I felt a swelling inside my chest that I could not then, and cannot now put into words.

"I sure did enjoy the teacakes, Miss Julia," I said. "An' the lemonade. An' ... an' ridin' Foster's scooter."

I looked at Foster's Uncle Jock, and I did not know what to say to him about ol' Sherman and the door and the hogs, but Uncle Jock didn't seem to expect me to say anything. He was lost in his own reveries, and I don't think anything I might have said would matter. So I said "Bye, Mister Jock."

He came out of the reverie, and smiled, sort of, and said "Well, you come again, Boy." I don't think my name ever registered with him. "You come an' play with Foster. You two boys make a pair all right. I mind when I was a boy about Foster's size." And Uncle Jock slipped again into reverie and into remembrance of when he was a boy, and Sherman came with the damyankees and ate all the hawgs.

The sun was setting when I got home. I still had time to close the door on the hen house door, but the chickens were all on the roost. When I went to help Papa, he said "The cows have done come home, but you can drive them back out to pasture when Willie and I git done milkin'."

When Mama called us to supper, she could see that I was still under the influence of my visit to Foster's Uncle Jock's house, and Papa looked at me and said "Well, tell it Son. I can see you're bustin' to talk about it."

"Papa," I said, while the glory of my hour before the nail scarred door was still on my face, and the memory of Sherman's pause in his March to the Sea to refresh himself on hawg meat and well water with silver in it. "Do you remember when ol' Sherman kicked down the door at Mister Jock's house?" Papa was sprinkling black pepper on his peas, and he was about to sneeze, and he couldn't answer right off. So I went on with my questions. "Did ol' Sherman come to your house too, Papa?"

When Papa had got the pepper out of his nose, he said to me "Well, I ain't quite that old, Son. I reckon ol' Jock's older than I am by a few years. But I ain't sure whether he remembers all them things about The Civil War, or if he's jest tellin' what's been told him so many times he thinks he remembers."

The glory began to fade under Papa's cynicism, and a cloud began to appear on the horizon of my dreams. I tried to hold onto the image of the nail scarred door though. "But ... but ... Papa. Ol' Sherman did come, didn't he? He was the mean ol' Yankee who come through Georgia in The War, wasn't he?" I was sure that if Generals Robert E. Lee and Stonewall Jackson had been guarding the approaches to Georgia instead of fighting in Northern Virginia, Sherman never would have burned Atlanta.

And now Papa had said something that called in question even the slanted histories which I had picked out of the library at Howard School. "Did ol' Sherman really come through Georgia, Papa? Back in The War. They didn't just make that up about 'im, did they?"

"Oh, he come through Georgia, all right." Papa sprinkled some more pepper over his peas and potatoes. Then he looked squarely at me in that way he had which made it hard for me to tell when he was teasing and when he wasn't. "Ol' War Is Hell Sherman, they called 'im back when I was a boy. He come through, and where he'd been it looked like a cyclone'd hit, they told me." More black pepper. Papa sneezed. "And he was man enough to deserve all they said about 'im. But then I heard a different story about them bootprints on ol' Jock's door."

I stopped eating. I stared at Papa. Mama stopped eating too. She just stared at Papa. Papa sprinkled some more pepper, and he sneezed again. Mama said "What did you hear?"

Mama had walked right into Papa's trap, and I was standing beside it without seeing it. Papa sneezed again and said "What I heard was that ol' Jock come in one night late an' pretty well lit up, an' Miss Julia had the door locked. She wouldn't let ol' Jock in, him bein' in that condition, as she would put it. And them's ol' Jock's bootprints on the door."

Mama said "Lord have mercy!" And she looked put out at Papa, because if Mister Jock had been lit up, and had to kick the door down to get in the house, Miss Julia would never have let the story get out.

Papa had now got so much black pepper on his peas and potatoes that he could not control the sneezing. I waited until Papa quit sneezing, and at last he quit, and I hoped he would say something more to soften the blow, but he didn't, and I looked down at my own plate. I was determined to hold onto something, even if it wasn't much, for what is a boy's life if there is no myth in it?

I said "Well, anyway, I'm glad they saved Miss Julia's silver. I'm glad that mean ol' Sherman didn't git Miss Julia's silver."

Once I get started telling these tales from my boyhood, they seem to keep coming like water from a spring. It seems to me that there was always something going on between me and my brothers and the black children who lived across the cotton patch from us. It also seems that boys, both black and white, can make a gambling game out of anything. Marbles, for instance. So while MarthaLee and I were talking about things to take our minds off the trouble in Shellman, Marbles became the subject, and Winnants the game.
WINNANTS

"Winnants?" MarthaLee said. "I've heard you use the expression, but I've never understood it. I know you got into trouble over it with the black children. And your Mama used drastic measures to correct your behavior. But what in the world is Winnants anyway?"

"Well, first of all, it was a bad time for Mama. She was pregnant, and she was too old to be having another baby. She'd had five, and bringing them up in the fear of the Lord was a difficult task. And Mama had certain prohibitions in her moral system. One of them was gambling."

"And Winnants was gambling?"

"In a way. In the way Mama saw things. Actually, it is a way of playing marbles."

"And I assume you played marbles when you were a boy?"

"Even when I was a very small boy, marbles fascinated me. Marbles fascinated Junior too. And he was really good at shooting marbles. James too. Only James, or Cliff as I have called him in my stories about boyhood, but he was not as good at marbles as Junior was. Junior had an unerring aim. He could knock a sparrow off a tree limb with a small stone, or break an insulator on the poles along the railroad. And at marbles... well ... there are two ways to play marbles. You can play for fun, or you can play for keeps."

"And Winnants was ... ?"

"For keeps. If you play for fun, it is just to show off your skill. You can outshoot your opponent and win the game, just as in any other form of sports. But if you play for keeps, it's gambling, according to Mama. A sin. And if you did something Mama said was a sin, you could expect punishment. The Bad Man would get you in the end, but punishment could come quicker than the end. I was afraid to do anything that Mama told me was a sin, so I was afraid to play Winnants."

Cliff - that's James - and Junior were not so scrupulous about avoiding sin. They were older and more learned in the ways of the world. And if it was something they really wanted to do, like playing marbles for keeps, they could handle the guilt, as long as they were not caught by Mama. So they would slip off and play Winnants, and I would tag along, afraid to play and even more afraid to be left out. So I was a spectator. I watched Junior and Cliff, and I had the thrill of sin without the full weight of the guilt.

So on a certain Sunday morning in Summer, when you would expect us to be in Sunday School like all God-fearing boys, we were with Seeb's boys, playing marbles.

=================

"Vinch!" Little Seeb exclaimed, and brushed aside a small clod of red dirt. He closed one eye and took steady aim at the big green marble in the eye of the ring. He shot the brown striped agate off the thumb of his pale palmed left hand, and whistled shrilly through his teeth. The green marble went flying out of the circle. Little Seeb was tall and thin and beginning to sprout some soft hairs on his upper lip.

Cliff watched the way Little Seeb shot. "Left handed," Cliff observed, half laughing but only half because that was the moment when Cliff's favorite, the big green marble, was knocked out of the ring and went into Little Seeb's pocket.

"Nuther one," Little Seeb said, grinning. His overall pockets bulged with marbles that had been in Cliff's pocket when the game began that Sunday morning in May. Little Seeb kissed his "shooting toy" and rubbed it between his palms.

"That was my shootin' toy," Cliff muttered unhappily. "I didn't aim for you to keep it. It was my shootin' toy."

"You don' wanta lose yo' shootin' toy don' put it in de ring."

"It's my shootin' toy." Cliff repeated. "I'll give you another one just as good."

"Naw." Little Seeb rubbed his hand over his bulging pocket. "Ah knock it outten de ring, Ah keeps it. You done los' it."

"I'll give you my jug and two pee wees."

"Doan' want no jugs an pee wees. Dis whole county made outten clay. Whut I want wid clay ma'bles?"

"The jug ain't clay."

"Ain't roun' nuther. Ol' jug plum wop sided. Cain't hit nuthin, wid it."

"How'll you trade then?"

"You want yo' shootin' toy back, you got to win it back."

"Awright." Cliff surrendered the idea of recovering the prized marble by barter. "I'll play you one more game. But you got to put my shootin' toy back in the ring."

"Not lessen you puts one in jest as good." Little Seeb's black face shone in the sunlight, the sweat glistening on his cheeks and brow. "Lemme see whut you gonna put up 'ginst it."

Cliff's face was not glowing. He thrust his hand deep inside his pocket. His fingers thrust aside what he knew were inferior marbles. He drew out a big blue and white agate. It was the companion to the one he had just lost. "Dat un will do." Little Seeb pitched the green marble into the ring.

"Junior's got to play too." Cliff was holding back the blue and white marble. Junior, red faced, freckled and sweating, swaggered to the edge of the ring.

Cliff was hopeful that Junior could help him win back his green marble. "Come on, Junior! You git in the game or we're goin' home to dinner. I heard Mama callin' us." Cliff had heard but he had not responded to the call, and this was making me edgy. Still, he was invoking Mama's authority to put pressure on Little Seeb.

Junior began fingering his own "shootin' toy". He was wearing overalls without a shirt. When the galluses slipped sideways, they revealed two white streaks crossing each other about the middle of his back, and running away from each other over his shoulders. Junior placed a reddish brown marble with white sworls in it at the very center of the big circle. Then he ran his left hand into his pocket and took out a large milk white agate, laid it gently in the red dust at his feet, then rubbed it against the coarse blue denim of his overalls. His high cheekbones stood out beneath his sunburned forehead.

Little Seeb watched every step of Junior's ceremcnial preparation for the game.

"Ra'Lee got to play too then." Little Seeb said "If Junior gonna play, Ra'Lee got to play too."

Robert Lee was about the same age as Junior. He was standing aside, pushing one bare big toe back and forth in the red dust. His hair had been cut close to the scalp. It was beginning to grow out again, curling tightly. His eyelids hid his eyeballs as he looked down at the pattern he was tracing with his toe in the dust. Robert Lee bore the name of the Confederacy's greatest hero. It was a proud name, and Robert Lee bore it proudly, but he knew next to nothing of General Robert E. Lee and his Army of Northern Virginia. He was Ra'Lee of Bibb County, Georgia.

Ra'Lee waved several smaller brothers and sisters back. Little Seeb spoke to the small fry. "Y'all git back outten Ra'Lee's way. Ra'Lee gonna play."

I watched this exercise of authority with awe. It was almost identical to Willie's rule over his underlings. I idolized Willie and accepted his primacy without question.

Robert Lee strode toward the ring. His face twitched. He touched me lightly on the shoulder as he came. I sat like a snowbird among the smaller brothers and sisters of Little Seeb and Ra'Lee. I smiled and hunched my shoulders, but I didn't answer.

Cliff spoke defensively. "Alfie ain't playing. He ain't big enough." My smile turned into a scowl. Cliff laughed nervously. "He don't know how to play marbles."

One of Little Seeb's smaller brothers, I believe his narme was Fenton but they called him Feenie, drew himself up closer and said "Shucks! Ah bet you do know how to play ma'bles too, don't you Alfie. You plenty big to play ol' ma'bles ef you wants to."

"I play at home all the time," I said, "But Mama won't let me play for keeps. Mama says it ain't no difference between winnants an' gamblin'.'"

"Yo' Mama won't let you play winnants Alfie?"

My face showed a mixture of prideful righteousness and disappointment. "Mama says winnants is the same as gambling."

"Shucks! Mah Ma doan keer nuthin' 'bout winnants. She say ol' ma'bles ain't wuth nuthin' nohow ef you loses 'em."

I felt a superior pride in my Mama's strict morality. "Mama won't like it if she finds out about Cliff an' Junior." I pushed out my lower lip and added with an additional touch of righteousness. "It's Sunday too."

"You ain't gonna tell yo' Mama, is you, Alfie?"

"Not unless she makes me tell." I fixed my gaze on the preparations for the game, secretly hoping that Mama might make me tell about the game.

"Shucks! Ah ain't telling even if Ma tries to make me tell."

Robert Lee and Little Seeb exchanged glances, and Robert Lee said "Awright, y'all ready to th'ow f'r taw." He did a hocus pocus over his marble. It was a red agate with white sworls. He sent it spinning into the dust for practice run, then retrieved it. The four players tossed their marbles at a line drawn on the ground about ten feet away. Junior's marble stopped a few inches short of the line. Cliff's overshot it, and Little Seeb's did too, Robert Lee's red and white marble rolled onto the line and stopped.

"Hot diggity!" Little Seeb exulted. "Ra'Lee, you fust. Now lessee you knock dere eyeballs out."

Robert Lee laid his left hand flat on the ground, and placed his right hand on top of the left in preparation for the first shot. "Hey! Knuckles down! "Cliff called out angrily. "No shootin' off the toppa your hand thataway. You got to put your knuckles on the ground."

"But it won't make no never mind. Ah'm gonna knock yo' big bluen white ma'ble to Kingdom Come."

"Do it an' then talk about it!" Cliff spoke with bravado. Robert Lee sighted carefully and fired his marble off his thumb. It sped toward the center of the ring, struck the big blue and white marble a glancing blow, bounded off it, and then struck the little yellow marble Junior had placed in the eye.

Both marbles spun crazily, and rolled out of the eye, the big blue one wobbling to a halt after a few inches. Robert Lee's shooting toy careened away, and rolled clear of the circle.

"Ha!" Cliff jeered. "All you done was mess up the eye. "Go ahead, Junior, an' show 'im how to knock it out of the circle." Cliff had placed great hope on Junior's ability to win back his marbles.

"Rounders!" Junior moved quickly about ninety degrees on the circle, and took aim.

"Vincher! No rounders!" Little Seeb moved to block Junior's shot. "You don' git no rounders on fust shot. You gotta shoot from taw same as Ra'Lee done."

"How come?" Junior bristled at Little Seeb's interference. "Long as I shoot from somewhere on the circle."

"Not on fust shot. You s'posed to shoot fr'm taw line on fust shot. Jes' lak Ra'Lee done."

"Tha's just if all the marbles are still in the eye. Robert Lee has done busted the eye."

"Ah don' keer ef Ra'Lee done busted da eye. You gotta shoot fr'm taw line jes' lak Ra'Lee done."

"Awright. I'll shoot from the taw line and I'll still see what the big green marble's made out of." Junior closed his left eye, took careful aim, and shot his marble off his thumb with the force of a catapult. It struck the big green marble a solid blow that carried it clear of the circle.

I sucked air into my throat and looked proudly about me at the black children on every side of him. Junior's feat was a victory for me. Junior's face was flushed. He grinned and picked up the marble and dropped it into the pocket of his overalls. His galluses moved, showing the white stripes again where he had not been tanned by the sun. I wished that Mama would let me go without a shirt so that I could get a tan, but whenever I slipped around and exposed my skin to the sun I blistered and peeled off.

"It ain't busted, so I'll keep it," Junior said, playing his role of victor with feigned contempt. He drew aim on another marble and missed it cleanly.

Cliff was encouraged by Junior's recovery of his treasured shooting toy. It was in Junior's pocket now, but that was closer to home than Little Seeb's pocket. Perhaps he could strike a bargain with Junior later. But he was now determined to get back the blue and white marble he had placed in jeopardy for the sake of the green one. Breathing hard, he thumped his marble at the target. His hand moved in a hunching motion to give the marble more force.

"Vinch!" Robert Lee's sharp eyes had caught the movement of Cliff's hand "Vincher no hunchin'!" But when he saw that Cliff had cleanly missed, and his shooting toy had rolled into the rough area beyond the ring, he jumped up and down with glee. "But it's awright! No vincher! You done missed evvything anyway."

"Awright Smarty!" It was Little Seeb's time to shoot and Cliff's turn to gibe. "Le's see you do better."

Little Seeb rubbed his shooting toy with a tattered shirt sleeve. The small black children on the porch step tittered and giggled. One of them said "Little Seeb he gon' hit 'at 'ol ma'ble sho as de sun goin' down dis evenin'." He turned to me grinning. "Whut yo' Mama gon' say when y'all come home an' Cliff done los' all his ma'bles. Whut she gon' say to Cliff, Alfie?"

I watched Cliff now with apprehension. And I remembered that Cliff had said he heard Mama calling. I had heard Mama too, but I was afraid to run off and leave Cliff and Junior. I said "She might whup 'im." Then I thought of something even worse. "She might tell Papa and he'd whup 'im." It was generally understood that to be "whupped" by Papa was a far more painful experience than to be given the relatively light "whupping" which Mama would deal out.

"Whut yo' Papa do to Cliff, Alfie?" The little boy knew but he wanted to hear the words again.

"Papa might whup 'im too if Mama tells Papa Cliff didn't mind her."

"How yo' Mama gon' know 'bout Cliff losin' his ma'bles, Alfie? You gon' tell?"

As the black children huddled near me, I ducked my head in an attempt to evade this line of questioning. "I ain't gonna tell unless Mama makes me tell."

Now Little Seeb spat on his marble, rubbed it again on his shirt sleeve, and fitted it carefully on his left thumb, with the forefinger wrapped around it. He spoke to the marble, quivering in his springlike grip. "Awright now Baby, you goin' out dere an 'git me 'at big ol' bluen white agate. He jes' settin' up fat an' sassy an' waitin' to be hit." Little Seeb's marble shot from his hand, struck the blue and white marble a glancing blow, causing it to roll slowly toward the encircling ring.

"Come on now Baby!" Little Seeb was coaxing the marble. "You jes' roll right over dat linean' inta mah pocket."

I turned to the little black children huddled around me, and said "I think I hear Mama callin' us."

The big blue and white marble rolled into a soft spot, slowed, and came to a stop less than an inch from the encircling line. "Dad gum it, Ma'ble!" Little Seeb addressed the uncooperative marble, urging it on. "Don' do dat to me!" But the marble had stopped.

"Mah turn!" Robert Lee was as excited by Little Seeb's failure to secure the blue and white agate as he was by Cliff's clean miss. "Mah shot now!" Then eyeing the position of the target critically,"Vincher! Rounders!" He began moving around the circle to a point more advantageous for knocking the marble out of the ring.

"Hey! No fair!" Cliff objected. "You can't git rounders. Junior couldn't git rounders. You can't neither."

"Ah gits rounders on second shot, jest not on fust shot. Tha's de rule."

Robert Lee's shot sent the blue and white marble spinning out of the ring. Cliff groaned. Robert Lee shot again and struck a glancing blow against a second target, but failed to carry it out of the circle. He snapped his fingers in disappointment at this, but he was happy about the blue and white marble now lodged in his pocket.

Cliff was downcast, but he said resignedly "Anyway, we got my green shootin' toy back." Junior gave him a sidelong glance that told him the green marble was still a long way from Cliff's pocket.

"Game ain't over yet." Little Seeb laughed. "Dey's still two mo' ma'bles. You gonna try to git 'em or not?" It was an open challenge.

"It's Junior's shot," Cliff said, and Junior fired at the small agate that Robert Lee had placed in the eye. He hit it a solid blow and knocked it out of the ring. Confidently, he aimed for the one remaining marble, but missed.

"One mo' to go!" Little Seeb announced. "Dis yo' las' chance, Cliff, You miss an' Ah cleans up." Cliff's hand trembled wider this threat and prospect of defeat."

Tense and sweating, he squinted at the one remaining marble, hunched and sent his shooting marble speeding toward the target. Two inches short of its goal, it bounced and leaped over the target.

"Vinch! Vinch!" Cliff cried in exasperation. "It musta hit sumpthin'. You saw how it bounced. Ain' s'posed to be nuthin' in the ring to make it bounce thataway!"

"Didden nuthin' make it bounce. You jes' hunch so hard it jump clean over. Yo' turn now Ra'Lee." Robert Lee struck the one remaining marble a solid blow, and knocked it out of the ring. "How 'bout it, Man!" Little Seeb exulted. "Y'all wanta lose some mo' ma'bles?"

"I'm quittin'," Cliff said, looking about him nervously. "I heard Mama callin' way back there. Junior can if he wants to."

Junior was hesitant. He had heard Mama too, but he was not satisfied with the way the game had gone. Then he made has decision. "Tell you what. I'll chase Robert Lee for the black and white marble.'"

"Fine wid me." Robert Lee was polishing his shooting toy on one leg of his overalls. "Ef you gon' chase wid yo' green 'un."

They cast again at the line to see who would go first. Or second. For the one who went first became a sitting duck for his opponent. Junior lost the throw. Frowning, he pitched the green marble out onto the rutted driveway. And waited. "Awright, Robert Lee. There it is. Go after it. Hit it if you can."

Robert Lee shot hard at the green marble. In case he missed, he wanted to roll well beyond it in order to make Junior's shot at him as difficult as possible. He missed. They shot and sat to be shot at, alternately, passing and repassing each other. They came to the end of the rutted driveway, and entered "the big road." The yellow clay surface of the road, called plating, had been scraped smooth by the blade of the road grader oper-ated by the chain gang. The work had been done recently, not more than a day or two earlier. There had not been much traffic to wear the shine off.

"Man! Lookit dat platin' shine!" Little Seeb stood admiring the road because of its possibilities for the game now underway. "Ra'Lee, you sho to git Cliff's green ma'ble out heah."

Junior and Robert Lee settled down to chasing one another on the smooth hardsurface of the road. Little Seeb's younger brothers and sis-ters crowded around me; we all followed the contestants at a respectful distance. One of the little blacks broke our silence.

"I seen nem chain gang men when dey scrape it yestiddy mawnin'." He spoke with mingled pride and awe.

"Yeah, I know. Tex come to our well for a drink of water. He drives a dump truck."

"He did?" The little black boy's eyes became as big as saucers and filled with fright as he looked into my face.

After a moment in which he decided I was telling the truth, he said "Wasn't you skeered of 'im?"

"Shucks! What was there for me to be skeered of? Tex is my friend."

"How come him on de chain gang ef he be yo' fren'?"

"They said he stole sumpthin' but he didn't do it. He was framed."

"Ah bet he did steal sumpthin' too. Or mebbe kilt somebody."

"Tex didn't do no such thing." I was feeling resentful because they were impugning Tex's character, and I wanted to strike back with a threat. "But you better not steal nuthin'. They'll put you on the chain gang. Tha's what they do when niggers steal sumpthin'."

"Shucks! I run away so fas' nobody ketch me."

"It wouldn't do you no good. They put dogs on your trail if you try to run away. Tex said they do. He told me."

The small black child's eyes grew even larger, and he began to blubber. I was enjoying the black child's pain, partly because his big brother had won Cliff's marbles, and partly because he was a small black child even smaller than myself. "Tex tol' me about a nigger boy who tried to run away from the chain gang and they put the dogs on his trail."

"Nem ol' dogs ketch 'im?"

"Yeah, they caught 'im an' drug 'im back. Hey! I hear Mama callin' us. We better go home." But Junior and Robert Lee were chasing marbles on the slick plated road.

Cliff intervened. "I hear Mama callin' us. We better go Junior."

"One more shot." But Junior missed again, and his marble rolled into the ditch. "Awright. Le's go." He picked up his marble, dropped it into his overall pocket, and looked toward the house. It was a rambling farm house with a big oak tree towering over it and dominating the front yard. Two chinaberry trees filled the back yard with shade. Junior, red faced and sweaty from the game, said "I hear 'er. We might be in trouble."

"Whut yo' Mama gonna say, Alfie?" The little black child was glad to get off the subject of the chain gang, the dread nemesis of Negroes in Georgia, and onto the subject of what might happen to Alfie and his older brothers who did not have to dread the chain gang because they belonged to the white race. "Whut she gonna do to y'all?"

I didn't answer. I didn't know. And when I learned it was a complete surprise. Junior and Cliff were trotting away toward home and I ran to catch up. "Wait for me!"

"Well, come on. Slow Poke!" Cliff was irritable with me because he'd lost his marbles to Little Seeb and Robert Lee, and already beginning to dread Mama's wrath.

"I ain't gonna tell," I replied breathlessly because it was hard to keep, up, "Unless she makes me tell. If she makes me tell I can't help it."

"You better not tell. She's liable to whup us all." He turned to Junior. "Anyway we got one of 'em back. One of my shootin' toys."

"I got one of your Marbles. You lost another one."

"It was my shootin' toy. I'll trade you for it."

"But I'm tellin' you, you better not tell Mama we were playin' win-nants."

"What?" Junior wanted to make Cliff's loss more painful. "What have you got left to trade?"

"That red marble I've got at home."

"Shucks, it's chipped. In two places."

"I'll throw in my jug."

"It's wop sided like Little Seeb said."

"It ain't neither. Not bad."

"It is too. Too bad to shoot straight."

"There's Mama standin' on the porch, waitn' for us. Alfie, you better not tell. You hear?"

Mama was standing on the porch, with her hands on her hips. That was a bad sign. Her lips were white too. Another bad sign. When she spoke, the signs became worse, taking on reality. "Where have you been?" she demanded. Her eyes held all three of us in their grip. "I called you twenty minutes ago. What were you doing?"

"Playin' marbles," Junior spoke. Cliff kept silent. I did too.

"Playing marbles with the niggers!" Mama's lips were drawn in a hard tight line. "Playing for keeps. With the niggers."

I thought: I won't tell unless she makes me.

"I said, you were playing for keeps with them, Seeb's younguns?"

Cliff ran his hands inside empty pockets. "Yes'm."

Junior was sullen. But his pockets were not empty.

I thought: Now I won't hafta tell. She made Cliff tell.

"Gambling! And on Sunday!" Mama's anger reignited by spontaneous combustion.

Cliff was thinking about Little Seeb's and Robert Lee's pockets filled with his marbles.

Junior was looking for a way out of the trap. "Is dinner ready?" It was what Papa would have said.

"Yes. It's ready." Mama focused her anger on Junior. "It's been ready for an hour." That was an exaggeration, but an hour is more impressive than twenty minutes. "It's ready and on the table. But you're not eating a bite 'till you wash yourselves all over and put on clean clothes." Her anger ignited again to a higher temperature. "Go wash the nigger off yourselves before you sit down to the table."

Cliff and Junior turned sullenly to the wash basin on the shelf by the well. Cliff lowered the bucket into the well, and started to haul up a bucket of water. Hand over hand. The wet chain glistened as the water dropped off it. The water sloshed over the rim of the bucket as he tilted it to set it on the shelf of the well housing.

I stared into Mama's face. My lips trembled. My eyes glistened with tears.

"Mama. It was just Little Seeb and Robert Lee an' ... an' all the others." I turned and fled, for I felt something I could not express, could not understand.

Mama went back into the house. She could not control her breathing. She sat down. Got up again. Went to the kitchen to look at the food on the table. Listened to the sounds of Junior and Cliff and me washing ourselves. "Lord have mercy!"

Looking down at her noticeably swelling belly, "Lord have mercy! I don't know what has come over me. I just don't know."

Chapter Eight

Mister Land touched off the spark that brought me into conflict with the elderly and retired Methodist minister, Reverend T. E. Davenport. Mister Land was a leader in the Methodist Church, and he operated a small grocery where I traded before the trouble started. He had been present at that Sunday evening service when I preached the sermon THE THREE HORIZONS, and on my next grocery shopping trip to his store, he handed me a copy of The Wesleyan Christian Advocate which contained an article by Mister Davenport on the segregation of the races. "Read this," he said, "and tell me what you think of it. Reverend Davenport is a highly respected Methodist minister." Mister Land customarily sought to engage me in the discussion of some religious matter or the interpretation of some passage of Scripture, and I fell into his trap this time.

The Davenport article heartily endorsed racial segregation and cited Scriptural authority for the position that segregation is ordained by God and that integration is a violation of the laws of God. In the opening words to his article, Mister Davenport said "You may examine all history; there has never been better treatment by a ruling race to a subject race than that of the Negroes in the South."

When I had finished reading, I wrote my rebuttal which I gave to Mister Land when I returned the magazine with Mister Davenport's article in it, and picked up my little bag of groceries from Mister Land's store. I wrote

"He (Mister Davenport) assumes that the question is to be discussed on the basis of ruling and subject races. This is not the basis at all; we are dealing with two races living side by side in a democratic republic which does not recognize ruling and subject races."

That should have been enough for me to say about the Davenport article; it was not all that I did say. And because I said more I had to quit buying groceries at Mister Land's store because I went on to say that the writer's prejudices in regard to race were exceeded only by his ignorance of the Bible. I believe that Mister Davenport had based his Biblical authority for racial segregation on the story of Noah who had cursed his son Ham because Ham had found him drunken and naked and exposed his father's shame to his brothers Shem and Japheth. Mister Davenport, as so many others had done, attributed Noah's behavior to God and thereby justified a curse on the black race. I considered this highly irresponsible, and I was caustic in my criticism. This was a grave mistake on my part because Mister Land showed what I had written about the Davenport article to other Methodists in town, and since Methodists and Baptists were intermarried, it made matters worse for me in the Baptist Church.

If it were possible for me to apologize to Mister Davenport for my treatment of his efforts at Biblical interpretation, I would do so, but he died, and if his hope of heaven was fulfilled, he may be bunked with black roommates there. If so, I hope they will treat him like a brother. A WHITE brother.

As for me, Julian Gill, the Methodist druggist paid me off. He called me on the telephone at midnight and gave me an eloquent cussin' which I probably deserved but did not enjoy. I had been roused from sleep, and I did not take it with grace. When I went back to bed, MarthaLee awakened and thinking there might have been an emergency involving some one of our family or friends, wanted to know about the call.

I started to tell her that Julian Gill had called, that he was drunk, and had "cussed me out", and she said "Oh, you mean the druggist?" Then she turned back to her pillow, but I was wakeful and excited, and I said

"If you have to get a prescription filled, you had better take it to Mister Jones. If you catch Gill sober, he might really do us in." Mister Jones was a Baptist who also had a pharmacy in town. He was a man of sobriety and he never made midnight calls to me to abuse me verbally for show-ing disrespect for the literary efforts of a retired Methodist minister who enjoyed the favor of the Shellman Methodists.

An unfortunate encounter with an elderly Baptist minister had been more direct in terms of our being face-to-face, but less direct in terms of the words that were spoken. Doctor John E. Martin - people in Shellman pronounced it Johnny - was a man of great renown and he was related to many of the people in Shellman. The Martins were numerous, and the Martins were intermarried with the Currys, which meant that about half the upper crust of Shellman claimed kinship with Doctor John E. Mar-tin, who had retired but was still active, and he was on a visit to relatives there. So I invited him to speak to the church on Sunday morning. He did, speaking mostly of memories of past experiences with friends and relatives, and making a plea for the unsaved to become more like himself He did not mention the issue of race relations.

At the evening session of the church, I did mention that issue. In fact, I gave a rather strong address which I called THE HURRICANE'S EYE, and because the congregation heard it, and Doctor Martin heard it, and I feel that it was germane to the subject of this little account of my ministry in Shellman, I will record here the salient parts of the sermon THE HURRICANE'S EYE.

"The position of the Christian today should be crystal clear. He is to stand at the very center of events. But he can never "stand" there until he first works his way through to the center. He is not one of the violent, destructive forces - just as Jesus was not a man of violence - but he must struggle with those forces be buffeted by them until, storm tossed, weary, and even badly mauled, he comes out in the "eye" where the peace of the Son of God is with him.

"That man who attempts to ignore the earth-shaking events of our age, to escape into some comfortable, smug corner of a sheltered life, hoping that the winds of world revolution will pass him by, that the storms that rend his nation will somehow leave him untouched, that the driving blasts that chill and drench our state will somehow go away and leave him as he has always been, that if he will shut his eyes and "make believe" the upheaval in his own midst will turn out to be a bad dream, that man is in for real trouble. For the storm will hit him, and his boat will be capsized so quickly that he will hardly know what has happened to him.

"A worse fate awaits only those who "huff and puff" and become a part of the raging wind and the tumult and the shouting, and become blinded by their own fury; they become a part of the storm, a part of the violence, the destruction; and their ultimate fate is to be spent, in the end, like the storm ....

"The whole world waits terror-stricken, not knowing where nor how, nor with what velocity, the storm of violent war between the two great giants, will strike. It is our responsibility to so carefully study and understand and chart the movements of these forces that we can tell men how to save themselves from destruction.

"The tragedy of our times in respect to the world struggle is that so many of our people do not know what it is all about. They know neither the real nature of communism nor the essential elements of Democracy. For them a Communist is any person whom they don't like, and Democracy is anything that works to their advantage. But what we are actually faced with is error's challenge of truth unproclaimed and unapplied - that is what makes communism such a menace to our way of life. The essence of true Democracy is lost if we fail to recognize first the sovereignty of God in our lives, the sovereignty of a God who demands that we give all if we would receive anything worth while ....

"Our state needs to know what is happening to it, for it is evident that unless something is done on the basis of enlightenment, the work of hundreds of years, the dedicated toil of men who gave their lives that their children might have a full and rich life, will be destroyed. It is the business of the Christian to battle through the thick mist, and stand in the light of the eye, and understand what is happening, and to tell men that in the face of the approaching storm they must be careful what manner of defenses they throw up, for they are apt to collapse of their own weight under the impact of the wind, and falling in upon the occupants of the fort, they will crush them as did the house of the Philistines which fell on the revelers there.

"The same is true on the local level where the issues are more apt to be muddied than anywhere else. It is the Christian's responsibility to know exactly what is happening, interpret the movements, and to warn men of the destruction, urging them to be prepared. We must stand where we can see the real issues, the obligation of the Christian to face up to the implications of a faith that is never so perfect in its embodiment as it is in its ideal; the necessity for that freedom of expression which makes the difference between a living faith and a dead hypocrisy; and the imperative of that tolerance of spirit which is able to tolerate even intolerance itself.

"And having battled the winds and the rains to achieve that position, we must cry to our fellows, and say "It is the hatred itself which will destroy you. Therefore love one another. It is your pride which will be your downfall; therefore humble yourselves. It is your unforgiving spirit which will leave in its wake the dead and the dying; therefore repent and forgive one another and be reconciled."

I can see now that what I said, couched in dramatic and symbolic and even highly charged language, could have been seen as a rebuke to the honored old gentleman who had spoken of happy memories of an idyllic past among his kinsmen and. friends. Still, no word of the local situation, so fatally charged with emotion, passed between Doctor Martin and me. And on the next day we were both invited to dine together at the home of my neighbors, his kinsmen, Mrs. John Denis and Mrs Nettie Wade. These two lived across the street from me. I walked over at noon. There was among us all a friendly interchange of ideas on matters theological and otherwise. I expressed myself, in reply to questions asked on some matters of Biblical interpretation, but the question of racial segregation was not mentioned.

It was reported to me a few days later that Doctor Martin had expressed his opinion that I was not orthodox in my beliefs, and that I ought to be silenced. Since he did not say this to me directly, I can neither confirm nor deny the report, and I saw that the opposition now had found the missing link in the chain they hoped to loop about my neck, ecclesiastical approval for what they wanted to do. When the deacons met on the first Sunday afternoon in November, and I started to present to them my program for the coming year, I was soon cut short, and the next two hours were devoted to an urgent attempt on their part to make me see that the majority of the church was against me, and I ought to resign.

I never knew, nor did I care, on what doctrinal or theological issues I had been found unorthodox by Doctor John E. Martin. I was concerned with the church's rightful role interpreting the love of God in Christ for all men, black, white and in between, and for my right, indeed, my obligation, to declare that message. I was well aware that some members of the Shellman Baptist Church, intended to keep me from proclaiming that message from the pulpit of that church. I realized that one local minister had said what the people really wanted to hear. When asked what he thought about the racial issue, he said "It is a good time to pray about it and a bad time to talk about it."

For my own part, I saw no point in praying about a question on which God had already given the answer and the go ahead for action. And I firmly believed that to refuse to speak when God had given me the word to speak, was to negate the call to preach and to make myself of no use to the Church in its time of need.

Acting on that conviction, I had won a vote of confidence back there in June. Now, after a long hot summer of bittersweet controversy, the pendulum had begun to swing, and I must now tell you what I believe was happening in Shellman.

Oh yes, I knew that Wilbur Smith, the school, principal, was unhappy about my version of the story of Jonah. But I didn't care if the whale swallowed Jonah, or Wilbur Smith swallowed the whale. It was the classic fish story. It would be the first in a trinity of great fish stories, when Herman Melville would write Moby Dick, and Ernest Hemingway would write The Old Man and the Sea. But the reason the deacons wanted me to resign was not that I didn't take the story of Jonah literally, but that I did take the words of Jesus literally.

So the pendulum was beginning its swing. My future, and the future of others would be profoundly changed by that swing of the pendulum.

In the Summer months of June, July and August, when the opposition was making its loudest outcry against me, it was, numerically, the cry of the minority. But those who supported me were less outspoken than those who were against me. Consequently, their numbers were not impressive except when the ballots were counted. But by September the pendulum had begun to swing noticeably. It teetered so near the fifty-fifty mark for several weeks that on one occasion the deacons had met to discuss the matter, but they came to the conclusion that to reopen the issue would not just alienate a few, but would split the church down the middle. So a balance of power existed for a while. But why was it moving against me?

My opponents worked harder against me than my supporters worked for me because my opponents believed ardently in separation of the races, and were determined to get rid of me, while my supporters did not believe in the mixing of the races, but only in my right to believe and preach integration. My enemies were "sold" on the principle, my friends only maintained personal loyalty to me.

I have mentioned the Mercer Extension Class which was conducted at the Blakely Baptist Church about thirty or forty miles from Shellman. This was an activity of my alma mater, Mercer University, and it was aimed at Baptist lay people who were interested in knowing more about the Bible's message than they were getting from the Sunday School lessons published in Nashville. I was asked to teach a couple of classes because it was assumed. that I knew more than was being offered at the Sunday School lessons.

At least I assumed that this was one of the purposes, but after I had stirred the waters in the pool of race relations, Mister Anderson, who was responsible for setting up and supervising these centers of Biblical learning among the laymen, took a closer look at what I was teaching, and he decided that I was not sound in doctrine, so I was notified that my services would not be required for another year.

Since I did not adhere to the line of literalists who were to become the Fundamentalists who would take over the Southern Baptist Convention, I was not surprised that Mister Anderson found my views unacceptable. I don't remember whether the issue was Jonah being swallowed by the wnale, or Peter trying to walk on water. Since I was teaching a course in old Testament and one in New Testament, it could have been either of these, or both. But what I was saying was an affront to Mister Anderson's faith, and so I had now been fired by two churches and one university extension school and was fighting to hold onto the Shellman Baptist Church which was where the issue was really being fought out.

They had a person, but no cause. There was a cause, the cause of freedom of speech, but some of my friends could never quite grasp that ideal and its implication for the future of the church. They kept coming back to the starting point, which was that they themselves did not believe that integration of the races would work in the South in our day. "Fifty years from now," maybe, but most of them did not expect to be around for fifty more years.

The "absentee" factor was having its effect. Most of those thirty seven who had voted against me had quit coming to church, but they were not moving their membership to some other church because they wanted to be eligible to vote again. They had quit giving too, and let it be known that they would not give to the church as long as I was pastor. The result of this was some who had supported me lost their nerve, thinking they would be stuck with the cost of running the church.

In fact, the church was in better shape financially than it was customary for it to be at this time of year when the farmers had not yet sold their crops. This was because of Mrs. Mae White, who had come up with money nobody expected. There had been a deficit of thirteen hundred dollars, and Mae White had paid it off all by herself. In explanation, she said "the money came from a money tree, but I have shaken it and there is no more on that tree." She did not say whether there were other trees, and subsequent events led me to believe that that there were other trees that were quite fruitful.

Still, the months August, September and October saw the pendulum swinging steadily against me, and it would continue in that direction until the fateful day that lay ahead of me when a second vote would be taken But I must say something here about the "fence sitters" because in political elections, the "undecided" are the ones who decide the outcome at the end.

These were people who liked me, and so were not against me, but they were for segregation. They would not come out actively in my support because they feared that others would identify them with my position. But they would not take a stand against me because of conscience, until they were forced to make a decision. In this group were some of my fellow ministers who feared the loss of their pulpits, but did not want to lose my friendship. So they were miserable, and their position in the community bears a remarkable resemblance to the condition of certain persons described in Dante's Inferno. The visitor, seeing these people hanging tormented between heaven and hell, asked the guide who they were. The guide replied:

"Speak not of them.
They are those who gave their lives to nothing.
Now heaven cannot receive them,
And hell will not have them."

Now I have spoken of them, only briefly, and I will say no more of them.

I will say, though, that Mae White had performed another miracle. The miracle of the Money Tree. But miracles are seen only by the eyes of faith, and devotion.

And now it is time to let the pot simmer for a while, and so some diversion in the form of another one of my boyhood tales will serve that purpose. The tale I have chosen for that purpose is the wedding of Dump, that much marriagable young woman who had run afoul of me, White Lightnin', and Mama.

DUMP GETS MARRIED

I believe I have told you about Dump's imaginary, or fantasized wedding that was interrupted by my dog's attack on her, and the resulting conflict between Dump and me, and then the head on collision with Mama over my indiscretion in calling Dump a Black Nigger. But fantasies become realities for teenaged girls who are standing on the rampart of womanhood, and so it was with great excitement that I both learned and announced the great good news to Mama.

"Dump's gittin' married, Mama! And Aunt Hattie said I could come to the wedding Mama? I really want to go. Can I go, Can I go?"

"Well, it's high time for Dump to get married. Before she gets in trouble... But I don't know about you going to the wedding. You're still awful little for that sort of thing."

I did not know what sort of thing might be going on at Dump's wedding, too advanced in its nature for my tender years. But Mama had aroused my curiosity on two levels. What sort of trouble was Dump in danger of getting into if she didn't get married in a hurry? And what sort of things happened at a wedding that I ought not to see because I was still "awful little"?

I was growing as fast as I could, because I hated being too little for the things that bigger people were entitled to enjoy. I begged "Aw Mama. Aunt Hattie's gonna have cake and ice cream. She said so. I wanta go!"

"Well, cake and ice cream are nice for growing boys." Mama realized that the emphasis on my diminutive stature could be damaging to my ego. But weddings are for grown ups."

I was beginning to wonder now if physical harm could come to me because I was too little to compete with grownups at a wedding. So I fell back on my hero, Willie. "Willie's goin' there won't be nothin' happen to me with Willie there. Nothin' bad." I was already beginning to suspect that bad things could happen at Dump's wedding.

Given a fertile imagination, I could think of bad things like Dump's temper, but the real danger never occurred to me. I just thought about the cake - chocolate, Aunt Hattie had told me - and ice cream - vanilla which Aunt Hattie pronounced "pernilla". So Mama had set me wondering, and this made going to Dump's wedding almost imperative, in order to find out whatever it was I was not supposed to know.

'Willie won't let nothin' bad happen to me, Mama."

Mama was not convinced. "From what I hear on the grapevine, there could be trouble, and I know how Willie loves a fight. It's really Willie that I'm worried about and just afraid you may be standing in the way when the fight breaks out."

"Aw Mama! Aunt Hattie said ... "

"I know what Aunt Hattie said."

"And Uncle Seeb's gonna marry 'em. He's a preacher, and he won't let no trouble."

"It may not be entirely in Uncle Seeb's hands, but I'll talk with your Papa about it."

Apparently Papa thought it would be a good idea for me and Willie to go to the wedding. "Be a good thing for 'im," Papa said. "From what I hear about his ambitions since he give up the idea of drivin' a Greyhound, he may need to see how it's done because he might be called on some day to do a weddin'."

Mama didn't think Papa was taking the matter seriously enough, but after considerable passing of the buck back and forth between Mama and Papa, it was decreed that I might go to the wedding if I promised not to ask for seconds of ice cream and cake. That was Mama's instruction; I don't think Papa thought the promise would be anything he could take to the bank.

Papa said "You stay close to Willie. That way you won't git hurt, and maybe Willie won't hurt nobody." I didn't understand his line of reasoning, but I didn't have to because I heard Mama telling Willie not to let anything bad happen to me, and Papa was saying he reckoned that Willie could put down any trouble that might arise. Later, Willy told me that he hoped there might be something more exciting than the "I do's" and that was one reason he wanted to go.

I also heard Mama telling Papa that it was already a bit late for the "I do's" but Papa said it wasn't ever too late to do the right thing. And Papa told Willie "If there's any trouble I reckon you're man enough to handle it." In fact, Willie liked nothing better than putting down a rebellion, unless it was starting an uprising of his own, just to liven things up. So it was finally settled that Willie and I would go to Dump's wedding.

Willie and I both dressed up for the wedding. Willie wore a new pair of mole skin trousers and a sharp looking blue shirt with a red neck tie that he said cost him fifty cents, but I think he said this just to let Cliff know what might happen to him if he borrowed it when Willie wasn't there. "If I see this tie on your neck, I'll use it to strangle you!" Willie told Cliff just in case his statement about the price was not enough to cause Cliff to leave it alone. Willie had put a shine on his brown shoes too. And I was wearing my best shirt and corduroy trousers that had caused the school bus driver to nickname me "whistle britches".

So Papa looked us over and said we looked "fit to kill" but this expression did nothing to allay Mama's concerns about the adventure.

It was getting on towards dark when Willie and I set off across the cotton patch. We knew the well worn path, and I was thinking about the ice cream and cake all the time, but Willie said "Aunt Hattie won't serve the ice cream and cake 'till after the wedding. It's called a reception, and I reckon that's the best part, when you receive the ice cream and cake, and the groom is lookin' forward to receivin' the bride so that he don't think much about the ice cream and cake."

Willie was so much older and bigger than I was that I figured he knew just about everything, and I made up my mind to just watch Willie and do what I saw him doing, unless Aunt Hattie got me aside and let me in on the goodies before all the grown people had a chance at them.

When we got there everybody was milling around, and Uncle Seeb was dressed out in his preaching suit; it was the first time I had ever seen him wearing it, all black with a white shirt and a blue neck tie. Sure enough, Aunt Hattie took me back to the kitchen and let me lick the ice cream paddle which she had just taken out of the ice cream freezer churn. She said "Can't give you no cake yet 'cause we can't cut it 'till the knot's tied."

I didn't see the connection between knot tying and cake cutting. I knew Willie was in the Boy Scouts, and they were teaching him to tie all sorts of neat knots, but I was so proud to get to taste the ice cream which I was licking off the paddle that I wasn't concerned about tying knots.

Anyway, I didn't see Dump anywhere, but Willie said "They always hide the bride until just before the wedding. She's prob'ly hidin' in a closet somewhere, but she'll come out at the right time. Don't worry none about Dump."

I recognized the groom because he was all dressed up and sweating more than anybody else, but I never did get his real name; everybody called him Buddy, and I didn't try to find out anything else to call him.

Uncle Seeb's booming voice brought about silence in the house, but I noticed some of the young men, Little Seeb among them, stayed out on the front porch. They were looking out toward the road, and I wondered what they might be looking for, and I was going to ask Willie, but Dump came out of hiding about that tine, and I had to watch the wedding. Dump was wearing a brand new flowery dress and high heels. I thought she was going to trip and fall on the floor because of the high heels, but she managed to stay on her feet, and then she was standing up there in front of Uncle Seeb, and I could tell by the way she looked up at him that she was both proud and scared at the same time.

Buddy was standing up there with Dump. He was sweating and looking just as scared as Dump did. But the wedding ceremony was going right along because Uncle Seeb knew what he was doing, and when he asked if anybody had any objection, nobody spoke, and he hurried on. But just as they got to the part about "Do you take this woman ... ?" I found out why Buddy was sweating.

Car lights shone down the driveway. I saw the beams sweep across the cotton patch as the car made the turn into the rutted driveway. It was coming fast, and when it hit the ruts, the driver almost lost control. Then he slowed down some, regained control, and swung in beside the front steps, coming to a sliding halt. Leaving the engine running, a young black man jumped out of the car. He hit the door steps with his feet and was on the porch, facing the group of boys and young men out there,

"Where Dump at?" he demanded of them, and Little Seeb shuffled to the front, stood facing the newcomer.

"Dump inside gittin' married." Little Seeb said. "Whut bizzness you got here? Ain't nobody invited you to Dump's weddin'."

"Dump's mah woman!" the young man said. "Ain't nobody gon' marry Dump. She mah woman!"

I heard the voices, and I ran to see Willie standing in the middle of the groupThere wasn't much light out there, but he stood out because he was white, and all the blacks sort of blurred together. Willie's blond hair was slicked down with water and vaseline, and his temples were flaring up the way I had seen them do before when he was getting ready for a fight.

"Willie!" I called, and tried to push in close to him.

"You stay back!" Willie said to me. "There's gonna be a scuffle here, and I don't want you in it."

The scuffle was going on though, because the young man had tried to force his way through the crowd into the house where he could hear the voices of Uncle Seeb and Buddy and Dump. Uncle Seeb's big voice was booming inside the house, and I heard Dump say "Ah sho' do!" But then Little Seeb noticed Willie standing there on the porch, and he said "Mist, Willie, you tell dis nigger to git on down 'at road. He ain't got no bizness comin' in heah an' tryna bust up Dump's weddin'."

Willie didn't need a second invitation. He waded into the bunch of boys and young men, and reached out to grab his share of the fight. He took hold of the newcomer's shirt collar with his left hand and drew back his right to land one on the newcomer's jaw, and said "Dump's in there gittin' married whether you like it or not. Now you just git your black ass outta here or you're gonna need a whole new face."

"You lookaheah, White Fokes!" the young man, whose name was Jimmy - at least that's what I heard some of them calling him - glared back at Willie. "Dis yere nigger bizness. You ain't got no right ... "

But the young black men hustled Jimmy Something off the porch, pushed him into his car, and told him to keep going. As he got it started, and lurched forward, one of the young black men kicked the right rear fender and shouted "Git on!"

By the time Willie and I got back inside the house, Dump was married, and she and the groom were cutting the cake, and some of the women were helping Aunt Hattie with the ice cream. Then Aunt Hattie got a slice of the cake and an ice cream cone, and she called out "You come 'ere,

Alfie. Lawd sakes. You standin' round out in the yard and you gon' miss out on evvything ef Ah don' look out after you."

I was still sticking close to Willie, but I heard Uncle seeb talking in a low voice to Little Seeb, "Now you stay 'way fr'm 'at bottle. You heah me? Ah don' want no trouble in mah house when Dump bein' married."

Little Seeb promised to stay sober and keep down all trouble. I didn't have to ask Aunt Hattie for seconds because she almost forced seconds on me.

Willie and I traipsed back across the cotton patch. We were happy about the wedding, but Willie seemed to be just a little bit disappointed that he didn't land one on the Jimmy Something's jaw. Mama met us at the door, and she said "I hope there wasn't any trouble. I heard some yelling and loud noise up there."

Willie said "There wasn't no trouble Mama. Uncle Seeb tied the knot tighterin' a Boy Scout couldha done, and I reckon Dump and Buddy are in bed together by now."

Papa said he didn't reckon that would be anything new for them, but that would not lessen the pleasure of the experience for either one of them, but Mama tried to shush Papa up, and to warn him that I was too young to hear such talk.

Papa said "I reckon he won't learn no younger, and I'm awful proud you two had such a good time. You sure there wasn't no trouble, Willie?"

Willie said there wasn't no trouble that he had seen, and Papa was satisfied. He said "Uncle Seeb bein' a preacher and a pillar of righteousness, I'd expect it all to go off smoothly and without no trouble."

I was just keeping quiet and hoping Mama wouldn't ask if I took more than one piece of cake. But then I thought she would be suspicious if I was too quiet so I said "I sure did enjoy Dump's weddin'."

CHAPTER NINE

Cuthbert is the county seat of Randolph County. It is where legal cases are brought to court and where the lawyer lived who told me that he went on a binge every time he won or lost a case. Cuthbert is a bigger town than Shellman but I think the percentage of college graduates and alcoholics runs a bit lower than Shellman.

The Cuthbert Baptist Church is bigger than the Shellman Baptist Church, and the turnover in ministers there is about equal to that in Shellman but it is done more quietly than was the case in Shellman when they were getting rid of me. Richard Allman was pastor of the Cuthbert Baptist Church, and he was a bigger man than myself; he was tall and gangly and rather impressive, and he did not talk about race in the pulpit. But Dick was a friend of mine. When you are in a tight fix like mine, you are grateful for friends, even though they keep quiet on controversial issues in which you are embroiled. Dick had invited me to go fishing with him one Saturday morning, and since I did not want to be one of Zack Crittenden's half wits, I accepted the invitation.

We had been sitting in the boat for a couple of hours, and had not caught anything, so I said "I was elected Chairman of Evangelism for the Association which meets in a week or so. I was thinking that instead of giving the usual clap trap type of report, I would talk about our mission to the black people of our community."

Dick furrowed his brow and said "Henry, people think you are crazy now. If you do that you will remove all doubt." Then he cast his line. It became entangled in a willow branch overhanging the water. He jerked, broke the line, and reeled in what was left of it. He said "Let's go to lunch."

The Bethel Baptist Association is made up of the Baptist churches in six or eight counties, and except for an occasional flash of humor, the two day annual meeting is pretty boring, although the food that is served is usually good. I managed to get through my report on Evangelism, leaving some of the mssengers undecided about me. And I began looking forward to the Georgia Baptist Convention which is made up of all the participating Baptist churches in the state, on a voluntary basis. The state meeting is usually a bit more exciting because this is where controversial subjects come up, and there is a weeding out process; Speakers who make rash statements are eliminated from the competition for larger churches and for selection for important boards of the larger Southern Baptist Convention which is made up of Baptists all over the Southland and some other parts of the country.

At the Southern Baptist Convention, the messengers deal with weighty matters like the Virgin Birth of Jesus and the Plenary Verbal Inspiration of Scripture. Controversial matters like racial mixing are handled with care by men who are capable of dealing with these things in a manner that will say as little as possible and promise to pray a lot about them. Virgin Birth and Inspiration of Scriptures get a big vote for them with little or no opposition, but racial matters could bring about a division among the brethren and sistern. I had not gone to the meeting of the Southern Baptist Convention; I was busy being hanged in Shellman, but I planned to go to the Georgia Baptist Convention meeting which would be held in Augusta, Georgia in the fall of 1954, and I was going to ride with Dick Allman and his wife who were driving to Augusta.

People in Shellman did not want me to go to the meeting in Augusta because they were afraid I would say something about racial integration and draw more attention to Shellman with more write ups in more newspapers. I was going anyway. I was not only going to attend the meeting in Augusta; I was going to say something there if the opportunity presented itself, and as Dick and I talked on the way I became convinced that the opportunity would arise, and I would seize it by the forelock. I might remove all doubt whether I had lost my mind, but I was convinced that somebody had to articulate clearly and forcefully the Christian theological position on Race, and that I was the man to do it.

At this meeting there were men who were ministers of Baptist churches from all over Georgia - no women pastors because Baptists don't let women preach - and they were all heated over the racial issue, and all eager to hear what the Social Service Commision would say when Judge Humphrey Dukes brought his report. Actually, the report was, I thought, rather weak and ambiguous, and more verbiage than content, but it did say something, so I am obligated to tell you what it said.

"... The issue of separate but equal rights, is a debatable question. The question of segregation is not new. There has been this issue before the public for many years in labor disputes, separate transportation facilities, right to vote. The Supreme Court's decision on the issue of segregation was not a surprise. The decision so far has only laid down principles to guide us. The Supreme Court recognizes the difficult problem of integration; and the necessity of coordinating the thinking of directors of school systems, civic groups and religious organizations.

"It is nearly unanimous among the ruling bodies of the Christian churches to preclude (strike down) segregation, and yet the pronouncements of such bodies do not determine the thinking of the individual members. The Supreme Court recognized these things when it put no enforcement time on its decision.

"We should strive to handle this issue as good citizens; calm and dispassionate. We should use all the faith at our command to act as God would have us to act when the final order comes. These issues should be met by Christian men and women on the basis of spiritual teaching that every man is embraced by the love of God, every man has value in the sight of God, and every man is included in the plan of God.

"We should urge all Christians to conduct themselves in the spirit of Christ. We should pray to God to guide us in our thinking, that in the end there should be justice and brotherly love.

"We should urge all Christians in positive thinking and planning so that all people, of all races, would have equal rights as God would have it.

"We, God's people, should be much in prayer, trying to find God's will, and seeking His guidance. There is not a united opinion on this problem, and we should try to find the answers as each issue presents itself. The important thing. is that we start out in the right spirit, in the spirit of Christ, and that we act in accordance with the will of God."

This report of the Social Service Commission at the Georgia Baptist Convention in Augusta Georgia on November 18,1954, was one that I believe I could have got by with in Shellman because it was so rambling and indefinite that nobody would have guessed what I was saying. Yet somebody did object to it in Augusta.

The man was Mister Hugh Grant, a resident of Augusta and a former U.S. envoy to Ethiopia. He wanted to offer a substitute motion, but when it was learned that he was not an official delegate or messenger to the convention, the presiding officer, Dr. James. W. Merritt, refused him permission to make a substitute motion. Mister Grant insisted on being heard though, and he was given five minutes to speak to the convention. I quote here from the Atlanta Journal coverage of the event on November 19, 1954.

"He said desegregation is a direct violation of the fundamental rules of the Baptist faith and philosophy and, was a political decision on the part of the court.

"He continued, It is the result of a conspiracy and propaganda campaign by radical elements, including communists and the NAACP It not only means integration of school children, but integration throughout our society.

Praising Governor Talmadge as a forthright state leader, he said If you approve this report, which in effect approves the Supreme court decision, it will mean direct repudiation of Gov. Talmadge's program."

I had two thoughts while Mister Grant was speaking. He must have heard something in the report that I had missed. And God have mercy on Ethiopia if this was what we had sent there to represent us. But mainly I was thinking that I must answer this man, and while I was looking for a way to get to the speaker's platform, Doctor James P. Wesberry, an Atlanta pastor got there first and said he was a friend of the governor, termed the report a "very fine statement" and said that he did not consider it a repudiation of Governor Talmadge.

I was still trying to get to the microphone, but I was like the lame man at the pool of Bethesda, and Doctor Henry Stokes beat me to it. Henry Stokes was pastor of the First Baptist Church in Macon where the Men's Bible Class had helped me pay my tuition at Mercer; by now the members must have been wishing they had left me in the corn field, but Henry Stokes admitted he was a member of the commission that had drawn the report and that he had "misgivings that it might not be strong enough."

This made me feel better about Henry Stokes and gave me the hope that First Baptist in Macon might have a future. But I felt that nobody had spoken to the issue, and I made it to the platform and asked for permission to do that. Doctor Merritt reluctantly granted me one minute, and I am a rather slow spoken man by nature, but I tried to crowd all my thoughts and feelings in that one minute. It maybe that I ran over the one minute limit a bit, but I had the mike and there was no stopping me. This is what I said:

"This is not primarily a political issue; it is primarily a moral issue. Therefore it is certainly a matter to be discussed and acted upon by men called to declare the Word of God. We are not here concerned with the repudiation or the non_repudiation of Governor Talmadge, but with whether we are to repudiate Jesus Christ by refusing to take a courageous Christian stand on an issue on which the Scriptures speak so clearly. To give way to popular opinion on this matter is to deny our calling as ministers of God's Word, and it can only indicate that we are afraid to vote our convictions lest we be fired from our positions when we get home. But if we are true to our calling we have nothing to fear, and shall have nothing to be ashamed of, except that we ought already to be ashamed that we have stood by and let the secular court of our land take the lead in a matter in which we ourselves should have been in the vanguard."

The motion, such as it was, was then put to a vote, and was carried easily. Then the Convention went on with its reports and its sermons and its prayers and with the preachers shaking hands with one another and telling about what wonderful things the Lord was doing through their ministry, in the hope that they would be recommended to some church larger than the one they were serving, and of course, at better pay. As far as I was concerned, the meeting was over. We had passed a resolution which said nothing and we would do nothing as a result of it. But it was better than publicly embracing the principle of segregation as the former envoy to Ethiopia wanted us to do. I had my say, and I knew that when I went home to Shellman I would pay the price for speaking my mind.

So while Dick Allman drove, and his wife entertained us with her impressions of the meeting in Augusta, my mind raced ahead of the automobile, for I was thinking.The news will be in the morning papers and all hell will break loose in Shellman. I was not surprised when I learned that a special meeting of the deacons was called for Sunday afternoon, and I was invited to attend.

I studied the faces of the men gathered there; I knew what they had come together to do; I knew they would do it. They did. They voted to submit a motion to the church, recommending that I resign effective January 1, 1955. The motion carried. There were ten deacons of the Shellman Baptist Church. Two of them, J.A. White, the husband of the Miracle Worker Mae White, was sick and did not attend the meeting. David Arnold was afflicted with a disease that caused him to jerk all the time. Claude Payne, an elderly worker for the city, had once told me he was the only pain in the church. These last two abstained from the vote.

Dr. F.M. Martin, a retired physician, was not there, but he sent a proxy vote against me. Claron Wooten, the Chairman who had been buried with me on the mound in town, did not vote. But I could see where his sympathies lay. Not with me. Of the ten deacons, six votes were cast, all against me.

The deacons said they would not submit their recommendation until the first Sunday of December. If I would resign in the meantime, the recommendation to dismiss me would not be offered to the church. I did not resign, and I must tell you why. I certainly did not expect another miracle like the one in June when Mae White turned the church around. I was accused of being perversely stubborn, but I don't think that was it. I knew these men. Except for D.K. (Doc) Bynum, the ones who voted against me that day had voted against me in June, so what was new? Doc was new. But what was new about Doc Bynum was that he thought he was putting me out of my misery, and he didn't want to see me humiliated, so he hoped I would resign before Sunday. His heart was full of confused love, but he simply could not see what I had been trying to reveal to him, that a principle of Right was worth a man's suffering, even dying for, and that to offer him a way of escape from facing the final issue does not do him a favor; it unwittingly comes between him and his God_given destiny.

So the action of the deacons did not represent anything new, and did not merit a reversal of my own policy. But there was a deeper reason for my refusal. I felt that what was happening at Shellman would mark a new era in the historical expression of Christianity, that it was therefore of eternal significance in the life of the Church, not just in the South, but in the whole world, for it was here, in Shellman, Georgia, that the issue was to be drawn along absolute lines.

Here the Church had a challenge to meet the ultimate test of her faith, and thereby enter into her glory, and neither I nor the deacons of the Shellman Baptist Church, had the right to take away that challenge, to rob the Church of the freedom to make that ultimate choice which would mean the difference between glory and shame, between Life and Death. If I had resigned, I would have relieved the people of the terrible task of firing me, but I would also have robbed them of the privilege of sustaining me. You cannot take away from a man the privilege of choosing hell without denying him the privilege of choosing heaven. For if there are no alternatives, there is no choice; if no choice, then no freedom; and the man who is not free is not a whole man.

The deacons themselves did not seem to realize that in refusing to resign at their request, I was delivering them from the greater weight of condemnation that they then would have had to bear, that of having fired me. The responsibility for that action must rest on all the members of the church, not on six deacons, one of whom did not appear in person for the action. And the Church? Even at the hour of eleven on Sunday Morning, the Church could redeem herself, if she found the courage. Meanwhile, I was thinking of three men who had faced such a challenge. They were the philosopher Socrates, the apostle Paul, and the Christ Jesus. Let me tell you about these three men while we are waiting for Sunday morning to come with the terrible necessity of the vote.

Socrates was condemned by a very large jury in Athens. But he could go into exile from the city, rescued by his followers, or die by drinking the hemlock. He chose death because to live anywhere besides Athens was intolerable, and to seek escape was dishonorable. So he drank the hemlock and died.

Paul could have listened to the warning of Agabus, and instead of going to Jerusalem where he would be bound and handed over into captivity, there was the whole Roman Empire for him to wander in. But that is what it would have been, a wandering. He chose to become a prisoner for the sake of his Lord, and at last to die in prison for what he believed.

Jesus could have saved himself if he had listened to Peter who tried to get him to turn back from his destiny in Jerusalem, but instead he went up, knowing what waited for him there. In his own words we have his lament which is not for himself, but for the people who had rejected him.

"O Jerusalem Jerusalem, killing the prophets and stoning those who are sent to you. How often would I have gathered your children together as a hen gathers her brood under her wings, and you would not. Behold, your house is forsaken. And I tell you, you will not see me until you say Blessed be he who comes in the name of the Lord. Would that even today you knew the things that make for peace. But they are hid from your eyes." (Luke's Gospel, Chapters 13 and 19.)

So I did not resign at the Deacons' suggestion. I waited for Sunday morning.

But I could not resist the temptation to have the last word in that meeting. I said "The duty of deacons is described rather well in the New Testament story of the early church. But examine it closely as you care to do, you will not find that it includes the hiring and firing of preachers."

And now, while we wait, another tale from my boyhood, this one about Papa, and my less than admirable part in Papa's trick on an old Negro.

A CORD OF WOOD

While I am telling you about Papa and his sense of humor, I have to tell you that he also had a mean streak in him. That mean streak expressed itself at times in the most surprising way, especially if a Negro was involved.

But there was a method in his madness. Just as Papa led me and Mama into his trap about Uncle Jock and Sherman's bootprints on the door, he would sometimes lead another man into a trap, especially if he knew the other man was unable to read and write.

Papa himself had only gone through the fourth grade in school, but he never stopped learning. He could read very well _ I don't know about his writing, for I never saw anything he had written _ but when he had spoken there was no need to write it. He knew his arithmetic and he did measurements very well. In fact, he knew everything he needed to know in order to live in an agrarian society and deal with the city folks when business required it.

Papa's assumption that black people of his own generation could neither read nor write, was generally correct, and he was not above playing on their ignorance in this respect in order to get what he wanted out of them. Or to get them to do what he wanted them to do.

So the story I am going to tell you here about Tobe and the cord of Wood will serve to let you know what you may want to know about Papa, and I will leave it to you to discern the influence he had on me. For we started out to say that if we would know why a man does the things he does, why he holds the values he holds, why he sticks his neck out for certain principles, it is necessary to know who the people are who influenced him when he was a boy.

And Papa definitely influenced my life and helped to shape my character, for both good and bad. I am more than genetically my father's son; I am the son he imprinted on. More often than not, it didn't turn out the way he expected, but still I am the man I am because as Papa's boy I was exposed to the foibles as well as the virtues of my father.

So then here is the story of TOBE AND THE CORD OF STOVE-WOOD.

Tobe was a short, squat, broadshouldered black man. In his forties? Fifties? Grizzled and bent from hard work in the fields and in the woods. Hungry. Definitely hungry, but no money to buy food. He could not read or write. He earned a meagre living at bard labor in the fields of white men. But when the harvest was in - the cotton picked, the corn in the crib - there was no work for Tobe.

It was that way when Tobe came to Papa, and said "Mister Buck. Ain't you got some work f'r me. Ah'm hungry. Ah could cut some wood f'r you."

Papa was a poor red dirt One mule farmer himself. But he was white, which in the Southern culture of my boyhood was a definite advantage, even if you were hungry and broke and looking for work and bread. So Tobe came to Papa, but Papa who did indeed have some work that Tobe could do, some wood that Tobe could cut, drove a hard bargain. He wasn't giving away anything.

"There's a cord of wood over there in the pines, other side of the creek. You chop it up into stovewood, and I'll pay you fifty cents." Tobe agreed because he was hungry. But there are two things I must explain for the modern day reader. First, fifty cents was a lot of money, in depths of the Great Depression. It was not what we would call pocket change. It was a day's wages.

Second, a cord of wood is a lot of wood to chop up into the size required for firing a wood burning cook stove. A cord is a pile eight feet long, four feet high, and four feet wide. Papa had cut down the pine trees, and split the logs to the above dimensions. Each log four feet long, then split into four pieces to dry and season out, then stacked between two saplings he had cut and driven into the ground eight feet apart. Now it must be split some more and chopped into small pieces about two feet long to fit into Mama's wood burning cookstove.

"When you're finished, I'll look at it to see that you've done the job right. I'll haul it to the house in the wagon and pay you the fifty cents for your work."

"Yassuh," Tobe said, and went off to sharpen his axe.

That was on Friday. Saturday, about noon, Tobe came to the house to announce that he had completed the job, and to collect his fifty cents. Papa was not there. Mama was not there. They had gone to town to peddle the farm produce, and to buy groceries for the next week. I stood facing Tobe. "Ah's done," Tobe announced. "Ah's come to c'llect."

I said "Papa's not here now, Tobe, and I don't know what time he will get home, but you come back in the mornin'. Papa's always here on Sunday mornin'."
Tobe went away. Negroes did not hang around a white man's house, waiting for him. Tobe went back home, and on Sunday morning he came back looking for Papa. In the meantime, Mama and Papa came home

early from town, I told Papa what Tobe had said, and Papa told me, "All right Son, catch the mule, hitch her to the wagon, and we'll haul the stovewood home."

When we came to the pile of chopped wood over in the pines, across the creek, Papa looked at the pile critically, walked all around it, and said to me, "It don't look as big as it ought to be, Son. A cord of wood oughtta chopped out more than this." He began walking about in the underbrush stomping in his wondering about the wood, and looking back from time to time at the pile. Then he stumbled over something at the edge of a honeysuckle clump, looked down, and said "God AlMighty! Son. Come 'ere!" Then he began poking under the honey suckle vines. When I reached him, he had dragged out several split logs of pine wood. He was piling them up at the edge of the honeysuckle tangle.

"That damn' nigger has hid the wood under these vines instead of chopping it up." We walked back to the empty wagon. "We'll leave it all here for the time bein'." Driving home in the empty wagon, I asked "Papa, what are you gonna do. Just leave the wood over there."

Papa said "I'm gonna fix Tobe's wagon for 'im." but when I asked what he was going to do to Tobe, he said "Never mind. I'll think of something. You just wait."

Next morning, Sunday, early, as soon as he had finished eating breakfast, Papa went to sit on the steps that led up to the back porch. He began rolling a cigarette from his little sack of Bull Durham. Tobe walked into the yard and approached Papa. "Mawnin' Mister Buck," Tobe said. "Ah done chopped up 'at pile a wood, an' Ah's come f'r my fi'ty cents."

"Mornin' Tobe," Papa spoke in a fairly normal tone of voice. "You got it all ready for me to haul to the house?"

"Yassuh. Ah's done chopped it all up."

I was standing on the porch, behind Papa. I still did not know how he planned to handle this situation. Papa turned and spoke over his shoulder to me. "Son, go fetch me the Bible. You know where it's at. Bring it here to me."

I certainly did know where the Bible was. I knew too that I was a more frequent reader of it than Papa was. I smelled trouble for Tobe, but I still had not guessed Papa's game. "Here it is, Papa." I handed the Bible over to Papa.

"All right, Tobe. It's Sunday mornin' and a good time for me to read you a Bible lesson. You ever read the Bible?'

"Nassuh, Ah cain't read. Ah heahs Preacher Seeb read it in chu'ch."

"You go to church, Tobe?"

"Oh yassuh, Ah goes when Ah can."

"You believe the Bible is the Word of God?"

"Yassuh, ever' word. Ah b'lievs."

"You believe it's all true, and all the prophecies in it will come to pass?"

"Yassuh. Hit all true. Jest lak Rev'ren' Seeb say."

"All right Tobe. I'm gonna read you a passage from the book of prophecy of Hezekiah. Let me find it here." Papa let the Bible fall open about in the middle, flipped a few pages back and forth, ran his work hardened, tobacco stained finger down the page, and said "Here it is. I want you to listen to what it says."

I had begun to guess what Papa was up to, for I not only knew where the Bible was kept; I knew there is no Book of the Prophecy of Hezekiah. Had not my Sunday School teacher at Mt. Zion Baptist Church required me to learn and recite the names of all sixty six books of the Bible?

And no Hezekiah. But Papa was preparing to read to Tobe from the book of Hezekiah.

Papa spoke now in tones that would make a sinner tremble at the prospect of hell's fire and brimstone. Papa's own father had been a circuit riding Methodist preacher, and Papa's hours in church were not wasted; they were spent in learning how to use the word to intimidate sinners. "Cursed be the man who hides the cordwood under the honeysuckle vines," Papa intoned. "Verily he shall be found out and punished for his sin. He shall answer for it on Judgment Day when all sinners are cast into the lake of fire."

Papa added a few more "curseds" and "verilies" to the extemporaneous "reading", closed the Bible, laid it on the top door step, and looked severely at Tobe.

Tobe was shaking in his broken down brogan work shoes. He was trembling in his faded and patched blue denim overalls. His few remaining scraggly, yellowed teeth were clacking together in amazement and terror. He was speechless in his guilt.

Papa said "Tobe, you rascal, you tried to cheat me, but I found you out. I know what you done. What's worse, the Lord knows what you done when you hid the cordwood under the honeysuckle vines to keep from cutting it."

Tobe said "Ah'm sorry, Mister Buck. You an' de Good Lawd f'give me, Ah go back and drag ever' log outten nem vines, an' Ah chop up ever' one of 'em. Please, Mister Buck, you an' de Lawd. Ah go back and chop nem logs up rat naow, befo' Ah sets down, today."

Tobe turned as if he were looking for his sharpened axe to begin work at that moment, but Papa stopped him.

"Not today, Tobe. It's Sunday. You can't chop wood on Sunday. You'll just add another sin to your load you're already carryin'. You wait 'till tomorrow, then you be there in the woods at sunup. You heah?"

"Yassuh! Ah be in nem woods at daylight. Yassuh. Ah sho' drag nem logs out an chop up ever' one of 'em. Yassuh."

"All right, Tobe. You see that you do that, and then you come to me for your fifty cents."

Tobe turned and hobbled away in his broken brogan shoes, jerking at the left gallus of his faded and patched overalls, mumbling "Yassuh! Ah be in nem woods fo' de sun come up, but Ah ain't choppin' no wood on Sunday. Nassuh!"

Papa handed the Bible back to me. "Here, Son, you put the Bible back where you keep it. I'm goin' to trim ol' Kate's mane an' tail. She's gonna have a full load of stovewood to haul in tomorrow evenin'." Papa stubbed out his home made cigarette, rose from the top step, and started to go to the mule's stable. But Mama flung open the screen door to the kitchen at that moment, and she stood on the porch, her cheeks flushed, her eyes blazing.

"You're not going anywhere until you hear what I have to say to you about what you've just done."

Papa stopped. He knew when he was caught in his own trap, and he knew there was no use to struggle.

"Say it." Papa tried to speak with bravado, but something was missing. "I know you're gonna take up for the damn' nigger, but go ahead an' say it anyhow."

"Blasphemy! That's what it is! Blasphemy! Pretending to be reading from the Bible. The Lord will punish you for it on Judgment Day, if not sooner." Mama turned to go back into the kitchen, stopped, and came back to face Papa again. "I reckon you'll go over there and search the whole woods and quoting from your book of Hezekiah every time you turn up another log."

"Ain't gonna search for 'em." Papa said. He was starting to roll another cigarette. "Ain't no need for me to watch Tobe now. The Lord'll be watchin' im."

I came, in after years, to see that even Mama had missed the real point herself. It was Tobe, not the Bible, that Papa had abused.

And in after years, when I was preaching at Shellman, and was conducting worship preaching services at one of the small Baptist churches in the county, we had finished and were standing around outside the church, talking and gossiping as people will do in country churches, when suddenly a new sound erupted. A black man and a black woman were walking along the road and engaging in a lively domestic quarrel. Their voices were loud and angry; I really don't know which was the dominant voice, the man's or the woman's. But the men of the church went out and stopped the quarrel, restraining the man physically until the sheriff arrived and arrested him. At the black man's trial I was called as witness, and asked if the man was interrupting a worship service; I said that the worship service was over when the event occurred. Then I was asked if the man had used profanity in proximity to the church, and I said "I really could not tell, because the deacons were cussing so loud I could not make out what the man was saying."

I was not considered a good witness by the all white court.

Chapter Ten

Sunday morning, December 6, 1954, dawned. It was like most December mornings in southwest Georgia, bright and sunny but cold, a cold that penetrates. It was unlike any other morning for me and MarthaLee and the people of Shellman Georgia. It was the Day of Destiny. The Day of the Lord, in both judgment and redemption.

After breakfast, MarthaLee walked across the lawn to the church where she was to meet her Sunday School class of ten or twelve year olds. They greeted her with sad, self conscious half smiles. A class of teen age boys met in the play room in the rear of the pastor's home. The ping pong table was the center of the room. While they were waiting for the teacher, who was one of the deacons who wanted me to resign, they struck the ball a few times,then they settled down.

I sat in my study, mulling over the sermon I had prepared and written out in full. It was not a happy sermon. No Good News in it. All bad news. I knew how the vote would go, and I had written the sermon accordingly

As the eleven o'clock hour drew near, I stuck the sermon in the Bible which I tucked under my arm, and walked over to the church. The pecan trees by the sidewalk were bare now, except for the empty outer husks still hanging on. The nuts lay on the ground. Some had fallen on the concrete sidewalk and were crushed by the feet of people hurrying to the church.

Mrs. Gladys Wooten was superintendent for the Sunday School. She was bustling about, getting final reports from the teachers, and trying to be cheerful when she spoke to them. Doc Bynum was standing outside the building, talking rather disjointedly with other men, some young like himself, some older than he was. Most of them were having a last minute cigarette. I went inside to the choir room where the choir members were waiting; they stopped talking when I entered.

We prayed together. I don't remember what I prayed for; I don't think it was anything God had not heard before. Maybe it was something different for me. We stood there waiting for the clock to reach the hour, and for Miss Alma to strike the first chord on the organ in the sanctuary. Romulus had not come to church that morning, so when Miss Alma sat down at the organ, there was no surprise waiting for her. The choir members and I were waiting. Mrs. Jennie May Curry came over to me. She tried to smile, but the smile failed. There were tears in her eyes, trying to come out; she was trying to hold them back. Her eyes searched my face. Her voice trembled slightly. She was a handsome woman in her sixties perhaps, but active. Miss Susie May Brown and she had gone with me and MarthaLee to the meeting of the Southern Baptist Convention in Miami the year before, and we had all flown over to Cuba together to visit the Baptist missions there. She was a great traveler, uncomplaining, untiring, even tempered, intelligent, probably the most highly respected woman in Shellman. Her two sons, Wistar the banker and Charles the merchant who sold me the first window unit air conditioner in Shellman; I had complained that I could not work effectively in the muggy, hot summer weather.

Miss Jennie May looked with pleading eyes, quivering lips, into my face. She said "No matter what happens here this morning, I want you to know that I love you... we love you."

Knowing what was going to happen, and how she was going to vote, I looked back into her eyes. I said "I don't believe it." My own voice quavered although I was trying to keep it level and steady. She gripped my hand, then turned away.

Miss Alma struck the first note on the organ. It was a true note. So Romulus had not followed me and slipped into the church. He probably sensed the mood of the people and stayed away on purpose. I walked to the pulpit. The choir members followed and took their places in choir. The house was full of people. More people than I could remember ever having seen there before. Even people who had moved away from Shellman, but had never moved their church membership. Now they had come back to vote. There were young children, boys and girls eight or ten years old who had joined the church during the summer. I believed their parents had urged them to this action so that they would qualify to vote. The place was quiet except for the sound of the organ.

The morning worship began. Organ music. Prayer. Singing. Scripture reading. Until the time for the vote.

Claron Wooten read the deacons' recommendation that I resign effective January 1955. I was to have the use of the pastor's home until then. My salary, which had been cut in half, would be paid for two months. That would be equal to one month's salary. There was no discussion of the motion when it had been seconded. Nobody made a speech. Not even Mae White. She had said she wanted to, but I dissuaded her.

The vote was taken and counted. It went against me, seventy eight to seventeen. I opened the book of church membership and wrote opposite my name and that of MarthaLee: "Cast out." I said I would accept no pay for services not rendered; we would move out of the house as soon as possible. I laid my sermon manuscript on the pulpit lectern, prepared to speak. People began getting up and walking out. Here is what I said to the people who remained to hear me.

"Now that you have completed the business which has brought many of you here for the first time in five months, permit me to use this final occasion for speaking to you as an opportunity to interpret your actions of this day, and point out to you the reasonable consequences to follow. For you have not merely "fired a preacher" this morning; you have done much more and much less than that.

"In the first place, by your rejection of your minister because of your antipathy to his views on the racial issue, you have gone far beyond the act of giving expression to your personal feelings on the matter; you have publicly declared that you will not tolerate the preaching of those views which have been endorsed by the Southern Baptist Convention, and have been embodied in the Convention's present program of education and missions. The very things which I have preached, and which you refuse to hear, are now practised abroad in our mission schools and at home in our theological seminaries.

"Now the Convention has no binding power upon you, but if you would be consistent in your conduct, you should withdraw from the Southern Baptist Convention, releasing yourselves from all obligations and depriving yourselves of all benefits of membership therein. And in fairness to all prospective future pastors, you should inform them in advance of your stand, so that they may not unknowingly become pastor of a heretical church.

"In the second place, by showing yourselves hostile to me in this matter, you do not only declare that you will not accept as binding upon you and your posterity those pronouncements of the Supreme Court which are not to your liking.

"But you also demand that the pastor who shall serve you shall give ecclesiastical sanction to your rebellion against the government of the United States of America. Now revolt against tyranny is not wrong. If this be tyranny against which you protest. But if you are in rebellion, then stand forth and declare yourselves. Your forefathers, when they found themselves in a similar position, had the integrity and the courage to secede from the union, and to assume full responsibility for their own government and for their own welfare. But you accept government subsidies, and you seek federal farm loans, and you even remain in the employ of the federal government.

"Moreover, your sons serve in the armed forces of our nation, where the program of integration which you say you will not accept, neither will you permit your preacher to speak of it, is already an accomplished fact. To be entirely consistent, you should secede from the union and openly declare that you owe allegiance to the sovereign state of Georgia alone, and from her alone will you accept the benefits of citizenship.

"But the foregoing considerations are minor by comparison with this third one. For in declaring that the man who has preached a doctrine which is unacceptable to you, although it is in keeping with the teaching of Scripture, must go, you deny the God of our Lord Jesus Christ and empty His word of its power. In saying that the principles which hold true for the Kingdom of God do not apply to the society of men, you deny that God has anything to do with human conduct, and thereby declare yourselves humanists. By erecting racial barriers between men who would share together the blessings of our Christian culture, you make of no effect the blood of Christ which was shed in order that the dividing wall of hostility might be broken down, thereby making of all true believers one new man in Christ Jesus.

"By renouncing a principle embraced by the New Testament church as the result of a heavenly vision granted to the prince of the apostles and verified by the apostle to the Gentiles, and by placing your own traditions and customs in direct opposition to the plain teaching of Scripture, you deny the Christian heritage and reject the leadership of the Holy Spirit. You therefore have forfeited the right to call yourself a church; you should adopt some such name as "the Shellman Community Club" and you should make it plain to all future leaders that they are to recognize no higher authority than the voice of the people, and they are to express no opinions other than those commonly held by the people. You should also inform all future "presidents" of this club that upon taking office they forfeit all rights of free speech as private citizens, and they can no longer speak for themselves in the press and at public gatherings.

"When I came to you three and a half years ago I believed that you were sincere seekers after Truth, and that you would hear the Word which the Lord had commanded me to speak. But when you were confronted with the Word of Truth, you could not accept it. Indeed, you declared that the spokesman of the Word must be silenced "for the good of the church." Therefore know that the Kingdom of God has drawn near to you, but you have rejected its demands and have closed your doors to the messenger of the Kingdom. I shall indeed leave your town, as you have requested, and in leaving I shall shake off the dust from my feet as a testimony against you, as the Lord has directed. But it is not I who will judge you; rather it is the Word which you have spurned; and this is the judgment which is decreed in the Word:

"You shall experience a famine of the preaching of the Word of God for you have commanded the prophet to be silent. Even the little Truth which you have shall be taken away from you and shall be given to another with more capacity for the Truth, for you have no eyes for the perception of spiritual Truth, and you have no ears to receive the Word of God, and your hearts are hardened so that you cannot receive him who comes to you in the name of the Lord.

"You have decreed that one man should become the scapegoat to bear away into the wilderness the sins of a people too proud to confess their own sins before God. But God has decreed that my blood shall be upon you and upon your children, and except you repent, you who so recently stood at the threshold of glory shall sink forever into shame, and your infamy shall spread abroad throughout the earth as did the name of Judas and Caiaphas and Pilate.

"Now let me reaffirm what I have said so often in the last six months, that I do not regret that I have drawn the issue on this point, for although we have all been plunged into the most tragic circumstances we have ever known, out of this experience have come three living, burning realities, etched in such clarity that I think no other stage could have brought them into the full orbit of our vision as we have seen them here.

"First, there has emerged the terrible power of evil thinly veiled in the robes of a false piety expressing itself in terms of a maudlin concern for the church and the town. By this entrance, Satan has marched abroad in our town, and has come to dominate at last the life of the church.

"I suppose that every man ought to have one experience in which he is permitted to view His Satanic Majesty exercising his sway in undisputed splendor, for only so can he come to rightly appreciate the humble reign of Christ and his saints, and to develop a healthy fear of the Devil's power. But blessed indeed is that man who is not deceived by the Father of falsehood, but resists him to the very end.

"Then there has been demonstrated in our midst the destructive power of fear over human lives, and it has been in such a terrifying manner that we can now see clearly how whole nations are enslaved by a few ruthless men. It is an unforgettable spectacle, this reduction of men and women to cowering, cringing non_entities by the application of economic and social pressures. Never before in my life have I felt such a flood of pity as I now feel for you who once were proud and strong in the knowledge of your own dignity, but who now must drag out the rest of your days in the knowledge that you have sold your birthright as free men for a mess of pottage served up by your enemies.

"But this experience has also called onto the stage those bright and shining, glorious ones, the true friends. I think that apart from this I might never have known the real meaning of friendship, for I might never have known how it was with the disciples of Jesus who found themselves cut off from their families, their neighbors, and their business associates, but who found all that was needed in that close fellowship with their true brothers and sisters in Christ. These new ties, forged in the fires of suffering, shall endure for eternity and though the heavens and the earth be removed, I know that one thing shall remain, the love that has bound me to the faithful ones among you.

"And now has come to pass in your midst the word of our Lord Jesus Christ; "I came to cast fire on the earth; and would that it were already kindled. I have a baptism to be baptized with; and how am I constrained until it is accomplished. Do you think that I have come to give peace on earth? No. I tell you, but rather division, for henceforth in one household there will be five divided, three against two and two against three. (Luke 12. 49_53)

"Think not therefore that your troubles are ended because you have got rid of me. For your troubles lie within yourselves, in your blindness to the light and insensitivity to the Truth. You will always be divided, as you always have been, because some of you can perceive the hand of God at work among you, and some of you cannot. On your behalf, I utter one final prayer: May God forgive you, for you do not know what you are doing."

There still remained in the sanctuary a few of those who had opposed me; most of them had left, either when I stood up to speak, or while I was speaking. I marvel that any of them remained to hear me. In fact, looking back on that experience in the light of fifty years, I marvel that they did not bodily throw me out of the building, so harsh had been my parting message to them.

The seventeen who had voted for me were still there too. I did not know how they were feeling about the words they had heard from me. I was to learn in the following days and weeks about their faithfulness and devotion. Now MarthaLee and I walked out, and faced an uncertain future, but one filled with such a challenge as we had not known before.

Miss Susie May Brown walked with us to the house which was no longer to be our house. She put her arms about me and MarthaLee and said "You two will come and live with me in my house for as long as you need to stay. Until you have found the place where you work next."

We put that pitiable little pile of furniture that had come with us by way of Texas in storage. We packed our clothes into a closet in Miss Susie May's comfortable house. And I began making some travel plans. We decided that MarthaLee should stay on and teach until I found a place for us. Then I got ready to drive to Louisville, where I would let it be known that I was looking for work. I went by way of Mama's house in Macon, taking Romulus and the Pointer Pup, now a full grown bird dog named Spots, to stay with Mama while I was gone. Everything went well with Spots, except that he pulled a Ghandi stunt of fasting until he realized that Mama would only offer food but would not force feed him. Romulus was a different story though.

Mama and I drove up town, with Romulus clinging to the back rest of the front seat. On the way we had a collision. Another driver, much under the influence of drink, simply ran head_on into us. This frightened Mama. I had hardly got the car stopped when she flung the door open and jumped out, fearing that even worse things were to happen if she stayed in the car. Romulus panicked too. When he saw an open door, he fled the scene of the accident. I stayed on at Mama's for two days, searching the neighborhood and calling in vain for Romulus. I never found him, but I became known as the Cat Man because I went about asking everybody "Have you seen my cat?" Perhaps it was better to be known as a crazy Cat Man than as a hanged "nigger lover." But by this time, both tags were very well attached to me.

CHAPTER ELEVEN

On the long drive from Macon to Louisville, my mind went back over the seventeen people in Shellman who had put themselves on the line for me. And the two at Brooksville and the six at Friendship. But I didn't know who the two and the six were. I only knew that two people at Brooksville and six at Friendship had voted for me to stay. But I never knew who they were. I did know the seventeen in the Shellman church. I was looking into their faces when they stood to vote for me.

And one of them, Miss Susie May Brown, had already taken us into her home. MarthaLee would be under her wing while I was away. Miss Susie May was a maiden lady in her sixties. She worked as secretary/book-keeper for Jim Curry, a Shellman business man whose business I never knew anything about. Miss Brown was a sort of second mother to Jim's two small boys, and unofficial missionary to everybody in Town and County, black and white.

Miss Susie May was on a tour of Europe when the trouble broke out in the Spring. She came home immediately to fight for me, and she continued the fight for the whole time and beyond. Opening her home to us was the big thing at the moment of our greatest need. Her generous heart had found ways to reach out to us all the time we were there. There was a humorous aspect about her; she was getting to be a bit forgetful, and the usual result was that she did the same good thing over a second time. But on one occasion her heart exceeded the action of her hand. She brought our Christmas present, handing me an envelope, and saying "I put a fifty dollar bill in it." I didn't open the envelope until she had gone, and when I opened it, the envelope was empty. Miss Susie May had forgotten to put the fifty dollar bill in it. I wrote her a Thank You Note for it, and never let her know it was an empty envelope.

I told you that she was one of my Lieutenants; she fought valiantly for me and when the war was over, continued, raising money to support us while we waited in Louisville. After we were settled in Lexington Miss Brown came to visit us. She was then about seventy, still very active and outspoken. She looked out the kitchen window one morning and informed me that a Linden tree I had planted in the back yard was in the wrong place and did not fit into the landscape properly. To her amazement, I went out and cut down the tree, and when she expressed surprise at my action, I said "Miss Susie May, your opinion carries a lot of weight with me. Even your opinion about a Linden tree."

Now I will mention a trinity of good people, Ernest and Jessie Landford, and their son Ernest Junior. And I won't leave out Evelyn. Ernest was a robust man in his forties, a saw miller who employed a gang of Negro workers, and was always loyal to me from the day I arrived. His wife Jessie taught in the Sunday School, and throughout the long struggle she stood staunchly by MarthaLee to let her know of her support. The boy, Ernest Junior, was sixteen, a slender, shy, handsome lad who was in the Boy Scout Troop, and he embodied all those good Boy Scout Laws. Evelyn, an attractive girl, had gone away to college in a little town in North Georgia, moved her church membership to a Baptist Church there, and was heartbroken because she had lost her voting rights in the Shellman church.

David and Euva Arnold, a remarkable old couple, lived over by the railroad tracks on the Southern edge of town, and he had a garden that would make you forget that a freight train was passing. He suffered from Parkinson's disease, or some related ailment that caused him to shake all the time except when he was asleep. I never saw him when he was not shaking, but he was unshakable in his loyalty. A visit with Mister Dave always involved a tour of his garden, some of Miss Euva's cookies, and a story of their son who was lost in World War Two. And concern for the church.

Mr. Claude Payne' was the one who claimed to be the only pain I would find in Shellman; he was wrong. He and his daughter Dorothy were anti- dotes for pain. Dorothy was an artist, and she wanted to do my portrait. I would not consent because I did not want to sit still long enough, so she did a painting of a flower, a Camellia, I believe it was, and I wish I had let her do the portrait because it would help me to know what I looked like to the people who cared about me.

Mrs J.E. Ellis was the wife of a mechanic at the Chevrolet garage and the mother of a large brood of children. I had baptized one of them, a little girl named Joyce. She had smiled up into my face when we stood together in the baptismal pool behind the pulpit. Now she stood with her mother, still turning that warm and spontaneous smile on me when the vote was taken.

Mattie Belle Thompson always wore a smile too. She could frown through it but somehow the smile stayed there. Her husband, a farmer, was named Phineas, and some wag had shortened that to Pig when he was a boy; he was the only man I ever knew who could wear a monicker like that with dignity. It was he who read that report to the Lions Club and was authorized to pay the bills although there was no money in the treasury. I don't know if he paid them out of his own pocket. I wouldn't be surprised. Although he was a member of the Rehoboth Baptist Church and could not vote in the Shellman Church, he helped to pay my salary and to support me after I was fired.

Mrs. W.C. Franklin was the mayor's wife, and the mayor was strongly opposed to me. He had expressed his feelings about me to her in very profane terms and she said "You better be careful what you say about Brother Buchanan. I will have him to preach your funeral when you die." This was not an empty threat; I learned that Mrs. Franklin carried a thirty eight calibre pistol with her when she went to the beauty shop for her weekly appointment. She would lay the gun out in plain view, lean back and relax while Louise Johnson did her hair. I was never informed about the mayor's death, nor called back to preach his funeral. So I assume he must have toned down his rhetoric after I left. I would have heard, certainly, if he had died at his wife's hand.

Mrs. James M. Wooten was superintendent of the Junior Department of the Sunday School. Miss Gladys was a vigorous, cheerful little woman in her sixties. On that Sunday in June, when the first vote was held, and I was very much concerned that it would go against me. I stepped into her Department on my way to the pulpit. She threw her head back, looked up into my face, and said "When you come into my department, smile." In December, she was not smiling because she knew the same thing I did, but she was undaunted, and she stood firm for me.

Mrs. Belle Curry was a frail little woman known for her devotion and faith. In some of my fictional tales, I have made her the model of religious devotion and unflagging faith. She is the mother in that story about the pair of new shoes. In real life she was the mother of Johnny Curry who was one of the alcoholics for whom Shellman was famous. But he was the smartest of the alcoholics and the most devoted to me. He was the hero of that tale about the trip to the asylum when he was to be admitted, but came driving home, having admitted his cousin who took him there. When things were at their worst in Shellman, Johnny came to me one night. He was pretty well soaked and his face showed deep trouble. "I've been in a fight," Johnny told me. "They said something bad about you and I got into a fight with 'em." He appeared to have lost the fight, but then I was a losing my fight too. We teamed up and drank coffee until Johnny was able to go home.

I have saved Mae White for last and will have the least to say about her because I have already told you about her. I believe it was Shakespeare who penned the line "Would you praise Caesar? Say Caesar." It is sufficient for me to say "Mae White."

So these are the Glorious Seventeen. If you add the two at Brooksville and the six at Friendship, we have a total of twenty five, but since I never knew who the other eight were, I can't tell you anything about them, except that they voted for me. They all were supporting my right to say something they did not necessarily believe on the race issue. They were not voting on the race issue though. In the face of popular disapproval, cutting across family lines, social ties, and business relationships, they were standing for a principle more basic than whether black children go to school with white children. They were standing for the principle of freedom. The Freedom of the Pulpit, where the Word is preached. The Word by which all human actions are judged. Without this Freedom even love and faith lose their peculiar meaning. These people stood for me because I symbolized and embodied for them the principle of Freedom to preach that Word of God in a time of great social unrest and upheaval.

So what happens to people like this who have stood up for a fallen leader? I believed that they would suffer abuse and slander and ostracism, but that they were destined to be the true leaders of the church in Shellman. I believed that their influence would reach beyond the small community there, and touch the life of the world. I urged them to stay in the church and keep their positions of responsibility, and stick to their guns. I believed that though others had asserted power, these humble servants would be the ones who would determine the course of the future. In thinking about this as I drove along, I fell back on words I had read and found to be a rock in a storm:

Truth is ever on the scaffold
Error ever on the throne
Yet that scaffold sways the future
For beyond the dim unknown
Standeth God within the shadows
Keeping watch above His own.

But how would these people feel toward me, the man who had been the precipitator of the immediate crisis in which they were caught up? What would they think of this man, now gone from their midst, who had presented the absolute claims of the Kingdom of God, leaving them no room for compromise? When they would have to face the daily grind of disapproval by their fellow townsmen, how would they see me then?

Now fifty years have passed. I cannot say what took place inside those people after I left. We maintained contact for as long as we could. Then the old were dying off and the young were moving away. Now I can only say how I feel toward the men who taught me and led me to the place where I could catch a vision of the Kingdom, told me of the absolute demands, pointed to the ultimate goal.

To those men who taught me and refused to accept from me anything less than the supreme effort, refused to listen when I wanted to bring down my sights or narrow the range of my vision. To them I am eternally grateful; they are my true friends.

Now I can only hope that that those who stood with me in Shellman, and in the outlying areas of the county, continued to feel the same way toward me. That so long as they lived, and wherever they went from Shellman, they were, and will always be, nobler because I made the supreme demand on them. And they rose to accept the challenge.

All these people were enough for my mind to feed on all the way to Louisville. In Louisville, I found a basement apartment near Cherokee Park. The woman who owned the house required letters of recommendation to assure her that I was a man of good character and safe to have in her basement. Since I was well known at the seminary, I was able to get sufficient certification. I rented the apartment and drove back to Miss Susie May's house in Shellman to get MarthaLee.

After we were settled into our place in the basement we learned that the character question was turned around backwards. I should have done a check on my prospective landlady. She was a young woman with a small child about a year or two in age. The little boy cried a lot, and when he cried she screamed at him, trying to make him quit crying. The more she screamed at him the more he cried, and the more he cried the more she screamed at him. This went on ad infinitum, and it was so hard to listen to that MarthaLee and I spent as much time outside as possible. We did a lot of walking in Cherokee Park and in Seneca Park as well. We would have walked on water if ... but more of that story later.

While we were there in Louisville the seventeen people back in Shell-man supported us with letters of encouragement and assurances of their prayers for us, and ... Money. That last part came in handy for rent and groceries, but I was eager to get work, and I had some offers, one of them from a whiskey distiller who much admired my courage and thought I might be just the man to stand up for his product in the face of the church's unreasoning attitude toward whiskey. I believe it was at this time that Martin Luther King called and invited me to join his Southern Christian Leadership Conference, and I had to turn him down because I wanted to be a pastor instead of a civil rights activitst. So the Registrar at the Seminary, Hugh Peterson, put me in touch with a couple of churches in the American Baptist Convention, thinking that I might fit in better in the North than in the South. The churches were in West Virginia. From seminary days I remembered that whenever a student applied to him for help in getting a place to preach, Doctor Peterson would first ask if the student had a car because the place he was going to send him was too far to walk and too isolated for public transportation.

I had a car, but Hugh Peterson was an Australian and he pronounced "car" the way I pronounced "cow", and the churches in West Virginia were not only too far away to ride a cow; they were too far to drive. The first was Old North Baptist Church in Parkersburg, and I rode the train, overnight, and arrived rumpled and bleary eyed on Sunday morning, to preach my "trial sermon". I did well enough for the pulpit committee to request a session with me in the afternoon, and the discussion seemed to be going along rather well until one of the members of the committee asked me if I believed in the miracles of Jesus. I said that I considered the life of Jesus Himself to be miraculous, but this was not what the man wanted. He said "Do you believe Jesus walked on the water?"

I said "Jesus comes to us in life's storms just as he did to his followers in his day. He comes to us and the storm subsides. He reaches out his hand to us and when our hand is in his, we can weather the storm."

I added "That's a miracle."

"That's not what I mean. Did Jesus actually walk on the water? And did Simon Peter walk on the water to meet him?"

I saw that there was no way out of this. Doctor John E. Martin had found me unsound in Doctrine because I didn't believe Jonah swallowed the whale. Now we were up against the real thing with Jesus walking water. I was going to have a long train ride home, but I thought, I may as well have this matter out right now, and I said "Well, if you put it that way, I guess it would depend on whether the Lake of Galilee was frozen over. I've heard of people driving their car across the Ohio River here when it was frozen solid, but no, I don't think that's what the story is about."

My answer did not go over very well, but apparently better than I thought because a few days later the chairman of the pulpit committee called to say "We won. The church voted to call you."

I could not believe what I was hearing. "What was the vote?"

"Fifty one to forty nine. Come on."

"One man changes his mind, and I'm in trouble. No sir. I can't come."

My next chance was at Hurricane West Virginia where I was told the town got its name because in early times a fellow named Cane operated a grist mill. The farmers would bring their corn to be ground, and it would be a slow job, with wagons waiting in line, and the impatient farmers would chant "Hurry Cane! Hurry Cane!"

But I was there because Hugh Peterson put me in touch with somebody in Hurricane. This time I flew and landed at the airfield on top of a mountain outside Charleston. The man from the church met me and I gave them my best shot at the Sunday morning worship service. The pulpit committee met with me in the afternoon, and the conversation went something like this "Why did you leave that church down there in Georgia?"

"Well, they asked me to leave."

"Asked you to leave?"

"To put it bluntly, they fired me."

"Fired you? Why did they fire you?"

"Because I preached that Negroes ought to be treated like White Folks."

I didn't see any Negroes in Hurricane. Certainly none came to the morning worship service. But the people of Hurricane were not taking any chances on a fellow who preached such doctrine. That ended my aspiration to go North with my Gospel. I and MarthaLee were stuck in the basement underneath the crying child and the screaming mother until I ran into Bill Mitchell in the seminary barber shop.

But time out now for some tales of my boyhood and how I became a preacher.

SEEB

It was long after my boyhood experiences. I was still hanging to the farm. Papa was dead. I had gone to college at Mercer University. World War Two had come. MarthaLee and I both were working at the Naval Ordnance Fuse Loading Plant in Macon. We were handling the sensitive powders that went into the fuses that fired the shells and the bombs that were sinking the Japanese Navy.

And when the War was over, we went to Louisville, Kentucky, where I began the six years of theological studies leading to a doctorate in Theology. MarthaLee had enrolled in the University of Louisville, and had begun studies leading to her teacher's certificate.

In the years at Mercer and the Seminary, we were doing what I called "my foreign mission stint", driving great distances each weekend to preach in little town and country Baptist churches. In all of this time I had eaten many chickens in fulfillment of Aunt Hattie's prophecy. We had known hardship and poverty in that period too. But I was so full of the excitement of preaching, that I hardly noticed the hardship. For the studies were challenging, the people were gracious, most of the time, and we were young and in love with one another.

But one day we were walking in Cherokee Park, and talking under the giant trees there. That was our favorite form of recreation because it didn't cost anything except a little shoe leather. And MarthaLee surprised me with a question that had not been in my mind for a long time. She said "I've heard you speak of the old black man you called Uncle Seeb, and you've told me how he had something to do with your becoming a minister. But you never told me what became of him. Would he be still alive?"

"Oh no!" I said. "Uncle Seeb died before I left home, long before you and I met. I was at his funeral."

"Tell me about it. I've never been to a Negro funeral. I have heard some things but I don't know what it's like."

"It's a long story of long ago, but if you'll listen ..."

I was remembering Seeb's gold tooth. And now Seeb is dead. Seeb will be buried tomorrow at the church.

Remembering Ol' Needmo'. Seeb's shining black face all wreathed in smiles at his mention of Ol' Needmo'. Thinking Ol' Needmo' might be the Bad Man in black disguise. A special disguise to hide him from whites and reveal him to blacks. But ever present in hard times when there is never enough of anything to meet the needs of men and women and their children struggling in the grip of poverty.

"Cain't buil' no screen porch, Alfie, on accounta Ol' Needmo'. Jest hafta put up with flies an, chickens an' jes' shoo .em off when they git too bothersome." And now Seeb is dead. He will be buried tomorrow at the Mt. Pisgah Baptist Church, Papa said.

Seeb has taken the secret with him. My secret. The secret I shared with Seeb. The secret kept close because of Mister Robb. And because of Papa. Ever since the humiliation of being subjected to Mister Robb's hard hands and his bad breath and his prying eyes, searching out the secret dream, until I exploded in anger at both Papa and Mister Robb. Crying out "ain't gonna be nuthin'. I'm just gonna be like my Papa."

But Seeb saying to me "You doan hafta tell me whut you goan be when you grow up. You doan hafta tell nobody. Hit jes' 'tween you an' yo' Lawd."

Then the great black shining face, the shining white teeth, the shining gold tooth, all shining beneath eyes opened wide in wonder at the discovery that I wanted to be a preacher like himself. "Like you, Uncle Seeb."

"Lawd God! A preacher! Praise God!"

Remembering Dump too. Dump's wedding. And Aunt Hattie's cake and ice cream. The ice cream made at home, in a churn, with ice and salt to make it freeze, by turning the handle on the churn. But Young Seeb had been drinking, and Old Seeb was angry. "You stay 'way fr'm 'at bottle, you heah!"

And the fight broke out right in the middle of the wedding ceremony. Because that young black buck showed up, claiming Dump for his own. "Ain't nobody gonna marry Dump!" he declared "Dump mah woman!" But Young Seeb and his friends threw him out, and Dump was married, and I ate the cake and the ice cream. And dreamed of being a preacher like Uncle Seeb. And being the hero in dramatic weddings like Dump's.

But the Dream. And Seeb's face. Would the Dream ever become Reality? Now Seeb is dead. Will the Dream be buried with him on the morrow?

"Papa." I looked into Papa's misty blue eyes. I had not seen them misty before. Well, once. When he came from the field because Mama sent Cliff (that's James) to tell him it was Margaret. When Papa came out of the room where Margaret lay, Papa's blue eyes were misty. Papa looked back at me now with misty blue eyes. "Papa, I'm going to the funeral. I'm going to Uncle Seeb's funeral."

Papa fixed his misty blue eyes on me. "You go, Son. You go an' see them put Seeb away. I want you to go." Then Papa took his hat from the hat rack, and he left the house.

I pushed aside the stack of books on the little table in front of me. I pushed the cane bottom chair back, and stood up. I was tall, and slender. Not as tall as Papa, and not as slender as Junior. But no longer the chubby baby faced boy I had been. "Where are you going?" Mama was watching me. She had not spoken when Papa told us that Seeb was dead. "What are you going to do?"

"I'm just going to see if my white shirt is clean. I'll need it for Uncle Seeb's funeral." I went quickly from the room.

The long black hearse moved slowly to a halt in front of the Mt. Pisgah Baptist Church. Two black men opened the doors of the hearse, and stepped onto the ground. One of them was a tall man in his forties or fifties. His closely cropped hair was showing a little grey. He wore a pencil line mustache across his upper lip.

It was evident in his face and in his movements that he was in charge.

The other man was younger. He seemed, in fact, a younger version of the first man. I assumed he was the son of the older, heavier man. He was nervous and eager to do the right thing, watching the older man for guidance and approval. Both men wore dark suits with white shirts, and with a red carnation in the coat lapel.

Another car, long, heavy and black, drew up quietly behind the hearse. Six men emerged from this car. They were all black. Some were blacker than others. One was light skinned, but nobody would mistake him for a white man. They were all wearing dark suits, white shirts, and red carnations in their coat lapels. They lined up behind the hearse, three and three, facing each other. They stood waiting, silent, watching for a signal from the man who had emerged from the hearse.

That man, the man in charge, opened the back of the hearse and began rolling out the casket, and as it came out the six men took hold of the handles, three on each side. Then the man in charge walked in front, and his son, the apprentice, walked behind, and they bore the casket inside the church. There they set it on a cart waiting in the aisle between the two sections of pews, and they rolled it down the aisle to the open space between the pulpit and the pews. Very respectfully, the man with the pencil mustache opened the casket. He and his son arranged the flowers on it, and then they stepped back.

Inside the casket was the body of Seeb. His eyes and his mouth were closed. Neither white nor gold was to be seen in his face. The face was black, but it was not the black that had once shone like onyx. It did not gleam like polished ebony. It did not have a light of its own like a black sun shining in a white heaven. It was simply black, for black Seeb was dead. And all the undertaker's art could not give to that visage the glow which had suffused it when he was alive and turned his great wondering eyes on me, and opened the great mouth full of white and gold to smile on me.

I stood and watched as the undertaker opened the casket and arranged the flowers on it. I heard, I felt, I was moved by a great sigh that went up from the people who were packed inside the church, and the sigh was like the wind in the tops of pine trees. The people sighed because Seeb was dead.

Then the sigh that went up from the people in the church became a humming, and the air inside the church vibrated with the humming. It became a moaning, and my heartstrings vibrated with the moaning. And the sighing, and the humming, and the moaning became a voice speaking. Words spoken first by one man, and then spoken in unison by all the people. I could not make out what the words were, but it did not matter, for I knew what they meant. I knew.

The words spoke, and the words said that Seeb was dead, and yet he lived in these people who had known him and had been inspired by him and lifted up by him. The words said that Seeb's gone now, but yet he was still there in the boy who had known him and had sat spellbound in his presence when his face shone and his voice spoke. The words said that the great voice was silent now, but in his silent journey he took with him the joys and the sorrows, the triumphs and the defeats, the questings and the restings of that great life that had been lived among the people there in the church. Then I felt my own lips trembling and I felt the moaning inside myself, and a shaking of my body.

After a great while the sound of the words died down for there was nothing more for the words to say. And yet I waited, listening for the word that was to be spoken to me. Waiting for God to speak to me out of the quiet that hung over the church and over the casket and over the people in the church. Then I remembered the morning after the storm. I saw again Seeb's great shining face with the eyes white and staring out of the blackness, and the gold tooth gleaming in the midst of the full mouth of white ones. I heard Seeb saying "Ol Massa, He git Hisse'f all ready to speak, an' He th'ow out a lightnin' bolt jest to git yo' 'tention. An' you know He fixin' to say sumpthin' 'portant. Now He open His mouf an' He speak an' His voice jes rumble all acrost Heab'n. Nen He say "Y'all look out down 'ere. Heah it come!"

I lifted my eyes to the pulpit where the preacher stood wiping the sweat from his brown forehead. His white shirt was wet with sweat, and even his dark coat was stained with sweat. And I remembered Seeb's words "'Lawd, Alfie, when mah union suit git all wet with sweat it cool me off lak a dip in the creek when a little breeze hit me."

The preacher and the people were in dialogue, in harmony, in agreement, togetherness. When what the preacher said called for a Yes, he got a Yes from the people. And when it called for a repetition of what he had just said, he got a repetition of what he had just said. And when what he said called for an Amen, he got an Amen. And all that the preacher said about Seeb was confirmed by the people. There was no denial, no refutation of what was said. No questioning of the promises. No doubting of the assurances offered to the people who grieved at Seeb's passing and celebrated his passage among them.

And I knew that what the preacher said found the Amen inside myself.

I saw Hattie and her children and her children's children. She wept aloud, and they wept with her. She wailed, and the sisters of the church wailed with her. She collapsed, and they supported her to keep her from falling. And I sat squashed between black giants who were sweating and keeping time with the motion of their own bodies. And I felt a wailing inside myself. I blinked back the tears but they would not go away. They kept forming behind my eyeballs, stinging and flowing outward. For Seeb was in the casket but the face no longer shone like a black onyx in the heavens. Yet the voice spoke inside me "look out down ere! Here it come!"

Then they came. The six black men in dark suits and white shirts and red carnations in their lapels. And they took up the casket to bear it away to the burial place outside the church. And Aunt Hattie flung her self on me. And the whites of her eyes stared out at me as she clung to me, and I knew the meaning of the language of her grief.

The six men bore the casket to the waiting grave in the cemetery beside the church, I rose and followed. I was engulfed in a river of blackness, for the black giants were on either side of me. And Hattie clung to me. I was like a white chip on black water; with Hattie clinging to me, she was part of the black water, but she was a chip too. We were a white chip and a black chip on the water.

I stood as far back from the grave as I could. but I was ever pressed forward, so that it seemed to me that I was in the very vanguard of the procession that moved to the very brink of the grave where Seeb's casket hovered, waiting. Then the preacher spoke, and all the people who were standing before the grave were silent, waiting. And the preacher said "Brothers and Sisters, our Brother Seeb goes even now, borne on wings of Angels, and as in a chariot of fire, but his mantle falls from his shoulders."

The preacher paused, and his eyes sought out my eyes, and he said "His mantle has fallen on the shoulders of the young white man who is with us today."

I heard the words of the preacher, but I felt that the words must be for someone else, and I wanted to look all around to see who it was, but the people said "Yes", and I could not turn to look.

Then the preacher said "Our Brother Seeb spoke to me even as he was leaving us, and he told me how God spoke to our young white brother. How the Lord spoke out of the lightnin' and the thunder, and laid His Hand on the head of the boy who has now become a man in our midst.?"

Then the people all looked at me and said "Yes."

The preacher said the Lord has laid His Hand on this young man, and the mantle of Seeb has fallen upon his shoulders. And now the Lord wants this young man to speak the Word that the Lord has laid on his heart as we lay our Brother Seeb to rest."

I stared dumbly at the preacher, and my legs would not move of their own accord, but I was carried forward on waves of blackness, borne to the side of Seeb's casket by the black giants on either side of me. Then I stood near the empty grave. I was looking down at the casket. It was closed now. It covered the shining black face, forever now, but I saw it against the wall of the little house where Seeb had lived, the great body thrown back in his chair as it tilted against the wall. The eyes were open and they roved about the world he had received from the Creator's Hand. The mouth was smiling white and gold in his pleasure with the gift. And the great booming voice was heralding the day that follows the stormy night.

Then the voice of the preacher was saying "our young white brother will say a few words to us."

Then my eyes were filled with tears, so that all the people gathered there in the graveyard, and facing toward the casket that hung suspended over the open grave, all their faces became a blur. My throat was tight and constricted, and when I thought I would speak, it seemed that I would choke. My throat muscles would not work, but it did not matter because there were no words in my brain. No words to be formed and spoken. I stood there, looking at the people, but they blurred into waves of blackness, and the waves of blackness moved forward toward me. They came and gathered about me, humming and moaning and chanting, until Seeb was lowered into the ground. Then they walked with me from the grave, supporting me on pillars of blackness. Then one said to another "You better take Mist' Alfie home. He done broke down with grief. He sho' did love Ol' Seeb, Mist' Alfie did."

And the other said to the one who had spoken "Sho'. Now doan you worry none. Ah take good keer of Mist' Alfie. Ah see he gits home awright. Doan you worry none 'bout him."

"You stayed and seen 'em put Seeb away?" It was a question, but Papa said it as a statement that a chapter of life was now closed. I did not speak, but Papa knew.

"I reckon he took it with him." Papa said, and I returned Papa's gaze without words, and Papa said "I reckon Seeb took the light with 'im." And I nodded.

CHAPTER TWELVE

Bill Mitchell and I had been students together in the seminary, and the way we became friends is this: Hugh Peterson had sent Bill to preach at a little church in the country near Owensboro in the bend of the Ohio River. The people in the church liked what Bill had to say, and the leading deacon said to him "Will you come and be our preacher?"

Bill said "I will pray about it and if it is the Lord's will ... "

The leading deacon said "The way I see it is this. You are a preacher without a church, and we are a church without a preacher. What more do you need to find out what the will of the Lord is?"

So Bill became the preacher there and Summer came on, the church wanted to hold a protracted revival meeting to win new members and revive the old ones, and Bill asked me to go with him and do the preaching for this meeting. I did, and the people liked me well enough that when the first week ended, they wanted to extend the protracted revival meeting another week. I was enjoying it myself, much more than mowing the grass on the seminary lawn and hauling off the garbage. I agreed to stay another week. I found that some of the best people I had ever known were hidden away in the woods down there; Bill and I became close friends; I went to Shellman where all those terrible things happened to me, and Bill went to a little country church near Lexington. But on the day I found him in the barber shop he had driven down to Louisville, to get his hair cut and talk with old friends. We began to talk, and he said "The Veterans Hospital at Lexington needs a chaplain. I could send you to see the Senior Chaplain there and you might get the job." I went, I got the job, and soon MarthaLee and I moved to Lexington.

The Veterans Hospital in Lexington housed and treated neuro_psychiatric veterans of our foreign wars. The hospital wanted a chaplain who would make no distinction between black and white patients. I wanted a place to work where the mentally sick people were locked up inside instead of running around outside firing the preachers. I was happy in the work, and it gave me a great sense of confidence to know that when I got ready to leave Ward Sixteen, which was the place where the most dangerous patients were kept, and go back to my office on the first floor, I had a key in my pocket that would open the door.

After a couple of years, the Central Baptist Hospital in Lexington wanted a chaplain, and I went there, struck up a friendship with Bob Brown, a local pastor, and we began writing controversial articles for national magazines. We wrote WHY THE CHURCHES DON'T INTE-GRATE, and the article was published in Ebony magazine. I am still writing controversial things in my retirement, but the biggest thing that happened to me while I was integrating Central Baptist Hospital and the Lexington Pastors' Conference was the birth of our son, Al.

I was inordinately proud of the boy, and each day I would tell him "You are the finest boy in all the world." He grew up believing that, I suppose, and he became a lawyer, practising in Chicago, and one day he became interested in what had happened to me before he was born, and he asked me about it.

"Dad, all these things that happened before I was born ... I have grown up in a different world. Tell me how you feel now about what you experienced back then, and what you said would happen as a result of it all. Has it been good or bad?"
"Who can say whether it is good or bad? It is different. As you have said, you live in a different world. I helped to make it different. It is the world we must live in now."

"But the things you said in Shellman. Have they happened the way you said?"

"Some of the things I said would come to pass, have done so. And some of the things my critics said would happen, have happened too. For good or bad."

My young lawyer son was not one to let things go, or to leave loose strings hanging. He said "What do you mean by that?"

"Let me change a couple of words. Instead of the things I said, let me change it to the things I believed. I believed then that what was happening in the church at Shellman would mark a point in time, in the life of the historical church. Yes, it would be a historical Day of the Lord, a Day of Judgment and Redemption within history. That from that point onward the Church would be different. And men would react differently to this moral issue; what I saw as the paramount moral issue of the day in which I was living and working because they would be forced by what had happened at Shellman to see Christ in a new light, and consequently they would have to see their world in a new light, and what is more to the point, they would see themselves in a new light. They would see themselves as having a moral responsibility which they could neither ignore nor escape."

"That is a rather long statement, using a lot of verbiage. Explain, in a few words, what you mean by that statement you just made."

"I believed that His Hand was on us and would be felt differently. That the Church was entering a new era of human relationships, a new dimension of faith in God and love for men, regardless of the color of their skin."

He was looking at me and I said "I felt the way I think the early church must have felt, and the way the men who wrote those letters to the early church must have felt. Especially Paul."

"And ... ?"

"I believed we would see a new realization of spiritual powers, a new experience of that freedom which is the very headwaters of the stream of life. I believed that the Shellman Story, the story of both tragedy and glory, would mark that point at which men would begin to enter into this new dimension of life."

"You never spoke to me of these things when I was a boy growing up. Have you seen some evidence that what you believed has actually been realized in the life of the Church and of the Nation. In America?"

"When you were a boy growing up, I was too filled with the joy and the pride and the terrible responsibility of your growing up as a boy. But yes. I have seen some of it. Perhaps I was too much carried away by the sense of the finality of it in my own experience. Perhaps not enough time has yet elapsed for me or you or any other man to see it. Human history, the history of the Church and of the Nation, is a big ship on the ocean of time. It takes a while for such a big ship to make a significant change of direction. I am coming to the end of my time, and I am impatient. Perhaps God is not so impatient."
I wanted very much to make this matter clear to my son who had not experienced what I had. And I wanted very much to look good in his sight. For this is why we write histories, to justify ourselves, to make our actions appear justifiable in the eyes of our children who must inherit and live with the things we have done. He said "Can you have missed something? Since you were so close to it."

"Yes. I overlooked the fact that mine was an unusual experience, one not apt to be repeated in every church. That the Shellman community was a town isolated from the rest of the world. That the experience of Shellman would not repeat itself in every town in our nation. That I, and Shellman, were not typical. That might just be unique."

"And what was accomplished? I don't mean the hanging and the burial and the votes in the church. I mean beyond Shellman."

"On a short term basis, I found that when I returned to Louisville, to the seminary there, to the students at the seminary, I found myself welcomed into the embrace of the many students there. They had a new awareness of the racial issue. There was a sharp realization that beyond the classes in Greek and Hebrew, there was an issue that could no longer be ignored by the Church. That young ministers, meaning themselves, going out to become pastors of the churches out there, in one year, or two, or three, they would have to face the same forces that I had faced. And they would have to put their ministry, their professional and personal future, on the line as I had done. They were both anxious about the future, and eager to meet the challenge the future held for them."

"But all of this was a matter of weeks. It is immediately after you left Shellman and went back to Louisville. What about the long range?"

"Long range. I'm afraid it is not dramatic, but then the long haul of history never is dramatic. I can see that the churches have not changed their emphases. The churches are still concerned with growth. Growth in numbers. In budgets. In the size and comfort of new and bigger buildings to accommodate the increased numbers of people coming to hear what the preachers tell them how to be saved and go to heaven, or at least what mistakes to avoid in order to avert hell and public disapproval. But yes, the churches that are predominantly white are accepting Negroes into their membership. They are welcoming Negroes to their worship services. And black churches are reciprocating. They are entering into some activities that are jointly sponsored and conducted by both white and black churches. Certainly the white men are not standing at the door to throw out blacks who may seek, to enter. So there is some progress."

"And what about the country itself? Has the Southland changed? Is it different in Georgia today? In Shellman?"

"Yes. The country has changed more than the churches. Negroes have been accepted into every aspect of our national life. True, I have not been back to live in my native state of Georgia. I have not yet been back to visit Shellman. And I certainly am not at the heart of things in Washington. When I have been back, then I will be able to say more truthfully whether I can see basic, elemental changes in the way people do business, politics. But from what I can see on Television and, in the movies, of sports, and what I read in the literature being produced today, yes, things are changing."

"All right Dad. Let's put that on the back burner for the moment. Tell me what the opposition to you in Shellman said would happen, or if you wish, what they feared would happen with integration. And whether it did happen."

"What they said and what they feared were nearly the same, because in their fear they spoke the truth. Yet their fears were deeper than what they said."

"Be more specific."

"The big bugaboo was intermarriage. And I guess they really did fear this because of the natural attraction. But they said going to school together would lead to dating, and dating to sex, and eventually to marriage. One spokesman at the Georgia Baptist Convention meeting in Augusta predicted that from these intermarriages would come black and white striped babies. Well, there has been some intermarriage, but I have not seen any zebra babies as the result of it. The children look very much like the children of illicit white/black unions we have seen ever since the Negroes were brought to this country as slaves."

"And did you respond to this expressed fear?"

"I said that marriage could come about only after the reason they feared the marriage no longer existed, and would mean that integration had ceased to be a matter of concern."

"That sounds almost convoluted, and I wonder if they understood you, since I am having some trouble with it. But what else?"

"And I presume that pulpits became empty all over the country." My son the lawyer was being ironical. But with a grin. "And that the Shellman church was unable to entice, another minister to come there."

I decided not to respond to his irony. "Some men did lose their pulpits; some lost more than their pulpits. They were beaten, publicly maltreated, thrown in jail along with the Negro protesters. The most notable was Martin Luther King whose fame is now so celebrated that I don't need to speak to you of what happened to him. And you will hear of his "Dream" over and over. It will be memorized and recited by school children along with Lincoln's Gettysburg address. I myself..."

"Yes, you. I believe you said the men never came to take you for the midnight ride in the country."

"I was spared some of the humiliations that others suffered. But I was not involved in the race riots of the sixties. I was the spokesman of the Fifties. It would have been, or certainly might have been, different for me as well after the matter had simmered and stewed for ten years."

The conversation was lagging at this point. I could see that we were not done with it. That there was another question. He asked it. "You believed ... How did you justify your belief?"

"Theologically. This is the mystery and the paradox of the cross itself. That tragedy may become glory when it is sublimated through divine grace and the human courage to break with error. This may be the very essence of the legend of Martin Luther King. That he paid the final, ultimate price because he had the courage to go all the way ... And because at some point the grace of God took over and transformed the rabble rousing to a victory parade."

Giving this answer, I could see that it did not satisfy my son. It didn't even satisfy me. I knew that I would never know the answer until I went back to Shellman. There, I believed, I would find it. But I had not determined to go back.

The way it happened was this: I had written a little book of Southern Tales. Humorous, witty, biting with satire. Essentially, truly folklore. And I had been out promoting that book. I traveled all over the Southland. I penetrated the Midwest. I even invaded Chicago. And the farther I got from home, the better reception for my book. So maybe things were not what they seemed to be. On the book signing tour I was an author. The people who came to my table to talk with me, and in some cases to buy my book, were not the people I had left in Shellman. The people, black and white, working in the book stores, were not the people whom I had known in Shellman. Yes, I would have to go back to Shellman. And the book signing tour provided me with the opportunity to go back to Shellman.

No, it was not to do a book signing there. It was a last hour, almost a last minute decision, when I was sitting at a dividing of the highways, one leading to some place in Alabama, and the other leading to Shellman. And I was going to take the one that led to Shellman.

Chapter Thirteen

I had spent the night in Griffin, the town my parents had left when they came to Macon. I had searched there for some cousins, only to learn that they were all dead. So when I approached Columbus, I was already in a reflective mood. I turned East onto Memorial Highway. Every five or ten miles the name of the highway seemed to change because of all the heroes who were honored on it. I felt like the apostle Paul at Athens when he saw the memorials to all the gods of the Athenians until he came at last to the one dedicated to the unknown God and started preaching Jesus Christ to the Athenians. Then I saw it. The marker by the roadside: Martin Luther King Memorial Highway.

"So this is Georgia's Unknown Hero," I exclaimed. And the highway stayed Martin Luther King right into Dawson, Georgia. Dawson, where I would have starved if I had been dependent on the grocer there to sell me food, and where my friend Fess Johnson had told the grocer to stick it. Dawson, where I delivered that radio, address in spite of the threatening telephone call, and the station manager said I could speak on the radio any time. "Wonder if I could go by the radio station and say a few words. But nobody would remember me, or care."

I turned West again on the highway that goes out of Dawson and past Shellman ten miles farther on. I looked for familiar landmarks, and saw none, but I knew I was on the right road because I had driven it many times. Still, I had the feeling I had never been there before. Yes, I was coming home. But would it be a homecoming? Would anybody be glad to see me? Would anybody recognize me? After forty four years, a man's face has changed. Odysseus came home from wandering for twenty years and his wife Penelope didn't recognize him until he described the bed he had built and where they had lain in their love. But there would be no Penelope waiting for me. I had even lost MarthaLee through divorce. Who would know me in Shellman?

Then I was passing the houses of the people I had known. There was George Robinette's house. Bet I couldn't even get in the front door there. Doc Bynum lived here on the left. Wonder if he still feels he was doing me a favor that day forty four years ago. Up ahead there, Miss Susie May's house. Look at those tall pines on the front lawn. I told her they would get so big they would dwarf her house but she wouldn't listen to that. Wait. On the left here. Mae White's house. It ought to be a shrine to an unknown goddess. An angel anyway A little farther on I saw Joy Wooten's house. People said Joy Wooten was the worst driver in Shellman. "What?" I said. "How many wrecks has she had?"

"None," they told me. "She's never had a wreck."
"

"But you said ... Why?

"She lives next door to the telephone operator, and when the operator sees her getting into her car, she calls everybody in town and says Joy Wooten is getting ready to drive downtown, and everybody stays off the street until Joy gets to the Post Office or wherever she's going."

Then the church. Good thing I was driving slowly. I could have missed it. Not called Shellman Baptist Church anymore. The sign read First Baptist Church of Shellman. Well, they didn't name it Shellman Community Club, but they did change the name. I guess that wipes out the bad publicity I brought on them.

Wait. There's where Miss Caro Martin lived, there on the left. She said her husband never made a mistake in his life. "Not even when he married me." He was dead though. He was the church clerk and he took the membership roll with him to heaven and they had to make up a new roll from memory. He probably still has it. Guess he had to revise when they threw me and MarthaLee out.

Here on the left at the corner is where Jim and Gladys Wooten lived. He had a heart problem and couldn't go to church, but she made up for it. She was plenty for two and all good. Railroad tracks just ahead. The Walls live right down there. Used to eat lunch at Mrs. Wall's. Joe Wall was the town policeman. I had him on the carpet once for beating up a black man downtown and he told me "I'd do the same to you if you needed it." But his son Walter advised him to be careful." I was bird hunting with the preacher and I saw him shoot a bird over his left shoulder." It happened, but it was an accident; I was never able to do it again.

Turn right, circle around through town. Lord, it looks dead. Wonder if I could find a coffee shop. There was one. Served fried chicken too, but all I wanted was a cup of coffee. I didn't recognize the middle aged woman who ran it. "Have you lived here in Shellman long?" I asked.

She said she had come there a few years ago, bought a house and opened this little business. I asked why she had decided to come to Shellman to live. "It's a quiet little town where nothing much ever happens, and I thought it would be a good place to live and bring up my children." I sipped my coffee and she repeated "Nothing much ever happens here in Shellman."

I asked her if she could tell where to find the Baptist preacher. "He's over there in the City Park," she said. "With the children." City Park? There was no City Park when I was there. But straight ahead. Over the railroad tracks again. And there was a man who must be the Baptist preacher. He was supervising a walking and running event to raise funds for a charity. Age seemed to determine whether the participants were running or walking. I saw a brick building on the edge of the City Park. A sign on it read City Hall. Much class. The one where I had been hanged was gone, and this was the replacement.

The preacher appeared to be friendly enough, and I introduced myself. He studied my face. "Buchanan," he said. "Seems I have heard that name somewhere, but I can't place you." He looked at me closely, and I thought: So much for immortality.

I said "I was pastor of the Baptist Church here forty four years ago."

He was quietly reflective. Then he said "I have told the people here that they won't have to fire me because I will retire when I am eligible for Social Security and the Baptist retirement fund."

I thought that he was hoping those good things would come soon. Then I asked him about the survivors in Shellman. As I ran over the roster of names he would say "Dead" or "Moved away." Then he said "Miss Mattie Weathers is still alive. Her granddaughter Byrd lives with her." Once when Mama had visited me in Shellman Miss Mattie had told her that she was born happy and had been happy ever since. But she had one disappointment in life; none of her numerous offspring had gone into the ministry, and this made Mama prouder than ever of me, her preacher boy.

"You will have to pound on the door," the preacher told me. "Miss Mattie is deaf." I pounded on the door and called out, but Miss Mattie was deaf, and she did not hear me. I opened the door and went in. Miss Mattie and Byrd were in a back room. Both of them smiled happily and hugged me. They had not voted for me but now they had forgotten that they did not vote for me. "Byrd has had brain surgery for cancer," Miss Mattie said. "She can't remember anything." Byrd looked at me as if she remembered everything. I do not know whether she had been born happy, but she was happy now.

"I bet you remember the time you took me to a bar in St. Louis," I said to Byrd. She laughed happily and I said. "You remember. You were the hostess on my plane, and when I got to St. Louis, you picked me up and took me to a bar where all the people were having a big time and we ate at the restaurant where they threw the bread at us." Byrd laughed as if she remembered every moment of that evening where she thought she was corrupting her pastor for a big prank. "Before that I thought bars were sinful places, but everybody there was having such a good time I was tempted to have a drink but I was afraid you would tell it on me." Byrd laughed happily again and Miss Mattie said "Byrd can't remember anything since she had brain surgery, and I am so deaf I didn't hear you at the door."

"I'm glad I came on in. I would not have missed seeing you two for the world." Miss Mattie told me that Brooks and Jane Wooten were still alive and that they still lived across the street from the church. We hugged again and I drove down the street past the new brick home for the pastor, and pulled up beside the church. Jane Wooten was putting the garbage out on the side of the street.

She recognized me and said "Brother Buck. Come in the house and see Brooks."

I followed Jane inside and found Brooks sitting in an easy chair. Wrapped in smiles. He was now suffering with some heart ailment and looked very much like his father of forty five years ago. Both of them had forgotten that they had voted against me. Brooks said "I tried to get hold of you for the church's anniversary." I believe it was the two hundredth but that is not what matters. They wanted me to come back, along with all the other pastors, to celebrate.

It would be an opportunity for reminiscing. I could imagine myself standing again in the pulpit and telling how I was the only minister in the two hundred years of the church's history to be hanged, buried in the public space in town, and driven away by the largest vote ever cast against a preacher. Then I would tell how I had scolded them and chided them and told them they should secede from the union and change the name of the church to the Shellman community Club. What a happy reunion. Brooks said "I tried to find you in the Southern Baptist Convention's Directory, and couldn't find you." So the convention had lost track of me too since I struck my name and MarthaLee's name from the roll of the church and had written "Cast Out" by them. What a madman I must have seemed to them that morning in December of 1954. And what a fool I must appear to the generation born after I was gone.

But Brooks and Jane were happy to see me. They liked their present pastor whom I had met in the City Park, and I saw no sign that they did not intend to let him stay until retirement. They were solicitous of my health, but they did not ask about MarthaLee. I guess the news of our divorce had gone ahead of me and they did not want to embarrass me by mentioning her.

They told me about Little Jane and Little Jim who must by now be in their fifties, and I can't remember it all. The church had been redecorated, but I did not ask to see inside it. It seemed the same from the outside, except for the sign that had been changed to First Baptist Church; I didn't see any sign of a Second Baptist anywhere in towm. I asked them about survivors, and they told me "Sarah Curry lives just up the street here. Alone. You must stop and see her. She will be so glad to see you."

We hugged again, Jane walked with me to the car, and I drove up Pearl Street, looking for Sarah Curry's house. It was not hard to find. Sarah was standing out in the front with a yard rake in her hands.

When I had last seen Sarah Curry she was a beautiful young red headed mother. Slender, intelligent, active in the life of the little town of Shellman. Now she was a frail old woman, doing what would have been called "nigger work" when I was pastor of the church there, raking up the debris of last night's rain storm on the lawn. But still beautiful, and radiant in her beauty. Because when she recognized me her face was wreathed in smiles and her eyes were filled with tears of joy. She threw her arms about me, praising God that the storm had spared her house, and the only effects of it now were the broken tree limbs and other trash on the grass. She told me that Shellman was very much like what I had said it would be. The racial tension was gone. My old friends and supporters were all gone though. She said "I want to ask your forgiveness. I know it's late, but what we did to you has bothered me all these years. Can you forgive us?"

I could. I did. I hoped that both Sarah Curry and God could forgive me for the harsh words I spoke on December 5, 1954. I stood there with her, and we were surrounded by the spirits of the heroic people who had stood with me so long ago. Miss Susie May Brown's house was just down the street with the tall pines, and Mrs. Mae White's house was across the street, filled for me with the presence of that great woman who stood for me against all comers. Sarah Curry and I hugged again, and she told me that she was happy that I had come back and had stopped to talk with her. I think she now felt as if she had cast that vote for me, forty four years late. But she was forgiven for the lateness. I drove on to Cuthbert.

Cuthbert is the County Seat Town. It is bigger than Shellman, and I believe it even has a little college there, and so it must have lots of college graduates, and some alcoholics. I guess the lawyer who got drunk after every case in court had died and gone on to the special reward that God provides for alcoholics who can bear neither victory nor defeat without some help. It was lunch time and I was hungry, so I drove about looking for a restaurant. If Cuthbert has a fine restaurant, it was well hidden, so I stopped at a place that served hot dogs and hamburgers. I sat at a table alone and watched the other people who were eating in there. At the next table I noticed a group of young men in rough workers' clothes. They were eating and talking and laughing and kidding and joking with one another in a spirit of camaraderie that made me feel lonesome there all by myself. I was tempted to go over and ask to sit with them, but I was afraid it would break the magic circle that they had woven about themselves. Some of them were white and some were black. I ate my hot dog, paid the cashier, and drove away. I had been to Shellman, and to Cuthbert. I would have to think about what I had seen and heard and felt.

Did I have the answers to my son's questions? Had I found what I had come to Shellman, bracketed on one side by Dawson and on the other by Cuthbert, to find? Dawson now sat at the end of Martin Luther King Memorial Highway. And in Cuthbert young workmen, black and white, sat eating together, and, the question of my sanity was still open, but there seemed to be light at the end of the tunnel. I was, in fact, forgotten, except for Miss Mattie and her grand daughter Byrd, the attractive, vibrant air lines hostess who had shown me St. Louis but now had brain surgery and couldn't remember. And Brooks and Jane Wooten who had willingly forgotten that they didn't vote for me, and wanted me to come back for the big celebration of the church's age and wisdom and caring for people. And Sarah Curry who wanted forgiveness for what was done to me forty four years ago, and was grateful that God had spared her and her house in the storm. I wish I had had that story to tell the people at the Old North Church in Parkersburg, Virginia when I was asked if Jesus did, in fact, walk on the water, and if Simon Peter, holding to Jesus' hand, did in fact walk on water with him. And I wish I could have told the people at Hurricane about Miss Mattie and Brooks and Jane and Sarah, and the Baptist preacher who seemed to remember having heard my name somewhere.

And the woman at the coffee shop who had brought her children to Murray because it was a quiet little town where nothing much ever happened. Yes, I wish I could have told the people at Hurricane and the people at Parkersburg about the little town of Shellman. But then they might have wanted me to be their pastor, and my whole life would have been different from then on. So I turned my face toward Alabama, to a book signing there, and I carried my memories with me.

And the Question. The answer I had given my son did not satisfy him. It did not even satisfy me. Maybe I had not even asked the right question. How can you find the right answer unless you first ask the right question? My words to him were, after all, rather theological, not very down to earth.

Oh, yes, I had learned something in Shellman, but was it what I was looking for? I had been all about over the Southland, and the people in the bookstores would receive me warmly, and then they would hide me away so well the customers coming into the stores looking for John Grisham's last book, or a thriller by Tom Clancy, would never even see me over there behind that stack of Southern Tales. The Goat might be Crying in my book, but the customers steamed past racks of books and headed for the coffee shop. I was invisible, still seeking the answer. Or the Question.

Then I came to Memphis.

Chapter Fourteen

At Memphis I found the Question and the Answer. It was in a bookstore there. I should have known it would be a man. Had not that been what God had said?

I was at a big book store in Memphis, signing the little book of tales called AND THE GOAT CRIED. The manager of the store came to the front to greet me. He was broad in the chest. His face was wide and friendly. His smile was a good one. His handshake was firm. A good grip, but he did not crush my hand. He knew I would need that hand again for writing. He ushered me to a table covered with many copies of AND THE GOAT CRIED. He said "Now I want you to sit right up here where everybody who comes in that door will see you first thing. Don't let anybody get past you without looking at your book. You are the man of the hour because you wrote that book. You know more about that book than anybody else does because you wrote it. I want these people coming in here to see your book ... and buy it ... and read it. You are here to sell your book." The book store manager was a black man.

Certainly I had had enough of being hidden away in some comer where nobody would find me. I wanted my book to be seen I wanted the people to talk with me about the book. I wanted them to ask me questions about the book. Most of all I wanted them to ask "Why did the goat cry? What made the goat cry?" for this gave me an opening to tell them just enough to want to read it and find out for themselves why the goat cried.

And the store manager had not waited for somebody else to show me where to sit. He was a man after my own heart. He knew what it was all about. My being there.

This man wanted people to see me, talk with me, and buy my book. For if people bought my book, the store would make some money. And beyond making money on this book, I was an Author, a person to be recognized, acclaimed, listened to. And who knows? If things went well, I might write another book that would go well. But surely, every person who came in that door must know about this book. Must be challenged to buy my book. Do I need to tell you that the book signing went well? It was great.

But then the darkness came on, enveloping Memphis. It was that time of year when it gets dark before sundown. Early in the afternoon I had checked into a hotel, a motel that is, on the other side of town, the first one I came to as I approached Memphis. The man at the desk gave me directions to the bookstore. The bookstore was a long way across town from the motel. But it was broad day light and I found it. That was hours ago though. Now it was the motel that was long way across town. And it was dark. And between me and the motel the city of Memphis lay in darkness, and I did not know which way to go.

It was time for me to fold up and go though. But how? Which way? I stood there seeing myself wandering all over the city of Memphis, unable to stop and ask for directions because of four lanes of bumper to bumper traffic that paused only at red lights. I turned to one of the workers in the book store. I did have the name of my motel. It was on the key. The store person started to tell me how to get there. Another worker came over and said "No. Here's the best way." Then everybody had a better way. They were all telling me the best way to get to my motel. Finally, they began to argue among themselves about the best way for me to get to my motel on the other side of Memphis. I was becoming more and more confused. Maybe I had better spend the night in the bookstore. Tomorrow, in daylight, it might be better. Right now, Memphis seemed a dark and threatening place. Then the manager of the bookstore came over to me.

He waved a big black commanding hand at all the people who were telling me how to get to my motel. "You folks be quiet," he said to them. Then to me he said "You just follow me. Get right in behind my car. Stay right on my tail lights. Follow me. I will get you to your motel."

We walked together to the parking lot. He got into his car; I got into mine. He started up; I pulled right up behind him. My headlights were almost touching his tail lights. He had told me to stay on his tail light and I intended to do just that. We drove away into the evening Memphis traffic. We wound through the maze of Memphis at night. I was clinging to his tail lights. My fear was subsiding. The anxiety was going away. Confidence was taking the place of panic. After a long while - it must have been at least twelve minutes by the clock on my dashboard - we pulled into the entrance to my motel.

He rolled down his window, leaned out, smiling, his white teeth shining in the darkness. He was the proudest looking black man in Memphis. I rolled my window down; I leaned out. I was the happiest white man in Memphis. He said "Here you are. Home. Thanks for coming."

I said "Thank you, Good Shepherd. Thank you, and Good Night."

"Good night," he said, smiling and chuckling at his Biblical monicker. Then he drove away. I pulled into an empty parking space, reached for my motel key. I said inside my head, Now there's man, a black man, made in the image of God.

Here then, was the most capable book store manager I had met in my travels as I went about the country promoting my little book of Southern Tales. He knew what he was there to do: to sell books. He knew that writers are the people who provide what he has to sell. He handled his role with authority. But most of all, he was a man who did not tell a fellow man lost at night in the city of Memphis how to get across town to his motel; he led that man to his motel. But fifty years ago, before I was hanged at Shellman, this man, if he had got a job in a book store, it would not have been as manager; he would have been pushing a broom.

Now this man who had brought over the best of the Negro whom I had known when I was a boy growing up on a farm near Macon, Georgia, and looking into the smiling face of Uncle Seeb, whom Papa had described as "the blackest man in the whole state of Georgia." And he had combined this gift which was on Uncle Seeb's face with the best that a man could become in the world that I had helped to create by declaring the Word, and by being hanged for declaring that Word in Shellman, Georgia, fifty years ago.

Yes, my Son, the real question with which you and I were wrestling, was this: Was it worth it? And the answer to that question must be seen, in the face of a Man standing there beneath that shining black skin, a Man acting out the role of the Good Shepherd who leads another man through the darkness to the safety of home.

A Man worth being hanged for. I thank God the hanging was in effigy only. Otherwise, you and I would not even be asking the question. And without the Question, there would be no Answer.

And what of the future of race relations in America and in the world? I believe the future of white men and black men living together in the American society hangs on two powerful realities of human nature: Anger and guilt. The black man's anger, and the white man's guilt. Both have their roots in the history of slavery. A heavy price was paid in the Civil War. It continues to be paid in Civil Rights. And human nature being what it is, we can expect that a great deal of unfairness and bitterness as well on the part of both white men and black men, will surface in the struggle to seek advantage in every relationship.

The black man will certainly act out his anger in making exorbitant demands on the white man, playing on the white man's guilt. And the white man will cover his guilt by ascribing to the black man qualities which he may not possess, and by giving to the black man privileges he has not earned and may not be able to handle responsibly. All of this because of the white man's need to assuage his own guilt in meeting the demands of the black man's anger. This is already evident in our present day tensions, and will become more prevalent in the future, as the anger of the black man expresses itself more and more, and the guilt of the white man requires more and more covering.

In large part, we have created this situation by equating Christianity with Democracy. Consequently, we have become the militant exporter of this new gospel, Christian Democracy, to the rest of the world. It is being done with the fervor that once drove the early believers in the Lordship of the Risen Jesus, to go out in to the Greaco_Roman world to proclaim Christ as the Lord of all. What is essentially different in the picture today is that our world mission is a militant one backed up by the most powerful military force in the world, even the most powerful in human history.

In war, as in peace, the whiteman's guilt, reacting to the black man's anger, results in the tendency to elevate blacks to prominent places in our society in order to prove that whites are not racially biased, and in actual case, give blacks a preferred status in their application to status law schools by saying that the purpose is a social one, to achieve racial balance.

An extreme example of the black man's anger being expressed, in exorbitant and unrealistic demands on the white man's guilt, is the demand for reparations for the slavery of their forefathers who were not adequately rewarded for their labors nor compensated for their sufferings in servitude to the white man. Both favoritism in the competition for place in schools, and the demand to be paid for the sufferings of forefathers, represent extreme attempts to deal with both the anger and the guilt. Or rather, to express the anger and to compensate for the guilt.

What we are doing in Iraq is an extremely violent and unusually humanitarian example of this same principle. We destroy, maim and kill. Then we feed, water and clothe. The first set of actions we call liberation; the second we call restoration. But both are thinly covered lust for power and control, and then the need to deal with our guilt accrued in the act of gaining that power and control. Again, what is different in this war is that we have drawn both blacks and whites into both the anger and the guilt, and the attempt to Christianize/Democratize the world, in order to prove to the world that we are not ruled by the greed and the lust which so obviously do rule our international relations. Morally speaking, this is a hazardous enterprize involving us in deeply rooted conflicts which have extremely high psychological toll.

A very important and highly significant factor ruling the future of this nation and the world is that the American society of today is no longer the Black and White one that existed fifty years ago. It is now both multi_racial and multireligious, and we must deal with it on an international level rather than just on a domestic scale. The American society is now made up of Orientals, Latinos, and Arabs, as well as the black and white people who have been here for a few hundred years. In Murray, Kentucky, the little county seat town where I now live and work, Chinese and Mexicans are a far more significant factor in the makeup of the population than the Negroes are. The Mexicans represent a very large part of the farm labor, and consequently, they largely determine what the land here produces, as much so as the black laborers did in the Shellman community. Both Chinese and Mexicans operate restaurants here, and so they are feeding the populace of Murray and Calloway County, but in a different manner from that in which Negro cooks fed white families in Shellman fifty years ago. Orientals make up a large part of the student body in the University here, and that has far reaching implications for the educational scene.

There is an essential difference in the equation here though. These people, I mean the Orientals, the Latinos, and the Arab or Islamic people, were never our slaves, while the onus of slavery of the blacks remains with us, both the whites and the blacks. But the issue itself is now both multi_racial, and multireligious, and vastly more complicated by our war on terrorists and Islamic or Arab nations viewed as threats to our safety and security. And into this maelstrom both black and white native_born Americans are inevitably drawn, but with sharply differing attitudes toward these other races that are being infused into the American stream of life.

We are now embroiled in warfare with the Islamic world, and our fears of the terrorists create suspicions of the people who are physically significant of this warfare. Developing hostilities with North Korea create the same sort of bias toward Orientals in our midst and throughout the world. And again, both blacks and whites in our armed forces are fighting these other peoples. So the game is ever changing on us, and we will have to find ways to bring the essence of the Christian faith to bear on a world situation involving men and women of other religious faiths as well as of different races. And the propaganda war continually confuses our values with the problems of our own physical and economic security.

So we now face an even greater challenge to the Christian faith today than what we faced fifty years ago when blacks were marching in Selma, Alabama, and whites were jeering and wielding truncheons and setting police dogs with bared teeth to face the bare legs of little black children with frightened eyes. The Messenger of God who faces this challenge today with the truth in both its Judgmental and redemptive aspects, could get hanged, symbolically if not physically. And the children of the hanged messenger from God will have to ask, and answer the question: Is it worth it?

It is my concern today that Baptists, at the leadership level, are allowing their fear of the terrors that face us in the modern world, and the propaganda about the evil forces at work in our world, to blind them to the challenge of this hour to proclaim a message of hope and redemption for the disenfranchised peoples of the world. The message of reconciliation and brotherhood of the redeemed through reconciliation is being drowned out by the sound of the guns, and the voice of military power stifles the cries of the angry men who hate us.

This chapter on the future is shorter than my chapters on past action, even those events that occurred fifty years ago. The reason is simple: I know less about the future than I do about the past, and I have attempted in this little book to tell you what I know and to stay away from those areas in which I am ignorant. But now at the very end of this book I am going to do what most people do at the beginning. I am going to tell you how it was when I was a child growing up on a red_dirt, one_mule farm in central Georgia. In order to do this, I will have to touch again on events already alluded to, but they are the events, the happenings that formed, molded me, made me what I am. And I am myself always drawing new and more meaningful lessons from them as they come up to haunt me, and sometimes to amuse me, when I look back to my roots to try to understand myself.

And it was my favorite philospher, Socrates of Athens, who was always saying to the youths who followed him in the search for wisdom and truth: Know Thyself.

CHAPTER FIFTEEN

An autobiography usually starts with three words "I was born". So I will conform at this point in telling the story of my life at Shellman by saying that I was born near Macon, Georgia, in a little house I dimly remember as the Bass house, in the vicinity of Midway Baptist Church. I remember that house because Granny Bass lived there when I was a small boy, and Granny Bass made tea cakes and muffins and she always had a tea cake or a muffin for me when I went to her house. Also, because Papa had planted a pea patch there, and he had taken me with him to pick peas. A terrific rain storm came up while we were there, and I hid under the seat on the wagon to get away from the rain storm, but I got soaked anyway.

Our mailing address was Lizella; that is where the Grammar School was, and I went to the first grade there, and Mister Redding was the principal. He had the reputation for being a strict disciplinarian, but he was kind to me and he found a marble some other kid had dropped on the school ground. He gave it to me and I have remembered that act of kindness for seventy five years. Mister Redding also was very particular about language. He grew Elberta peaches, and when people said "Alberta" it upset Mister Redding. Papa said that he went to buy some "Alberta" peaches from Mister Redding, and that scholarly gentleman refused to sell him the peaches until Papa said "Elberta."

I believe I had already learned to read before I started to school through daily exposure to the "funny papers" which appeared in the Macon Telegraph which Miss Maggie Haygood saved for us. Learning to read had nothing to do with phonics. I studied Little Orphan Annie, Moon Mullins and Andy Gump. I associated their actions and facial expressions with the words in the floating bubbles which appeared over their heads. By a very similar method, I came to know what the proper relationship was between black people and white people, by the actions and facial expressions when they talked with one another.

About ten years ago a feature writer for the Macon Georgia Telegraph called me. He was writing a story about my Shellman adventures, and he asked me who had influenced me in the shaping of my views on race relations. I said "Mama and Miss Florrie." I don't think he understood that neither Mama nor Miss Florrie, my grade school teacher, Principal of the Howard Elementary School, and my in_house mentor during my first year in High School, believed in racial mixing or integration of the races in the educational process. Their influence on me can best be defined in one word: Justice.

When I encouraged the dog White Lightnin' to attack Dump, the black girl with the basket load of washed and ironed clothes on her head, and Dump dumped the clothes on the ground while she was trying to kick the dog, Mama washed my mouth with Octagon soap because I had called Dump a "big black nigger". But she also switched my bare legs with a limb stripped from the peach tree because I had abused the black girl by encouraging the dog to attack her. White people and black people occupied different levels of society. The Whites were at the top and the Blacks were down below, but Whites could not misuse their superior role by abusing the Blacks. That was morally wrong, and a worse sin simply because the Whites were superior and ought to both "know better and do better." So much, for the moment, about Mama; now for Miss Florrie P. Searcy, Teacher.

I told you about throwing the shelled corn out the school bus window and the black children, and the school bus driver threatening to put me off in the midst of them. He did not eject me from the bus, but when we pulled up in front of Howard Elementary School, Fred Powers, bus driver, told Miss Florrie, Principal, who was also his sister, what I had done, and Miss Florrie warmed my buttocks with the Orange Wood Paddle, which was also known as Miss Florrie's Board of Education, all the time delivering a very clear message that it is criminal for little white boys who enjoy the privilege of riding a bus to school, to throw corn and yell "Black nigger. Black nigger" at little black children who are walking in the dust thrown up by the bus because the Bibb County Board of Education did not provide bus transportation to school for black children.

Miss Florrie had other valuable lessons to teach me, and I will not go into detail on them, but I will mention the fact that when I was debating whether to study Latin, "a dead language", she informed me that I would not only study Latin, but Greek as well, and German too, because God had called me to preach, and it behooved me to both have something to say and know how to say it when I stood up to preach. As a result of her teaching, nobody ever claimed that he did not understand what I was saying, but most of the trouble I got into in Shellman was the result of people understanding exactly what I was saying.

So neither Mama nor Miss Florrie ever dreamed, as far as I could tell, that white and black children would go to school together. Mama did not even approve of white boys playing marbles with black boys, though I suspect that she felt that it was divine judgment that the black boys had won all our marbles in the game of "winnants on Sunday", but she would require more than a bath in cold water to "wash the nigger off" if we had cheated the black boys at marbles.

Mama was not a racial integrationist. She respected Negroes, but she required the outward signs of a higher degree of respect from them for herself. But there was something else; I guess the word for it is compassion or concern. This last lesson I learned from her while I was still a student in the seminary. I had come home for Christmas. Mama, MarthaLee and I were going to visit John Reeves, a friend from early boyhood school days. John lived on a dairy farm about a half mile off the main road, and. the little track that led back to the Reeves Dairy Farm was mud, mud, mud. We were churning along through that mud, and I was feeling some concern about getting the mud all over my car which I had washed shortly before I started out because I wanted John to see my shiny clean car, even though it was only a second hand Ford, and we passed an old Negro woman going in the same direction. When we had got past the old woman, Mama said to me "That was Carrie. Why didn't you stop and offer her a ride, Son?"

I was thinking of all the mud on Carrie's shoes, and how the mud would get all over the inside of my car, and at that time I had not given much thought to the moral implications of white people riding past black people who were walking and I said "What? And get mud in the car?"

Then Mama turned her big brown, accusing eyes on me and said "You care more about your car than you do about another human being."

So you will see that when I told the feature writer for the Macon Telegraph that Mama and Miss Florrie influenced my racial views, I was not just playing the old game of giving credit to Mother for all the good one has done in life. I was acknowledging something real, but also paradoxical, even contradictory. And it will require a bit more explanation to become adequately clear.

Here, then, was the contradiction, certainly the paradox, in race relations in the South where I grew up and in my own life as I grew up. Whites were not allowed to associate, with Blacks on even terms. But Whites were not allowed to abuse Blacks because of their different social status in the Southern social system. This may seem to the modern mind a difficult concept for a small white boy to understand. But a sharp switching with a stripped branch from the peach tree, on bare legs, and the threat of being put off the school bus to face the angry, insulted black children, then the threat become a paddling at Miss Florrie's hands, all this is a form of education far more effective than a classroom lecture on race relations. So I grew up knowing what my status was, and knowing too what the Negro's proper place was in the white dominated society.

Not all of my lessons were painful though; there were some pleasant ones. And Uncle Seeb provided them, with Aunt Hattie's assistance.

But you must know two things here. The terms "Uncle" and "Aunt" were forms of respect shown by little white boys for respectable older black people who were not blood kin to them, and I have used the fictional names of Seeb and Hattie here as I have done in many of my short stories now in print. Uncle Seeb was a black preacher whose ebony face glistened and shone with sweat as he expounded to me the wonders of the Lord's governance of the world. It was a bright and shining morning following a night of storm with lightning, thunder, wind and rain. Uncle Seeb looked out with admiring eyes upon this new washed world after the storm, and he said to me, the little white boy about ten or twelve years old, "Ol' Massa He say y'all look out down 'ere. I goan teach you sinners a lesson. But then when He done teachin' us a lesson, He smile on us an He say Now y'all behave yo'se'fs an' I be good to you."

Uncle Seeb said that he was awful proud when he learned that I was going to be a preacher. And Aunt Hattie cast her eye on a half grown rooster who had ventured near the back door steps to pick up crumbs she had thrown out. Then she proposed to give me my first lesson in being a preacher of note by providing a dinner of fried chicken. The young cockerel was given a combination of both warning and high privilege when she informed him that his imminent sacrifice was really an honor because "You goin' inta the ministry soon, so you pick up them crumbs fast as you can. They be yo' last."

So I was born and I grew up on a red dirt one mule middle Georgia farm, accepting without question both the nearness and the inequalities of the two races. Whites enjoyed privileges denied or forbidden to blacks. But whites were also forbidden to "lower themselves" by engaging in intimate relations with blacks. Blacks were subservient to whites, and any attempt to elevate themselves above the level assigned to them was forbidden. There was nothing worse for a stable and well ordered society than an "uppity nigger". But there was something immoral about a white man taking advantage of the Negro's lower social status. It was considered good fun to black one's own face and put on a minstrel show. Or to take an unsuspecting black boy - was he really unsuspecting? - on a snipe hunt. But the limits were always there. Limits on both the whites and the blacks.

Undergirded by Mama's unwavering sense of right and wrong, and urged on by Miss Florrie's Orangewood Board of Education, I went away to school at the Southern Baptist Theological Seminary to learn what I need to know in order to become an effective preacher of the gospel of Jesus Christ. It was then I began to get a new vision of black and white relations, and to feel that in preaching the gospel of Jesus Christ, I would have to come to grips with this issue in Southern society. This led me ultimately to Shellman, and to conflict with the people there over the racial issue, and to my being hanged in effigy, and fired by three Baptist churches, and to my return to Kentucky, where I became a chaplain, to both black and white veterans in a mental hospital, and to my efforts at removing the racial barriers between the black and white patients at the Baptist hospital, and to cooperation between black and white ministers in the churches of Lexington, Kentucky.

So it may seem trite to say that we are what our mothers make us. But it is true. Mama taught me to be just, fair, and respectful of black people. She herself held to a fine line of difference between white people and black people. It remained for me to make the connection between respect and the erasure of that part of the line which had resulted in unfair treatment of blacks by whites.

Once that erasure had taken place through a developing sense of what the Fatherhood of God and the Brotherhood of men in Christ Jesus, meant for race relations, I was ready to take the stand I took at Shellman.

And to be hanged for it.

EPILOGUE

After I had turned down Martin Luther King's invitation to join him in the Southern Christian Leadership Conference, saying that I felt that my role was to be a pastor, I found that the churches were not eager for me to be their pastor. I did serve a short while at the David's Fork Baptist Church between Lexington and Winchester, Kentucky, but I found my true niche in the hospital chaplaincy.

First at Veterans Hospital, and then at Central Baptist Hospital in Lexington, with a training stint at U.S. Public Health, known as the Narcotics Treatment Center in Lexington. And it was in this work that I found a new dimension of meaningful ministry to both blacks and whites in their deep trouble.

The most attractive aspect of this work was that in deep trouble and suffering men forget what color they are. Some even forget what color the chaplain is. In any case, it was for me an area of ministry that made some people wonder what I was doing. At Central Baptist, a deeply concerned woman working in the Gift Shop came to me and asked "just what does a chaplain do anyway, besides go around and hold people's hands?"

This made me think for a while, and at last I replied "What else is there to be done?" Because it does come to this: The Man of God represents the Presence of God to the man who is suffering pain, fear, and anxiety accompanying illness. For the Man of God to hold his hand while he

267

goes through the dark valley is the most helpful thing that can happen to him.

And at Veterans, where my ministry was to neurotic and psychotic men, I found still another dimension of the universal role of Christ in the life of sufferers. I was talking with some of the men on Ward 16, which was the sickest and the potentially most dangerous in the hospital, when a big fellow came to me, draped his arm over my shoulder, brought his face close up to mine, and said "Chaplain, do you know why we like you so much up here on Ward Sixteen?"

I found myself surrounded by men sick in mind and body, all looking into my face, waiting for my answer. I said "No, I don't know why. Tell me."

And the big fellow with his arm about me and his face close up, said "It's because we feel like you are just one of us."

That statement is capable of two meanings, and I admit I did feel about in my pocket to make sure the key was there. But here too we find the essence of the relationship in which Christ became one of us, that we might experience the presence of God in our life here. That is the ultimate KEY to the matter of race.

ABOUT THE AUTHOR

When Henry Buchanan was a little white boy growing up on a one mule, red dirt farm near Macon, Georgia he was taught white people and black people are very different and those differences must keep them apart. But God called him to preach - God had some help from Uncle Seeb-and Henry became Pastor of the Baptist Church in Shellman, Georgia. He said and wrote and did some things the white people of that little town could not accept because he had challenged the Southern Tradition. So the people of the Church fired him, and he and his wife MarthaLee who taught the second grade in the all white Shellman School had to leave town and seek another life in another place.

But he had written down everything he said and all the events that led up to his firing, and he remembered all the people, those who fought him and those who stood with him in the eight months long battle. So we now have this little book which tells the story just as it happened.

THE SHELLMAN STORY is Henry Buchanans twentieth published book - the first was AND THE GOAT CRIED, but it tells of events that antedate all the others. The author now lives alone in Calloway County near the little town of Murray, Kentucky. But not entirely alone. Spirit, the little white dog, and Max the big yellow cat live with him, unaware that he is a controversial figure in the world where other people live.